Original Sin
and Everyday Protestants

To Michael,

I've enjoyed conversing with another sinner-saint,

All Best,
Andrew

Original Sin and Everyday Protestants

The Theology of

REINHOLD NIEBUHR, BILLY GRAHAM,

and PAUL TILLICH *in an Age of Anxiety*

Andrew S. Finstuen

THE UNIVERSITY OF NORTH CAROLINA PRESS
CHAPEL HILL

© 2009

THE UNIVERSITY OF
NORTH CAROLINA PRESS
All rights reserved

Designed by Kim Bryant
Set in Whitman and
Bickham Script Pro by
Keystone Typesetting, Inc.
Manufactured in the
United States of America

The paper in this book meets the guidelines for permanence
and durability of the Committee on Production Guidelines for
Book Longevity of the Council on Library Resources.

The University of North Carolina Press has been a member of
the Green Press Initiative since 2003.

Library of Congress Cataloging-in-Publication Data
Finstuen, Andrew S.
Original sin and everyday Protestants : the theology of
Reinhold Niebuhr, Billy Graham, and Paul Tillich in an age
of anxiety / Andrew S. Finstuen.
p. cm.
Includes bibliographical references and index.
ISBN 978-0-8078-3336-0 (cloth : alk. paper)
1. Sin, Original—History of doctrines—20th century.
2. Niebuhr, Reinhold, 1892-1971. 3. Graham, Billy, 1918-
4. Tillich, Paul, 1886-1965. I. Title.
BT720.F56 2009
233'.14—dc22
2009022448

13 12 11 10 09   5 4 3 2 1

for

JOHN N. FINSTUEN

(1948–2009)

and

KAPPY A. FINSTUEN

Dad and Mom

CONTENTS

ACKNOWLEDGMENTS

I have incurred many debts during my work on this book. Writing fellowships from the Graduate School of Arts and Sciences at Boston College and from the Louisville Institute at Louisville Seminary provided financial support that allowed me to finish the dissertation in a timely manner. The friendly help of staff members at the Billy Graham Center Archives in Wheaton, Illinois, assisted my navigation of their collection. Chris Larson, surrogate parent, provided housing, food, and transportation during research trips to the Library of Congress, the repository of Reinhold Niebuhr's papers. Francis O'Donnell, curator of archives and manuscripts at Andover-Harvard Theological Library was exceedingly helpful as I waded through Paul Tillich's papers there.

A host of scholars and professionals have offered their encouragement and expertise at various stages of the project. At Boston College, Paul Breines, Seth Jacobs, David Quigley, and Stephen Schloesser, S.J., gave expert advice and much encouragement. Jim O'Toole, my graduate adviser, has shepherded me and this book through the ups and downs of academic life. His generosity of spirit is simply extraordinary. From the first conceptualization to the final composition of this work, Mark Noll has supported it and made cogent suggestions to improve its quality. Grant Wacker has been a wonderful, boundlessly giving source of help and intelligence as the book has taken shape. Elaine Maisner, my editor at UNC Press, has been a responsive, astute, and patient guide through the entire publication process. Paul Betz ably oversaw the editorial aspects of the production phase, and Rick Huard copyedited the manuscript with exceptional skill.

The Lilly Fellows Program in Humanities and the Arts at Valparaiso University provided a stimulating intellectual environment and a reduced teaching load that allowed time for revision of the manuscript. Mark Schwehn, the program's founder, and Mel Piehl, my program mentor, read and critiqued the book with their razor-sharp editorial and historical sensibilities. Mel, a true mentor if there ever was one, deserves an extra word of thanks for modeling such a high degree of academic excellence, integrity, and professionalism. In addition, I wish to thank my fellow Fellows at Valparaiso, Franklin Harkins, Matt Hedstrom, Joanne Myers, Stephanie Johnson, and especially James Skillen, for creating a genial scholarly community that made my time there so enriching.

Friends and family were indispensable to the completion of the project. Adam Chill, Anthony Daly, Zach Hiatt, Josh Leech, Chad Smith, Todd Romero, Scott Starbuck, and Brian Tierney, listened to many versions of the project and all the while contributed to my general well-being. My brother Peter, sister-in-law Jessica, and sister Katherine have been great sources of good humor and love. My in-laws, John and Mary Lindeblad, have shown interest in my work and have been unreservedly generous in their support of it. My parents, John and Kappy, to whom this book is lovingly dedicated, cannot be thanked enough. Their influence in my life is wide and deep. My dad had a special engagement with this book, and, in one sense, it is a long letter to him. He died on July 17, 2009.

My wife, Ingrid, has endured it all with grace, smarts, wit, and love. I humbly thank her for that and wish her to know that the completion of this book would not have been possible without her. Our son, Carl, also would not have been possible without her. He is not yet aware of his father's work, and that has been one of the many wonderful gifts of his presence.

Original Sin
and Everyday Protestants

INTRODUCTION

The appearances of Reinhold Niebuhr, Billy Graham, and Paul Tillich on the cover of *Time* magazine after World War II publicized their religious thought; and although the images were somewhat like caricatures, they captured the distinctiveness of each figure's Christian ministry. With foreboding skies and a distant cross in the background of his 1948 cover, Niebuhr's station as America's prophet was communicated clearly by his stern visage and by the accompanying caption—doubtlessly inspired by his vivid sense of original sin—which read: "Man's story is not a success story." Six years later, a Garden of Eden scene, complete with a naked Eve and a menacing serpent coiled around the tree of knowledge, provided the backdrop for Graham's cover portrait. Graham is depicted in midsentence, with an intense gaze and a finger pointed at the viewer. The message is plain: Graham is an evangelist doing what evangelists do, confronting humans with the reality of their sin. Tillich's cover of 1959 is equally somber as those of Niebuhr and Graham. He sits in deep thought with a human skull resting on a table in front of him. A bookshelf filled with leather-bound volumes fills the space behind him. The portrait, complete with its reference to Shakespeare, also evokes the theme of the human condition, as the consummate theological scholar contemplates anew Hamlet's existential question, "To be or not to be?"[1]

Scholars have rarely portrayed Niebuhr, Graham, and Tillich as anything but utterly distinct and contrasting figures. Indeed, their very names conjure definitive images of their careers and disparate audiences, as the differences in their respective *Time* covers demonstrate so vividly. As a consequence of these characterizations, Niebuhr the neo-orthodox prophet,[2] Graham the popular evangelist, and Tillich the learned German émigré theologian seem to have nothing in common save their contemporaneity. Yet the *Time* covers also feature a foundational unity, one hidden in plain sight. The covers, in fact, are all of a piece, showing each figure's deep concern with the human situation and his grave, religiously grounded assessment of it. The cross in Niebuhr's cover picture, the serpent in Graham's, and the skull in Tillich's ought to have signaled their shared roots in a sober, critical Protestant Christian worldview. But the conventional intellectual and cultural portraits of each thinker, both then and now, have proven so powerful as to obscure this obvious point of theological convergence. Beneath all the apparent antitheses, Niebuhr, Graham, and Tillich anchored their theology to a common core theological belief: the doctrine of original sin.

This intersection of mass media and traditional theology was not simply a consequence of the religious concerns of *Time's* publisher Henry Luce, the son of Protestant missionaries. Rather Niebuhr's, Graham's, and Tillich's cover appearances both reflected and enhanced the influence they wielded and the attention they received in the mass media and among everyday Protestants for their articulation of the doctrine of original sin in the post–World War II era. The "original sin moment" that reached its zenith between 1945 and 1965 is the subject of this book. Indeed, the discussion of original sin that circulated widely among American Protestant communities in this era owed much to Niebuhr's, Tillich's, and Graham's interpretation and revitalization of this doctrine. While the three men conceptualized original sin differently—Graham's interpretation, especially, contrasted with that of Niebuhr and of Tillich—their appearances in mainstream magazines, on radio and television, and on speaking tours reopened American eyes and ears to the centrality of original sin to the Christian faith.

Historians generally have overlooked the significance of original sin in mid-twentieth-century American Protestant culture.[3] The doctrine's importance to belief in this period has remained almost invisible for at least three reasons. First, even though some scholars have noted quite rightly that the Great Depression, World War II, and the cold war provided the context for the renewed relevance of sin and evil in America, the discussion typically ends there, and how and why this historic doctrine emerged with such force among Protestants and within American culture is left unexplored.

Second, studies of postwar Christianity have focused almost solely on the extent to which mainline Protestantism and Catholicism became captive to American culture. These accounts overemphasize the transparent "culture-religion" exemplified by such figures as Norman Vincent Peale and his best-selling *Power of Positive Thinking* (1952) and by such kitschy phenomena as the Dial-A-Prayer telephone network and *The Power of Prayer on Plants* (1959). Studies beholden to this view of mid-century Protestantism ultimately conclude—as did many contemporary commentators[4]—that most believers practiced an optimistic, progressive, complacent, and materialist faith unconcerned with sin. In these ac-counts, Niebuhr's and Tillich's theologies of original sin are viewed as both anomalous and isolated from the experience of ordinary believers. They become exceptions that prove the rule of America's faith in an optimistic Christian gospel. Graham, meanwhile, is often erroneously linked with Peale as a proponent of what some have called the captive revival of midcentury. On the rare occasions when he is distinguished from Peale, his pronouncements on sin have been explained as at best moralistic and at worst the occupational hazard of a smooth-talking evan-gelist more concerned with buttressing the American way of life against the threat of "Godless" communism than a heartfelt appeal for repen-tance. In short, Niebuhr, Tillich, and Graham have been presented, to borrow from Jon Butler's metaphor, as "jack-in-the-box" figures,[5] popping up momentarily with their talk of sin but lacking real traction in an era of self-satisfied Protestantism.[6]

Third, scholars often have divided midcentury white Protestants into received, often bifurcated historical categories. In this approach, believers are distinguished along a continuum, which resembles such schema as highbrow versus middlebrow versus lowbrow, liberal versus conservative, or popular versus elite. While such categories have been serviceable up to ⋅ a point, lay and pastoral relationships to Protestantism in general, and of Niebuhr, Tillich, and Graham in particular, seldom conform to these standard classifications.[7] Alleged "highbrows" often favored Graham over Tillich or Niebuhr, just as "middlebrows" or "lowbrows" at times favored Tillich and Niebuhr over Graham. Furthermore, some Protestants were not so single-minded in their loyalties; appreciation of both Graham and Niebuhr or both Graham and Tillich was not unheard of. Finally, tracing the rich conversation about sin among Niebuhr, Tillich, and Graham and the ordinary Protestants who engaged them complicates the notion of popular religion as being somehow devoid of theological concern. Quite simply, the highly publicized ministries of Niebuhr, Graham, and Tillich suggest that a great many midcentury Protestants must have been recep-tive to their theologies of sin.

The doctrine of original sin penetrated postwar American Protestant culture to a greater degree than any of these explanations allow. This study tells that story by yoking together Niebuhr, Graham, and Tillich and by gauging the reception of their theologies of sin within the pulpit and the pew. Consequently, it brings together men who came from very different backgrounds while taking seriously the theological imaginations of everyday Protestant pastors and parishioners in an age of supposed theological complacency.

It would be hard to imagine three figures more distinctive than Niebuhr, Graham, and Tillich. As a midwesterner and former parish minister, Niebuhr approached the question of human sin rather pragmatically. Although erudite and quite capable of abstract theological speculation, he often appealed in his analysis of human nature to what he understood to be the voluminous empirical evidence of sin in history.

Raised in North Carolina and schooled in the revival tents of the South and the lecture halls of Wheaton College, Graham ministered almost exclusively as an itinerant evangelist of the "old-time" religion. Graham had little time for sustained theological reflection, not least of all on the question of human sin; he was too busy spreading the Gospel.

Tillich, the German émigré steeped in continental theology and philosophy, had trained and taught at the most distinguished universities in Germany. Accomplished as he was in the realms of ontology and theological abstraction, he consistently returned to the problem of sin, something he clearly expressed in his *Systematic Theology*: "One should always be conscious of the fact that 'sins' are the expressions of 'sin.' "[8]

Despite their varied backgrounds and occasional sharp criticism of one another, these three men not only shared leadership of postwar Protestantism but also emphasized the doctrine of original sin. To be sure, Niebuhr, Graham, and Tillich interpreted the doctrine differently, but in a basic way, each understood humanity to be irrevocably sinful and desperately in need of redemption. Beyond this fundamental point, their explanations of the operation of original sin within humanity were sometimes strikingly and revealingly convergent.

Their articulation of the doctrine of original sin moved easily through American culture. All three men wrote for popular consumption, and their work was frequently written about in such periodicals as *Time*, *Newsweek*, *Life*, *Look*, and the *Saturday Evening Post* as well as in the three most influential Christian publications, the *Christian Century*, *Christianity and Crisis*, and *Christianity Today*. These magazines had a combined circulation in excess of 20 million and were central to the formation of American national culture from the 1940s through the early 1960s.[9] Never before or since have circulations of popular periodicals reached such heights. From this unique position of strength, they benefited from an undiluted pool of skilled writers and a nation of readers who had not yet exchanged their magazines, books, and newspapers for the television dial.

The content of these newsweeklies was "popular," but not in the simplistic and pejorative sense. The stories were highly literate and thoughtful when it came to matters of religion and theology. The most remarkable illustration of this level of discourse was the Adventures of the Mind series in the *Saturday Evening Post*—the reputed magazine of record for Rockwellian America. The series consisted of articles from America's leading philosophers, scientists, writers, and theologians with the goal of introducing millions of readers to the latest advances in their areas of intellectual concern. Tillich and Niebuhr, for example, contributed articles to the project in 1958 and 1961 respectively.

Their articles not only demonstrate the intellectual nature of Adventures of the Mind but also indicate the extent of Niebuhr's and Tillich's presence in popular culture. In addition to the close attention they received in the mainstream press, their books enjoyed steady sales. Tillich, for example, achieved best-seller status with *The Courage to Be* (1952). Their message reached audiences through other media as well. Radio stations across the country—from San Francisco's KPFA to New York's WRVR—broadcast sermons and lectures by Niebuhr and Tillich. They were no strangers to television, appearing on the National Educational Television Center's *Search for America* project and Edward R. Murrow's *This I Believe* program.

Billy Graham enjoyed an even greater public profile than either Niebuhr or Tillich. For instance, his *Peace with God* sold more than 2 million copies in 1953 and was heralded as theology for the "common man." His crusades received sweeping coverage among the nation's newspapers and magazines and were attended by millions in cities across America. Graham's New York City crusade of 1957, for example, stunned even gruff New Yorkers, attracting more than a million people during its eighteen-week run at Madison Square Garden. He also created a media blitz through his *Hour of Decision* radio program, his My Answer syndicated newspaper column, and his magazine ventures, which included the founding of *Christianity Today* in 1956 and *Decision Magazine* in 1960.

The everyday Protestants and pastors who carefully studied the writings of Niebuhr and Tillich and thronged to Graham's crusades were a diverse lot. Lay persons and pastors from a wide range of denominations appreciated the ministries of these three leaders of Protestantism. They were not strictly defined by denomination, gender, class, profession, or region. Indeed, these lay men and women[10]—whom I will call "lay theologians"—ran the gamut of education and social position. Everyone from high school dropouts to medical doctors could and did read and appreciate Niebuhr's, Graham's, and Tillich's articulations of the doctrine of original sin at midcentury. Lay theologians, in other words, came from all walks of life and wrestled with the meaning of sin in their practice of the Protestant faith.

Conceptualizing a group of Protestants as "lay theologians," however, is not an arbitrary designation or merely another label for "middlebrow." The term emerged from two collections of letters from everyday Protestants. The first, published letters to the editor that appeared in the most influential mainstream Christian and secular periodicals of the day, revealed a constituency of thoughtful ordinary Protestants concerned with the concept of original sin. These findings were confirmed by the substantial collections of unpublished letters from everyday Protestants in the personal papers of Niebuhr, Graham, and Tillich housed respectively at the Library of Congress, the Billy Graham Center in Wheaton, Illinois, and Harvard Divinity School. These Protestants proved to be a fascinating group, far too diverse to conform to the customary analytical typologies that have been employed to separate believers by any number of standard criteria.

The category of "lay theologian" crystallized for me one day in the Tillich archive at Harvard Divinity School. As I paged through yet another box of Tillich's vast correspondence, I came across a letter from a pastor in Dallas who referred to one of his parishioners as a "lay theologian." My search for an appropriate category to define this interesting constituency of Protestants ended that day. "Lay theologian" avoids the value-laden and typically hierarchical models often used to distinguish Protestants, while simultaneously conveying a serious theological disposition among a substantial number of believers. I encountered the term again in a 1959 article by John C. Bennett, a colleague of Niebuhr's and Tillich's at Union Theological Seminary. Bennett's use of the term is doubly important for this book. Not only did it further validate the category as a descriptor of a post–World War II community of believers, but it also occurred in the context of what Bennett called the "theological revival." This project explores and expands upon Bennett's notion of a theological revival in chapter 1 and later in the text through the voices of the lay theologians who wrote thoughtful letters about matters of great concern to them.[11]

As with any category of analysis, the concept of "lay theologian" is imperfect. Identifying lay theologians on the basis of their contemplative dispositions may not be the most precise classification. The range of interpretation of the concept of sin by these ordinary Protestants was quite broad. Some were certainly more sophisticated than others. Yet, whether they asked basic questions or offered challenges and criticism about the nature of sin as conceptualized by Niebuhr, Tillich, and Graham, they were included within the category. Niebuhr and Tillich had a similar litmus test for defining mature faith, and both had great respect for the wisdom that emanated from the pew.[12] Tillich, echoing Martin Luther's doctrine of the "priesthood of all believers," articulated the point simply: "The priest is a layman, and the layman can become a priest at any time. To me this is not only a theological principle, but also a position I have maintained professionally and personally."[13] In other words, the story of America's lay theologians is a story about the range of thought among midcentury American Protestants concerning what they understood to be the sinful nature of human beings.

While these lay theologians wrote regularly of sin, they rarely wrote of hell. On the one hand, this is a curious omission, since traditional Christian thought maintains that the consequence for living apart from God's will—sinning, in other words—is damnation to hell. On the other hand, the absence of hell from the letters of these everyday Protestants makes perfect historical sense. Western Christians had become less concerned with the orthodox doctrine of hell as early as the eighteenth century and most certainly by the late nineteenth century. As the twentieth century advanced, the reality of hell had become, in the words of the non-Christian British philosopher Bertrand Russell, "neither so certain nor as hot as it used to be."[14] Yet the dearth of specific references to hell in the correspondence of lay theologians and the obsolescence of a "hot" hell do not necessarily indicate that the concept of hell was irrelevant to midcentury Protestants. On the contrary, Billy Graham's sermons at times still provided a vivid sense of the unbearable temperature of hell. At other times, the idea of hell, even if unmentioned, was likely assumed both by Graham and by his audience.[15] Despite these realities, most scholars of hell concur with Russell's view, if only because it is true that that kind of literal hell has been replaced by a kind of metaphorical hell as separation from God, whether in this life or the next. From this perspective, then, the lack of "hell-talk" from lay theologians and especially from Niebuhr and Tillich, in spite of the abundance of their "sin-talk," is both unsurprising and inconclusive as evidence of the fate of hell in post–World War II American Protestantism.

What is clear from the study of the lay theologians who responded to the ministries of Niebuhr, Graham, and Tillich is that they participated in an alternative revival—a theological revival—that existed alongside the culture-religion, or captive, revival of the era. Because scholarly attention has focused only on the captive revival, little is known about the collection of lay theologians who, guided by the prophetic ministries of Niebuhr, Graham, and Tillich, constituted the theological revival. Niebuhr provided an apt summary of the coexistence of these revivals in his *Pious and Secular America* (1958): "Perhaps we are so religious because religion has two forms among us. One challenges the gospel of prosperity, success, and achievement of heaven on earth. The other claims to furnish religious instruments for the attainment of these objectives."[16] To be sure, as Niebuhr acknowledged, strong currents of complacency and captivity swept up significant portions of Protestant culture into a gospel of optimism and success. But as Stanley Rowland, the religion editor for the *New York Times*, also argued in 1958, much more lay below the surface of Protestant cultural accommodation, which he suggested was simply the "top of the iceberg" of the revival.[17]

Beneath the exposed "top of the iceberg" was a mass of scholars, clergy, and lay people attuned to human limitation, moral ambiguity, and conceptualizations of human sin. While Niebuhr, Graham, and Tillich led this alternative theological revival, they were not alone. Other critical examinations of the postwar religious scene—including Will Herberg's *Protestant, Catholic, Jew* (1955), A. Roy Eckardt's *Surge of Piety in America* (1958), and Martin Marty's *New Shape of American Religion* (1959)—pointed to a deeper theological revival below the top of the iceberg, even as they characterized the Christian expressions of this period as fundamentally captive to American culture. This is an irony all but missed by later studies that cite these works solely as evidence of the superficiality of belief in this era.

The book is divided into two parts. Niebuhr, Graham, and Tillich anchor this story of the doctrine of original sin and American Protestantism. The significance of these three men, however, derives as much from their influence in the everyday lives of thousands of lay men and women as it does from their larger-than-life public personas. Indeed, the book is dialogical in its assessment of each figure's conceptualization of sin and of the extensive interaction between these three Protestant giants and their large and diverse audiences. The narrative opens with a review of the political, social, and cultural forces that created the conditions for the relevance of the doctrine and locates the theological revival within the larger context of an anxious post–World War II Protestantism. Thereafter, the focus returns to Niebuhr, Graham, and Tillich, who remain the protagonists of the story throughout the final five chapters. Chapter 2 revisits the personal and intellectual biographies of Niebuhr, Graham and Tillich. Chapter 3 provides an analysis of sin from a theological perspective, comparing each thinker's interpretation of the doctrine of original sin. The remainder of the story, in chapters 4, 5, and 6, illustrates how their articulations of sin shaped the theology of their sizable constituencies.

Freeing Niebuhr, Tillich, and Graham from prevailing assumptions about their work and their connections to ordinary Protestants has rich implications for the study of midcentury Protestantism. By recovering the doctrine of original sin as the theological center for all three Christian leaders and by recovering its importance in the lives of lay theologians, this work intends to illuminate that important theological common ground—not simply theological difference or theological apathy—existed in an era conventionally defined by a culturally captive faith.

Part One

CHAPTER 1

Protestantism in an Age of Anxiety

The Captive and Theological Revivals of Midcentury

From 1945 to 1965, Americans experienced a time of immense promise and equally immense peril, one that inspired W. H. Auden's 1947 poem "The Age of Anxiety." Social and cultural commentators quickly adopted Auden's phrase to describe the postwar mood, making "anxiety" the buzzword of the era.[1] Leonard Bernstein, for example, read Auden's poem in the summer of 1947 and composed a symphony to capture the feelings of anxiety pulsing through the culture. At the heart of the composition, Bernstein wrote, was "the record of our difficult and problematic search for faith."[2]

Contrary to the self-satisfied, placid image of the postwar era—especially the 1950s—Americans in these years, as Auden, Bernstein, and others noted, were an anxious people. The sources of their anxiety ranged from the possibility of World War III—including the prospect of nuclear holocaust—to the health of the postwar economy. These abstract worries mingled with the lingering emotional toll of World War II and the outbreak of actual war in Korea just five years after V-J day. Upheavals caused by mass migration to the suburbs, questions about equal citizenship for African Americans, and the timeless search for meaning amid the mystery of existence also occupied the attention of the citizenry. Consequently, halcyon portrayals of American life after the war neglect the palpable cultural uncertainty of the period. As Robert Wuthnow has argued, "The prevailing mood, then, was by no means one of untrammeled optimism. Some rays of hope had broken through at the conclusion of the war, but much of the sky remained dark."[3]

Amid the anxiety, Americans flocked to Protestant churches, hoping that some light might penetrate the threatening darkness. The result was an astounding renewal within Protestantism, the twentieth-century equivalent of the First and Second Great Awakenings. Polls indicated that

13

more than 90 percent—at times as many as 98 percent—of Americans professed belief in God in the late 1940s and 1950s. In 1954, the *New York Times* noted the recovery of church membership after the "religious depression" of the 1930s. From 1940 to 1954, Americans joined churches at three times the rate they had from 1928 to 1940. Protestant churches received the majority of the new members, pushing the Protestant share of American churchgoers to nearly 59 percent. The most solid evidence—literally—of this religious awakening was the abundance of new churches popping up across the country. *Newsweek* called the construction boom "the most extensive church-building job in history." Protestantism had, it appeared, rebounded from its depression.[4]

Within this rising sea of Protestant belief, however, two revivals set its tidal patterns. In 1959, theologian John Bennett described these dominant trends within Protestantism in an editorial simply but aptly titled, "Two Revivals." Bennett, a friend and colleague of both Niebuhr and Tillich, looked back over the 1940s and 1950s and identified both the "revival of interest in religious activity" and the "theological" revival as primary influences within postwar Protestantism. He defined the first broadly: a movement typified by a "vague religiosity" that sanctioned American cultural values and stressed "a gospel of love without the Cross, of 'acceptance' without judgment." The other revival, Bennett noted, drew from theologians like Karl Barth, Dietrich Bonhoeffer, and Emil Brunner in Europe, and from Reinhold Niebuhr and Paul Tillich in America. The effect of their collective theological endeavors was to recover "the profound Christian diagnosis of the human situation and the gospel of God's forgiveness." Ultimately, he distinguished the two revivals by assessing their respective relationships to American culture: "The one [theological] has encouraged the independence of Christian faith from culture; the other [religious activity] has encouraged the assimilation of the faith to culture." As Bennett saw it, while the theological revival was less widespread than the religious activity revival, it nevertheless kept pace with its competitor.[5]

This analysis employs Bennett's categories for the two dimensions of the revival, though with some revision. While Graham was no theologian, he joined Niebuhr and Tillich in their advocacy of the "independence of Christian faith from culture." When discussing the "assimilation of faith to culture," the term "captive"—used at the time to describe this process—will serve as a shorthand designation for Bennett's rather awkward phrase, "revival of religious activity." Norman Vincent Peale, author of

The Power of Positive Thinking (1952), figures prominently in the analysis of "captive" expressions of Protestantism.

Placing Billy Graham on the side of the theological revival challenges conventional readings of his ministry. Graham is often erroneously seen as Peale's ally in the captive revival. To be sure, Graham at times preached a Gospel captive to the culture, but his ministry did not end there, as Peale's did. In fact, as a consequence of his evangelical theology of sin, Graham could and did offer trenchant criticism of American culture. Thus, although theologically pedestrian in comparison with Niebuhr and Tillich, Graham nevertheless advanced a definite theology of human nature, one that drew from such church fathers as Augustine and from his own interpretation of Scripture.

Though the theological revival was without doubt the principal bearer of the original sin moment, its full character is thrown into sharper relief by contrasting it to the captive revival. After all, both revivals emerged out of the same ambivalent postwar mood, the same Age of Anxiety. Their responses to the paradoxical and harrowing context of the era were predictably quite distinct. Protestants within the captive revival, most notably Peale, offered a triumphal message in the face of the anxiety and ambiguity of the period. It was as if they took their theological cues from the popular 1945 song "Accentuate the Positive," literally encouraging believers to "Eliminate the negative; Latch on the affirmative; Don't mess around with Mr. In-between."[6] By contrast, Protestants within the theological revival, with Niebuhr, Graham, and Tillich at the helm, placed the promise and peril of American life in the context of sin. For them, the anxiety within the culture was a function of sin writ large, but it was also a reflection and consequence of individual sin.

✣ Bennett's two revivals had roots in the paradoxical American cultural climate that followed World War II. For a quarter century after the war, although America had risen to political and economic preeminence, its citizenry was steeped in the tragic dimensions of the new character of American life. Many Americans were touched by promise, to be sure, but the perilous international and domestic context in which they lived was an ever-present corrective to any unbridled optimism about the future.

Tensions abroad quickly terminated the prospect of a longstanding peace after the war. The jubilation of V-E and V-J days was short-lived as Americans witnessed the world move from a hot war to a cold war. Truman's pledge in 1947 to intervene in Greece and Turkey to counter communist advances raised the possibility of another global conflict. Thereafter, the Czechoslovakian coup (1948), the Soviet detonation of an atomic bomb (1949), the "loss" of China to communism (1949), and the outbreak of the Korean War (1950) heightened concerns about American national security. The Soviet possession of a nuclear weapon was of course the most dramatic threat to American peace of mind. The specter of an atomic mushroom cloud haunted the sunny forecast of post–World War II American prosperity.[7] Taken together, these events induced nightmares in the midst of the popularly imagined heyday of the American dream.

The domestic situation, while not as strained as the fragile stability of the international community, nevertheless contributed to the anxieties of postwar Americans. In the first place, the idea of "postwar America" was a misnomer. The war lived on as Americans processed the brutality of World War II and the soldiers themselves reckoned with their homecoming and reintegration into society. The violence of the war affected millions of Americans who mourned the loss of more than four hundred thousand fathers, brothers, sons, and friends to the battlefields of Europe and East Asia. The horrors of the Holocaust and of Hiroshima and Nagasaki confronted still more millions with the magnitude of humanity's capacity for inhumanity. In the latter case, John Hersey's bestseller, *Hiroshima* (1946), challenged Americans to contemplate the full significance of the decision to annihilate that city with a single bomb. In that same year, William Wyler's film *The Best Years of Our Lives* also attended to the complexities of war with his illuminating depiction of the GIs' return to American soil. The film won best picture honors in 1946 for its portrayal of battle-scarred veterans—one of the main characters of the film was played by an actual veteran who lost his arms overseas—facing the difficulties of relationships, work, and happiness in civilian life.[8]

The experiences of the troubled protagonists of Wyler's film mirrored those of many former soldiers after the war. In particular, many veterans exhibited less certainty and patriotic fervor about the war than retrospective celebrations of their sacrifices have allowed. For instance, *Time* magazine reported the results of one army poll taken in early 1946, which found, "A lot of G.I.s are wondering why they ever had to fight the war."[9]

Other veterans were simply and understandably traumatized. Even Sloan Wilson's quintessential suburban novel, *The Man in the Gray Flannel Suit*, captured the mental consequences of the war. The novel's main character, Tom Rath, is haunted, not unlike Wyler's characters, by the bloodletting of World War II. Flashbacks of his war experiences intrude on Rath's suburban existence. Rath, after all, had accidentally killed his best friend, Frank Mahoney, with an errant hand grenade toss while fighting in the Pacific theater. Wilson recounts the memory of this horrible event in stark detail. Rath rushes to his friend's aid only to find "Mahoney's entire chest had been torn away, leaving the naked lungs and splintered ribs exposed." Momentarily deranged, Rath fights on, carrying Mahoney's corpse as he disposes of several "Japs." When finally he releases his friend's body for burial, he notices that several of his comrades at arms are collecting mementos, "making necklaces of teeth and fingernails." Later he hears that others had boiled Japanese heads "to get the skulls for souvenirs." Unfortunately, these ghoulish practices were not limited to the pages of fiction but were in fact a regular occurrence. In 1944, *Life* magazine published a picture of a young woman with a Japanese skull sent to her by her fiancé, and treated it as a human-interest story.[10]

Rath strives to forget such "incomprehensible" facts of his war experience as he faces life in 1953. He ruminates on the idea that just as the army begins with basic training, it ought to end with "basic forgetting." Rath's experience was not an isolated one. Several advice books and numerous articles in such popular periodicals as *Collier's*, the *Saturday Evening Post*, and *Life* offered strategies for relating to America's troubled veterans.[11]

The legacy of the war was but one powerful force that contributed to the dark shadow of midcentury America. Economic concerns troubled Americans as well. The health of the postwar economy was by no means certain. Rising inflation stirred rumors about the possible return of the Depression, while recession threatened in 1954 and became a reality in 1958. As the war overseas concluded, a labor war stateside began. During late 1945 and early 1946, strikes in the auto and coal industries slowed the nation's economy, while the railroad unions sparked "pandemonium" by threatening full stoppage of service. The various walkouts in these years amounted to the largest labor protest in American history (5 million workers in all) and left doubts about the endurance of wartime unity.[12]

Despite the nation's recession and its labor problems, the war had jumpstarted the economy. Many Americans were flush with wartime savings and ready to treat themselves to more comfortable living after four years of rationing. Yet it seemed that the newfound prosperity created as much anxiety as it alleviated. Postwar wealth, according to an article in *Time*, brought "millions of new homes dotting the countryside, and the tangle of TV antennas atop them; the ribbons of superhighways and the relentless stream of flashy new autos flowing down them." But, *Time* concluded, "wealth has also brought problems." Overproduction, rampant consumerism, and an accelerated pace of life contributed to feelings of dissatisfaction in spite of the material abundance. In addition, the article noted the postwar increases in poverty and crime, foreshadowing Michael Harrington's dismal appraisal of the fortunes of Americans in *The Other America* (1962).[13]

The economic vertigo was, however, only part of the problem. The suburban migration—the second "Great Migration" of the twentieth century—exacerbated these socioeconomic tensions. Eighteen million people moved to the suburbs between 1950 and 1960. By their design, the suburbs greatly reduced the opportunity for social interaction and support within the neighborhood. This massive exodus replaced neighborhoods centered on the corner market and city park with atomized housing developments. The isolation of the suburbs was enhanced by the mobile and transitory nature of the communities, as 25 percent of the population in America moved at least once a year in the midcentury era. The automobile was now king: garages reduced curbside conversations, and residents drove to anonymous shopping centers to purchase goods and services. While suburbanites carved out their slice of the American dream, they hardly could have expected that this radically altered lifestyle would augment feelings of anxiety and alienation.[14]

Suburban malaise was especially acute among women. Women endured an oppressive domestic ideal and, as they joined the labor force at unprecedented rates, worked in uninspired clerical jobs. Women, then, worked a double shift, putting in their nine-to-five only to return home to cook, clean, and care for children. The situation left many women frustrated and bored. For some, alcohol, drugs, and social clubs filled the void. Researchers compiled startling statistics charting the surge in consumption of alcohol and tranquilizers. One suburban woman, as recorded by historian Stephanie Coontz, summarized her experience of the times with a description of "the four b's . . . booze, bowling, bridge and boredom."[15]

While suburban anxiety was certainly a concern, leading postwar intellectuals worried more about American conformity. David Riesman's *The Lonely Crowd* (1950) chronicled the transformation of American character from "inner-direction" to "other-direction." Perhaps more than any other individual, Riesman captured the widespread notion that postwar America was mired in conformity, sparking a whole slew of articles and books concerned about the loss of the American entrepreneurial spirit. William Whyte's *Organization Man* (1956) advanced Riesman's critique with its focus on conformity from the perspective of the "organization man," the corporate cog caught in a mind-numbing bureaucratic career.[16] Although both books were subtler than simple indictments of American conformity, such phrases as "other-direction" and "organization man" quickly caught on and became shorthand for social critics describing the unimaginative masses—often including the religious herd.

Riesman and Whyte, it is important to remember, were part of a larger golden age of public intellectuals. Rarely before or since had intellectuals so powerfully influenced Americans' impressions of themselves and their country. The postwar years saw publication of, among others, Arthur Schlesinger Jr.'s *Vital Center* (1949), Perry Miller's *Jonathan Edwards* (1949), Lionel Trilling's *Liberal Imagination* (1950), William F. Buckley's *God and Man at Yale* (1951), C. Wright Mills's *White Collar* (1951) and *Power Elite* (1956), J. Kenneth Galbraith's *Affluent Society* (1958), Vance Packard's *Status Seekers* (1959), Dwight MacDonald's *Against the American Grain* (1962), and Richard Hofstadter's *Anti-intellectualism in America* (1962). Some historians have classified this intellectual atmosphere as one of consensus and conservatism.[17] Yet these "consensus" scholars cast a critical eye on virtually every aspect of American life. In particular, they stressed themes of human limitation and the dangers of both undue optimism and facile belief in progress. In short, while they may have been careful to avoid rocking the boat, they thoroughly inspected its seaworthiness.

This intense, critical self-consciousness about America also extended to literary spheres. As Russell Lynes, a reviewer for the *New York Times Book Review*, argued in 1959, "I doubt if there has ever been a society as eager as ours to find out what it is, who it is, what it thinks its doing, where it came from and where it belongs." Literary critic Morris Dickstein later echoed Lynes's contention, writing, "Relentless self-criticism, not complacency, was the key to postwar culture." In the same spirit, David Castronovo's *Beyond the Gray Flannel Suit* chronicled the exceedingly rich literary landscape all but forgotten among characterizations of an era supposedly "smug and absorbed with its own splendors."[18] Ralph Ellison's *Invisible Man* (1952), Saul Bellow's *Adventures of Augie March* (1953), Bernard Malamud's *Magic Barrel* (1958), Jim Thompson's *Killer inside Me* (1953), Patricia Highsmith's *Talented Mr. Ripley* (1955), Philip Roth's *Goodbye, Columbus* (1959), John Updike's *Rabbit, Run* (1960), and

Richard Yates's *Revolutionary Road* (1961) are but a few of the titles Castronovo resurrected.

Within this context of self-appraisal, disappointment, and disillusionment, it is little wonder that darker European intellectual traditions became fashionable in America at midcentury. Hannah Arendt, who fled Nazi Germany in 1941, offered a series of provocative titles, including *The Origins of Totalitarianism* (1951) and *The Human Condition* (1958). In 1963, however, she created a stir with her coverage of the trial of Nazi mass murderer Adolf Eichmann for the *New Yorker*, in which she coined the phrase "banality of evil."[19]

Arendt's arresting and controversial investigations into human tyranny and atrocity raised questions about the rationality of human civilization, a question pushed even further by European existentialist philosophers. The existentialist critics Jean-Paul Sartre, Albert Camus, and Samuel Beckett enjoyed wide audiences in the United States. Through their popular novels and plays, the concepts of existentialism—alienation, despair, nothingness, and estrangement—saturated both American and Christian culture. Their renown, coupled with the work of such domestic counterparts as William Barrett, fostered renewed interest in the father of Christian existentialism, the nineteenth-century philosopher Søren Kierkegaard. The popularity of this philosophical import was yet another confirmation that Americans were concerned with the basic questions of human existence.[20]

American exposure to ideas about human alienation and anxiety grew with the rise in the influence of psychology within American life, prompting *Life* to declare the era "The Age of Psychology."[21] Apart from the wounded psyches of many veterans, increasing numbers of men and women found themselves "on the couch."[22] And for those not acquainted with counseling, self-analysis was possible through translations of Sigmund Freud's work and the popular books of such psychologists and psychoanalysts as Erich Fromm, Karen Horney, Abraham Maslow, Karl Menninger, and Harry Stack Sullivan. In fact, by the 1950s, as the business community increasingly adopted psychological techniques in management of employees and in advertising, and Hollywood offered thrillers such as *Psycho* (1960), psychological concepts were a common feature of everyday conversation.[23]

This cultural and social web of psychological awareness reinforced Protestant interest in psychology. Although the Protestant encounter with psychology dates to the early twentieth century—William James's foundational *Varieties of Religious Experience* (1902) spawned a generation of inquiry—the height of the cross-disciplinary dialogue occurred after World War II. Professional journals such as the *Journal of Pastoral Care* and *Pastoral Psychology*, both founded after the war, became leading forums for religious-psychological inquiry. Meanwhile, scholars like Seward Hiltner, Paul E. Johnson, Wayne E. Oates, David E. Roberts, and Carroll A. Wise guided the development of a new, psychologically informed specialty in ministry, pastoral theology.

Taken together, these intellectuals, novelists, psychologists, and pastoral theologians contributed—some more critically than others—to the midcentury American predilection toward careful scrutiny of the social body and the self. And in their different critical approaches to corporate and individual life, they nevertheless raised some common themes. They conveyed skepticism about and suspicion of notions of progress, optimism, and certainty while stressing the ambiguity, limitation, and evil that seemed to govern human affairs. These themes were not at all foreign to the doctrine of original sin, and this critical context partly explains why the doctrine fell on fertile cultural ground after World War II.

⁜ Outside of such intellectual circles, the burgeoning religious self-help movement further popularized or, as its critics argued, vulgarized the dialogue between psychology and religion. Rabbi Joshua Loth Liebman almost single-handedly created the postwar religious self-help movement with *Peace of Mind* (1946). The best-selling book opened the door for Protestant imitators of Liebman's message. Several of these texts jumped off the presses in the postwar era, including, among others, Claude Bristol's *Magic of Believing* (1948), James Keller's *You Can Change the World!* (1948), Harry Overstreet's *Mature Mind* (1949), Peter Marshall's *Meet the Master* (1949), and Charles L. Allen's *God's Psychiatry* (1953). These books and their message of religious optimism embodied the spirit of the captive revival.

Norman Vincent Peale, however, was the undisputed leader of the Protestant self-help movement and consequently of the captive revival. Influenced by his collaborator, psychoanalyst Smiley Blanton—the last of Freud's students—Peale offered a version of Protestantism consistent with his colleague's first name: faith coupled with "positive thinking" produced smiles and success. Peale, a former journalist and midwestern transplant to New York City, arrived at the Reformed pulpit of Marble Collegiate Church in Manhattan in 1932—the same year Niebuhr pub-

lished his landmark *Moral Man and Immoral Society*. Peale's gospel of optimism departed from the usual strict Calvinism of the Reformed Church
and drew more from his own brand of Methodist perfectionism, although
John Wesley would have hardly recognized Peale's Methodism. Peale's
view of sin was the telltale sign that he had little use for either Calvin or
Wesley. For him, sin was not an intractable condition, but a defect in
personality that could be improved upon by positive patterns of thought.[24]

Peale's rise to the pinnacle of Protestant culture in postwar America
came after years of crafting his message. In the 1930s, though his radio
broadcast, *Art of Living*, boasted a large audience, sales of his book by the
same title were disappointing. But Peale found his voice and his vast
audience after the war. His breakthrough came with his founding of
Guideposts magazine in 1945. Peale modeled the publication after the
popular monthly *Reader's Digest*, but *Guideposts* focused almost exclusively on inspirational human-interest stories. Its pages teemed with first-
person accounts of businessmen, sports figures, and occasionally housewives whose lives were transformed by the power of Christianity. The
stories followed a similar pattern: individuals plagued by feelings of help-
lessness and meaninglessness discovered Christ's healing answer and experienced renewal and personal success. Perhaps encouraged by the success of *Guideposts* and by the strong sales of Liebman's *Peace of Mind*, Peale
joined the self-help book industry with *A Guide To Confident Living* (1948).
Unlike *The Art of Living*, the book sold well, and Peale soon came to
dominate the captive revival.

By the 1950s and 1960s, Peale controlled a well-being empire. Circulation of *Guideposts* surged: by 1953, five hundred thousand Americans
subscribed. Its pages revealed that Peale had mastered the religious rags-to-
riches message he had been cultivating since the 1930s. The spiritual
reversal of fortune, according to Peale, materialized into literal fortunes:
from abundant health and well-being to financial security to improved
social and familial relationships. The spike in readership of *Guideposts*
correlated to the publication and record-breaking sales of his *Power of
Positive Thinking* in 1952.[25] At the same time, Peale added a syndicated
newspaper column, an advice column in *Look* magazine, and a network
television show, *What's Your Trouble*, to his media résumé. Meanwhile, his
radio program, *The Art of Living*, remained popular. Somehow, to his credit,
he still found time to preach twice on Sundays to his four-thousand-
member Marble Collegiate Church in Manhattan. A reporter for *Look*

captured Peale's tremendous presence within the culture by calling him the "Minister to Millions."[26]

In all of these media, Peale's status as the foremost preacher of American cultural values was unmistakable. He openly and uncritically celebrated the American Way of Life. For Peale, the United States was a beacon to the world, and capitalism was the backbone of the nation's greatness. More than any other postwar Protestant leader, Peale advocated free markets, aggressively pursuing contacts with businessmen and favoring ministry to the white-collar world.[27] His books and articles resembled a business model, manufacturing positive-thinking Christians with an assembly-line methodology. No personal struggle was too great for Peale's essential message of optimism and its corresponding three-step plan: "(1) Prayerize, (2) Picturize, (3) Actualize." For Peale this formula resolutely solved any number of problems, even the problem of sin. He argued that this "one-two-three how procedure" changed "people whose lives were very bad" into "very good people."[28]

The renown of Peale's message within American culture was indeed impressive. His emphasis on the joy of Protestant belief even caught the eye of the entertainment industry. Columbia studios filmed *The Norman Vincent Peale Story* in 1963, starring Don Murray (*The Robe*, 1953) as Peale. Peale's iconic status inspired another entertainer of sorts, a stripper who dubbed herself Norma Vincent Peel.[29]

Peale's omnipresence and his popularity explain why scholars, both then and now, have largely classified postwar piety under the heading of cultural captivity. At the same time, secular and Christian commentators alike blasted Peale's sunny optimism and utilitarian gospel. The "Peale debate" as it came to be called, reached its climax in the mid-fifties when publications as diverse as the *Atlantic Monthly*, the *Reporter*, *Religion in Life*, *Saturday Review*, the *New Republic*, *Redbook*, *Time*, and *Life* all published rather scathing reviews of his work. Critics called him "God's Salesman" and "the Confidence Man," and they identified him as the "high priest" of the "Cult of Reassurance." One article compared him to the sin-denying fifth-century theologian Pelagius, asking "is Pelagius the Latin spelling for Peale?"[30] The most frequent charge leveled at Peale was that his see-no-evil, hear-no-evil approach offered nothing but a pseudo-Christian Pollyanna Gospel unfit for the ambiguous realities of midcentury life.

The commentaries were brutally direct, none more so than an article in the *Reporter* entitled "Some Negative Thinking about Norman Vincent Peale," by William Lee Miller, who later became a religious ethics professor. In preparation for his piece, Miller read five of Peale's books, including *The Power of Positive Thinking*, and advised: "Let me say, in the unlikely event that anyone else would undertake this redundant inspirational feat, that it isn't necessary. If you have read one, you have read them all." *Time*'s customary tongue-in-cheek editorial bias went beyond friendly sarcasm when it reviewed Peale's "prayerize, picturize, actualize" method. Such advice, the editors concluded, deserved a "fourth possible heading, Pasteurize."[31] Peter Williams's article in *Redbook* "The Case against 'Easy' Religion" outlined by then familiar denunciations of Peale's ministry and marshaled the quotations of several Christian leaders to illustrate the positive thinker's shallow Gospel. According to biographer Carol George, Peale was surprised and dismayed by this disdain for his work. He took such offense at Williams's treatment of his ministry that he considered resigning as pastor of Marble Collegiate Church and thought of pursuing his evangelism outside the confines of mainstream liberal Christianity.[32]

Niebuhr and Tillich agreed with Peale's critics and would have welcomed Peale's departure from Marble since they considered him an apologist for Americanism, not Protestantism. Although Niebuhr and Tillich rarely bothered to comment on Peale's ministry, they nevertheless distinguished his version of the Gospel from Graham's more authentic Christianity. This distinction irritated Peale, and in one instance, he dashed off a letter to Tillich in protest. Peale questioned Tillich's honor as a gentleman for his preference for Graham, and Peale objected to Tillich's characterization that he catered exclusively to businessmen. He argued further that Tillich was obviously not familiar with his work, clarifying that he "certainly [did] not teach this superficial sort of thing." Tillich replied respectfully, but stood firm and noted that his view of Peale was "obvious if one analyzes your writings and your work."[33]

For his part, Graham, always ecumenical and cordial, acknowledged the tremendous success of Peale's ministry. But Graham was otherwise careful to distinguish his work from Peale's. Peale did not reciprocate, remarking in the early fifties—apparently without a sense of irony—that Graham was "of the sensational type which I never took to much myself." Their most visible cooperation occurred during Graham's 1957 New York City crusade. Peale sat on the board of the Protestant Council of New York City that had invited Graham to conduct his campaign. Peale's wife, Ruth, partnered with the Graham Evangelistic team and oversaw the training of the lay counselors for the crusade. And in a dramatic, if somewhat curious moment, Peale strode up to the podium one night in response to Graham's usual invitation to accept Christ. Peale hardly seems to have felt that Graham "saved" him, as he later characterized their relationship as friendly, though never close.[34] Graham's polite attitude toward Peale was not mirrored by contributors to *Christianity Today*, two of whom asserted that Peale's message was un-Christian.[35]

This chorus of protest has been either overlooked or misinterpreted by those who proclaim Peale's dominance of Protestantism and, by extension, the superficiality of belief at midcentury. These critical voices were not crying into the wilderness. The publications that aired their critiques —especially *Life, Time,* and *Redbook*—were read by everyday Americans. And while many readers defended Peale in letters to the editors of these and other periodicals, at least as many congratulated the magazines for their skeptical articles about his message.[36]

Most contemporary scholars have missed another significant point in their analysis of Peale as a representative of large swaths of American Protestants. His ministry and the captive revival as a whole were similar to the theological revival in one respect: both were responses to the Age of Anxiety. To be sure, proponents of the theological revival—especially Niebuhr, Graham, and Tillich—offered an answer that differed radically from the one propounded by Peale. But Peale's followers were no less representative of the anguished search for meaning in an uncertain era.

Some of the more balanced accounts of Peale's ministry from the 1950s recognized that underlying spiritual distress was a motivating force behind Americans' interest in his gospel of optimism. Writing for *Life* in 1955, Paul Hutchinson, editor of the *Christian Century*, disapproved of Peale's "cult of reassurance," yet he also reproached mainline Protestantism for neglecting the needs of average believers. Peale's popularity revealed that large numbers of Americans were filled with anxiety and searching for answers to individual crises. For Hutchinson, Peale's success called the churches to more effective ministry, lest Protestantism be overrun by reassurance instead of redemption.[37] Kenneth Hamilton made a similar point in a less critical piece for *Theology and Life*, a United Church of Christ journal, in 1959. He argued that Peale and Tillich shared some "common ground." Although the comparison was misguided in many respects, Hamilton correctly pointed out that both Peale's and Tillich's work targeted the rampant "soul-sickness" of the postwar era.[38]

Carol George echoed these contentions in her biography of Peale three decades later. She noted that the "archetypal reader" of *Guideposts* was "the beleaguered middle-class victim of the crush of modernism." George further surmised that *The Power of Positive Thinking* sold so well because, according to her survey of the avalanche of letters to Peale, readers "felt they were leading shriveled, diminished lives."[39] Pealeites, it would seem, were not all happy-go-lucky individuals, ignoring the pain of life through the narcotic of Protestant good cheer.

What Hutchinson, Hamilton, and George described was the general cultural malaise of the Age of Anxiety. Like Peale, Niebuhr, Graham, and Tillich ministered to the anxieties of Americans. Unlike Peale, however, they explained the situation as a function of sin, and their respective teaching and writing in this vein placed them squarely within the theological revival.

✠ The theological revival arose in part as criticism of and a reaction against the captive revival and the likes of Norman Vincent Peale. Indeed, both revivals, by virtue of their competition and intersection within the culture, made for a complex Protestant landscape in which each wielded influence over the spiritual lives of Americans. Reinhold Niebuhr, Billy Graham, and Paul Tillich were, to be sure, the stars of the theological revival. The "crisis theology" of Niebuhr and Tillich resonated with the atmosphere of the period, from the crisis of meaning and individuality to the crisis of nuclear proliferation. For his part, Graham preached an evangelical version of crisis theology. True to the evangelical tradition, Graham focused principally on the crisis of the self and the need for individual repentance. But he, like Niebuhr and Tillich, located the wider national and international crises, albeit with less sophistication, in the context of the doctrine of original sin.

The theological revival, however, has been largely overlooked in studies of the period. Pealeism, the popularity of peace-of-mind religion, and the abundance of religious kitsch have suggested an undiscriminating Protestant culture to most commentators, both then and now. Several conspicuous Protestant artifacts—including the best-selling *Pray Your Weight Away* (1957), the Dial-A-Prayer telephone network, pop songs such as *The Man Upstairs*, and drive-in worship services—were and are easy targets for those who decry the inanity of postwar Protestantism.[40]

No aspect of American religious life, however, drew as much criticism as suburban Christianity. Throughout the postwar decades, critics blasted the oppressive, conformist atmosphere of the bedroom communities and often dismissed the suburban church as little more than a social club, where parishioners worshipped a domesticated God. Stanley Rowland of the *New York Times* provided a particularly acerbic account of suburban faith in his 1956 article "Suburbia Buys Religion." He openly mocked "the homogenized suburbanite" who, as he put it, "likes his religion, unlike his martinis, diluted." Gibson Winter, professor of ethics at the University of Chicago, later completed the vilification of suburban religion with his publication of *The Suburban Captivity of the Churches* (1961).[41]

Though there was certainly evidence to support this criticism, the conventional narrative of the "captivity" of suburban Christianity has been overplayed. In fact, Rowland offered in the same article a counter-argument to his own stinging critique of the suburban religious situation. Although he colorfully described the banality of suburbanite faith—heaven was "scrubbed in detergent" and the mood of Sunday services was like "that of a fashionable shopping center"—Rowland also reported, consistent with his "top of the iceberg" analysis, that suburban church-goers attended services "at least partly because they want to learn something about God, not because they want a sophisticated emotional bang or a lesson in the power of positive promotion." Moreover, he observed, the "suburban church worries the living daylights out of [the clergy]."[42] Rowland's suggestions of a sincere interest in God and a clergy troubled by a supposedly "diluted" suburban Protestantism thus cast doubt on the convention of suburban captivity even as he sought to confirm it.

Rowland was correct in reporting that the suburban church worried the clergy. Several articles in *Time*, the *Christian Century*, and *Christianity and Crisis* indicted these congregations as the locus of captive religiosity. Predictably, *Christianity and Crisis*, the mouthpiece of American neo-orthodoxy, led the charge in 1956 with its front-page article "Euphoria in Suburbia." The author, Pastor Waldo Beach, declared that in the suburbs, "No one hears any thunder"—instead, everyone considers Jesus largely "as a friend and helper, kind and good." Beach further argued that the suburban church featured only generalized sermons and had become a site of respectability instead of redemption.[43]

Beach's article and others like it struck William Farmer, a professor at Drew Theological Seminary, as excessively cynical. Fed up with characterizations of the suburbs as a spiritual wasteland, Farmer challenged the assumptions of critics like Beach and accused them of irresponsibly fostering clichés about the suburban church. With an "air of superiority," Farmer asserted, the religious commentators, church leaders, and theological professors of the day critiqued the religious scene from "behind their polished desks," seemingly "completely out of touch" with the happenings of the average parish.

The cynics' favorite pastime, wrote Farmer, was taking "potshots at the Grahams and the Peales" without attempting in the least to understand their popularity. While Farmer distinguished Graham's biblical ministry from Peale's self-help approach—he had "very serious reservations about Peale"—he noted that critics of their work showed disregard for the spiritual hunger of the average American. The vast popularity of both Graham and Peale, Farmer argued, revealed not just a desire for "easy security" among believers but also an openness to the true Gospel of judgment and mercy. Smug critics of Graham and Peale were missing an opportunity for evangelism. In fact, the cynics failed to recognize the ironic truth revealed by their very criticism: Peale's popularity was less a reflection of the average Protestant's superficiality than a sign of the failure of "our ministry, our preaching, our worship services." In short, though Farmer appreciated the need for critical evaluations of Protestantism, he hoped for assessments free from preconceptions and for a constructive program of evangelism from the readers of Christianity and Crisis.[44]

Farmer's challenge to Beach and his fellow cynics exposed their reliance on the myths of suburbia and the straw men of Graham and Peale in their attacks on midcentury Protestantism. A suburban pastor from California reinforced Farmer's point in a letter to Christianity and Crisis. He argued that what the churches needed was guidance: "Pray for us, brethren, help us—don't just slam us!"[45] The critics' "slam" of suburbia distorted as much as it clarified. It unfairly damned the faith of large numbers of American Protestants, erroneously conflated Graham and Peale, and did so without consulting the laity beyond a few opinion polls.

Farmer's call for an end to hearsay and cynicism in evaluations of suburban religion applies equally to discussions of the religious kitsch of Protestant-themed weight loss and other sensational ephemera of the period. Unfortunately, perhaps because of their novelty, these images still permeate the history of Protestantism after World War II. Consequently, a majority of American Protestants has been grouped under the "captive" label and unfairly portrayed as superficially devout. The Dial-A-Prayer telephone network is a case in point. Although perhaps not representative of refined spirituality, the network nevertheless proved tremendously important for untold Americans.[46] The point here is not to recover the hidden profundity of Dial-A-Prayer, or any of the spiritual kitsch of the period, but to push beyond these clichéd artifacts and to probe the theological revival that heretofore has been marginalized by an overwhelming focus on the captive revival.

Although perhaps less noticeable than the captive revival, the theological revival was readily identifiable in the postwar years. To be sure, some of the strongest indicators of the theological revival were less conspicuous than captive material such as *The Power of Prayer on Plants* or Peale's "one-two-three how" approach to Christianity. For obvious reasons, signs of the theological revival like the increase in the number of lay-driven organizations and especially the widespread "Liturgical Renaissance" that followed World War II have merited less attention than the more eye-catching aspects of the captive revival.[47] Still, manifestations of the theological revival were numerous, some of them even quite striking, within the vast corpus of commentary on Protestantism in the 1940s, 1950s, and 1960s.

The most obvious indicator of a theological revival—literally—was the publication of the Revised Standard Version of the Bible in 1952. It topped the nonfiction best seller charts in the 1950s, with millions of copies sold. Whether the Bible was more than a paperweight in most households was another matter. Critics doubted both the worth of the new translation and the average Christian's commitment to study of the text. Appalled by the trend toward popularization in the 1950s, the unapologetically highbrow critic Dwight Macdonald likened the easier language of the new Bible to "taking apart Westminster Abbey to make Disneyland out of the fragments." Will Herberg, of course, had made much ado about the American inability to name any of the four Gospels. Subsequent scholarship, though, has shown that knowledge of the Bible increased in these years, due in part to a surging evangelical population that boasted an excellent command of the Scriptures.[48]

The theological revival, however, both preceded and followed the publication of the Revised Standard Bible. In fact, in each of the decades of the 1940s, 1950s, and 1960s, the print world of mainstream magazines—both secular and Christian—and publishing houses chronicled its existence both as an independent movement within Protestantism and as a corrective to the captive revival.

As early as the mid-1940s, a general theological awakening had taken root in America, at least according to the German theologian Emil Brunner. Comparing his impressions of the religious scene in America in 1946 to those from his previous visit in 1939, Brunner observed that a vital theology had tempered the "social-service Christianity" he had noted seven years earlier. He reported further that this lively theological disposition, while most obvious among seminarians and intellectuals, had reached into the lives of the general public as well.[49]

Other sources confirmed Brunner's view and indicated that the issue of human nature was a chief theological concern of many Americans. In the thousands of letters that poured into the office of National Radio Pulpit preacher Ralph W. Sockman each week in 1946, many writers expressed worry over "free will and their ability to control their destiny." Concern over the freedom or the bondage of the will resurfaced a year later in 1947, when *Time* pondered the possibility of a "Calvinist Comeback?" The article noted that the theology of Niebuhr, Tillich, and others had vindicated the "Pauline-Augustinian-Calvinistic view of human nature," leading the author to wonder whether Calvin's doctrine of the "total depravity of man" had made a comeback. He was satisfied that it had, writing that Calvin's call for men to repent from idolatry, the "greatest and root sin," carried new weight in postwar America.[50] A decade later, the importance of sin to American culture was still making news. Under the headline "Sin's Return," *Time* again carried a story on the doctrine's relevance. It came in a review of historian Arnold Toynbee's multivolume *Study of History*. The reviewer highlighted Toynbee's contention that "original sin has come back with a vengeance, after several centuries of apparent banishment."[51]

Time's sister publication, *Life* magazine, also bore witness to and even participated in the theological revival in the 1940s. In 1947, for example, editors at *Life* printed what amounted to a sermon for the periodical's millions of readers. Its text was John 3:3: " 'Except a man be born again, he cannot see the kingdom of God.' " Careful to disabuse readers of the idea that faith correlated simply to the idea of the Golden Rule, the editors stressed the transcendence of God: "Without that Fatherhood, man's efforts to live by the light of altruism have always landed him in its dark opposite."[52]

Dark themes continued to preoccupy *Life*, which published an exposé of the devil in 1948. The author, Whittaker Chambers—who later gained notoriety as the key witness against Alger Hiss—argued that any apparent meaninglessness in the world could be traced to the devil. Chambers wrote the piece in dialogue form, a conversation between the devil and the "pessimist." As the conversation proceeded, Chambers noted that since the advent of the "Age of Reason," the prince of darkness had succeeded in making "men think he doesn't even exist" and thus was able to practice his handiwork freely.

Chambers intended the dialogue as a dramatic warning to his readers to wake up to the crafty power of evil. For the devil wrought destruction not only overtly but also, still more devastatingly, covertly. At one point, the devil revealed his master plan to the "pessimist": "I saw that Hell must write Progress on its banners and Science in its methods." The devil further explained the brilliance of his plan: "To destroy man by seducing him through good." In short, what man considered good, including progress, science, rationalism—and according to Chambers at his most conservative, "liberalism and universal compulsory education"—were the most efficient tools for the demolition of civilization.[53]

Hope, however, was not lost. Chambers's pessimist challenged the devil's pronouncements with the works of Reinhold Niebuhr and C. S. Lewis. Niebuhr's two-volume *Nature and Destiny of Man* (1941, 1943), for Chambers, had fully chronicled the exploits of sin, the failures of liberalism, and the forces of evil. Lewis's international sensation, *The Screwtape Letters* (1941), had humorously yet profoundly depicted the ministrations of evil. Both books, in other words, would serve as an obstacle to the devil because of their clear acknowledgment of the reality of sin and evil in the world. By the end of the piece, the pessimist had joined Niebuhr and Lewis in predicting Christianity's ultimate triumph over the devil, reasoning that God would perennially create good out of evil. To make his point, the pessimist quoted from Arnold Toynbee's magisterial *Study of History* (1946): "In the language of Mythology, when one of God's creatures is tempted by the Devil, God Himself is thereby given the opportunity to re-create the World." Shaken for a moment, the devil recognizes that man, by the grace of God, has the capacity to work creatively toward goodness despite his suffering. Yet the devil regains his poise and, noting the implausibility of such faith, remarks, "I have never felt my chances [for success] to be so good."[54]

For all his melodrama and conservatism, Chambers's concern about the reality of evil and his admiration for Niebuhr were genuine. In March 1948, one month after the *Life* article, he wrote the piece in *Time* that accompanied Niebuhr's famous "Man's Story Is Not a Success Story" cover. Historian James Hudnut-Beumler has made much of this twenty-fifth anniversary cover, contrasting it with the prior anniversary edition of *Time*, which had featured John Dewey. Dewey's faith in the goodness of humanity and Niebuhr's deep convictions about sin and the ambiguity of human nature—issues the two New York scholars had sparred over—were, according to Hudnut-Beumler, symbolic of an intellectual, if not cultural, transformation.[55] Neither goodness nor progress was assumed in American society in the postwar era.

Also in 1948, the problems of human nature and progress captured vividly by Niebuhr's and Dewey's *Time* covers were just as dramatically, if less popularly, addressed in the pages of the Methodist periodical *Zion's Herald*. In "A Plea for Human Nature," Pastor Charles G. Girelius implored his fellow Methodists to recognize the goodness of humanity. He allowed that humans had "shortcomings and limitations" but continued, "human nature has proved that it is changeable, that it has capacity for unlimited progress, that it is adaptable to circumstances, that it can be trained and educated." Several of the *Herald*'s readers disagreed. One layman vigorously disputed Girelius's malleable view of human nature: "The writer did an excellent job of proving the obvious fact that man has been able to make great advancements in the areas of science, industry, economics, social action, etc. Yet this begs the point. It doesn't prove that the heart of man has improved morally—it is still as sinfully wretched in its nature as it ever was, in spite of what has been accomplished in other ways. The devil himself is most intelligent and can make progress in many ways, but his evil nature too would motivate him to use the atom bomb."[56]

In the 1950s, the captive and theological revivals continued to coexist and often shared space in articles and books on midcentury Protestantism. A 1950 article in *Look* about the "new look" of the Presbyterian Church, for example, unwittingly reported on both phenomena. The author detailed the shifting of the Presbyterian Church's focus away from "gloomy sentiments" about man's nature and precarious position before a wrathful God and toward God's love. The transition produced an "atmosphere of optimism" and an "aura of alert well-being," not to mention growth in church membership. At the same time, according to the article, sin continued to occupy the attention of the church; the emphasis, however, was not on "'worldly sins'" such as smoking, drinking, dancing, and "gayety in general," but on corporate sin. The church's deemphasis of God's wrath and its concern with social problems bore the hallmarks of early twentieth-century "liberal" theology. This focus on the social matrix of sin demonstrated a less moralistic understanding of sin, one not obsessed with individual transgressions but rather concerned with the wider context of sin. But, as one midwestern pastor noted in a letter to *Look*, the article had generalized too freely: "Presbyterians still know from the ample evidence in the world today that man—outside of [a] right relationship with God and his fellows—is either a proud sinner or a vicious one."[57]

Look returned to the theme of sin a few years later in 1952. A banner headline announced that America was "losing the battle against sin." The "sin" in this case was prostitution. More sensationalism than religious discussion, the piece ranked American cities on a scale from "Good" to "Fair" to "Poor" to "Bad," depending on their degree of "open toleration of sin [prostitution]." The lurid account of America's sex trade—complete with a dramatized photo of an American serviceman being ogled by a seductively posed young woman—was somewhat anomalous in comparison with *Look*'s substantive coverage of sin in religious contexts.

For example, *Look* published two intensive, multiyear studies on religion in America that ran from 1952 to 1955 and from 1958 to 1960. Both series consisted of lengthy stories on upward of a dozen Christian denominations and sects. The articles outlined the basic tenets of each denomination, including its view of sin. Not every major Protestant denomination accepted the doctrine of original sin—for example, the Disciples of Christ—but Baptists, Congregationalists, Episcopalians, Lutherans, Methodists, Presbyterians, and even the Disciples of Christ, according to the articles, shared a basic belief in the inescapable sinfulness of humanity.

Look's studies were by no means conclusive or entirely accurate. The editors received correspondence from both clergy and laity correcting errors in the periodical's representations of the different Christian expressions (yet another indication of a dedicated church community). The articles also described, usually unwittingly, some tendencies toward captivity within mainstream Protestantism. Sin, though, had an unmistakable presence in each article.[58]

The mixed messages in *Look*'s surveys of postwar Protestantism were hardly unique. Two important reviews of Protestantism after the war, the Methodist Murray H. Leiffer's *The Layman Looks at the Minister* (1947) and J. Paul Williams's *What Americans Believe and How They Worship* (1952), chronicled definite captive trends within the church. Both studies, however, revealed that Protestants expected more than a peace-of-mind gospel. The Methodist study, though rife with moralistic conceptions of sin—for example, parishioners frowned upon dancing at church socials, alcohol, and overweight ministers—nevertheless indicated that the church's congregations objected to "Pollyanna" presentations of the faith.[59] Though somewhat contradictory, the survey's conclusion regarding the undesirability of Pollyanna Methodism matched the view of another commentator writing on the denomination. In a retrospective of Methodism from 1900 to 1950, a theologian writing for *Zion's Herald* highlighted the church's share "in the general theological trend of a new emphasis on a God-centered gospel," one that replaced "superficial optimism and secular confidence in man's unaided power, and an immoral belief in automatic progress."[60]

Like the Methodist survey, Williams's more widely respected and cited portrait of Protestant belief generally reinforced the notion of a captive revival. He characterized the majority of Protestants as beset by "mild," "middle-of-the-road" convictions. Yet Williams also observed that this same majority believed "that men are more prone to do evil than to do good."[61] This curious statement, sandwiched between comments about the placid faith of American Protestants, leaps off the page. Apparently, according to Williams, this majority of Protestants possessed of only a "mild" faith nevertheless believed in original sin. He explained this phenomenon by noting the rising influence of neo-orthodoxy, the theological movement associated with Niebuhr, Tillich, and others and known for its reemphasis on the doctrine of sin. As he put it, "Neo-orthodoxy is the current theological rage."[62]

Williams's hypothesis was plausible in light of the continued references to original sin in periodicals of all types. Writing for the *Christian Century* in 1953, Winthrop Hudson echoed Williams in a tribute to the renowned social-gospel theologian Walter Rauschenbusch. Hudson concluded that Rauschenbusch's articulation of the reality of original sin and his grave warnings against ideas of human progress in the early twentieth century were now commonplace. "Today," Hudson suggested, "we no longer need to be cautioned against undue optimism."[63] A year later, an editorialist in *Christianity and Crisis*—the periodical founded by Niebuhr and others—corroborated Williams's and Hudson's views, opining that Protestants were more concerned with "Sin" than they were moralistically preoccupied with "sins."

By the mid- to late fifties, a host of articles continued to draw attention to the theological revival that ran parallel to and was often intertwined with the captive revival. Writing for the *Reporter* in 1955, William Lee Miller observed that Henry Luce's *Life* and *Time* magazines liked religion and "especially like[d] the doctrine of original sin."[64] Although Miller intended to criticize the faddishness of these popular periodicals in their theological leanings, his skepticism was overdrawn. *Time* and *Life*, while not flawless in their religious coverage, "liked" original sin because it was a doctrine relevant to and reflective of the beliefs of a large segment of midcentury Protestants.

That same year, Eugene Carson Blake, president of the National Council of Churches, kept sin in the public eye in an article for *Look*. In reference to "peace-of-mind" religion, he queried, "Is the ancient sin of idolatry once more among us?" Drawing on Will Herberg, he continued his interrogation of idolatry, commenting that if Christians confused "the American Way of Life with the kingdom of God, a preacher feels like asking: 'Do you really think God is an American?' "[65]

According to a major feature in *Newsweek*, the answer to Blake's latter question was yes. The piece rather uncritically documented certain indices of Protestant strength, conflated the contributions of Peale and Niebuhr, and asserted that Protestant principles were "embedded in America's historical base . . . woven into its national conduct, and . . . implicit in the voice with which it addresses the world." Despite these highly dubious judgments, the article credited a dedicated corps of preachers and parishioners for Protestantism's resurgence and praised the "new and powerful grip" that believers had on Christian "theology and its gospel." Furthermore, its explanation of the union between America and Protestantism, while self-congratulatory, named the doctrine of original sin as the reason for American success. Indeed, the "first principle" of Protestant America was the Puritan contention, inspired by John Calvin, that "human nature was inherently evil." So crucial was this Calvinist insight, according to *Newsweek*, that without it, "the government of the United States of America would have been neither as stable nor as just as it has turned out to be."[66] Whether read as complacency with the virtue of America or not, the article tied the nation's destiny to the doctrine of original sin.

This renewed theological interest in sin was an unwelcome development for some Protestant liberals. Writing for the *Christian Century*, Roy A. Burkhart bemoaned the renewed emphasis on sin in a lively article. Consistent with at least one strain of liberal theology, Burkhart accepted human sin as a fact of life, but he believed that humans were born "good" and could progressively realize that goodness. For Burkhart, the corruption of humanity was not a function of some inherent defect but of unjust environmental factors. In short, Burkhart argued that improved efforts toward cultivating love and stability ensured human goodness and ultimately freed humans from "anxiety and fear."[67]

Fellow liberal Lloyd J. Averill Jr. roundly criticized Burkhart's position in a subsequent issue of the *Century*. Averill defended neo-orthodoxy and Reinhold Niebuhr—Burkhart's unnamed target—though he stressed his own continued allegiance to theological liberalism. Averill argued that Burkhart had misrepresented the current emphasis on sin as defeatist, and he lamented his peer's unabashedly optimistic theology that, as he put it, "we liberals had long since left behind." Averill contended that Niebuhr's theology was both optimistic and pessimistic about human nature, cognizant of both humanity's self-transcendence and its finitude. Downplaying one at the expense of the other jeopardized not only communication with the ordinary believer—who, he contended, felt the sting of sin acutely—but also the integrity of the Gospel. "Whether liberal preachers like it or not," wrote Averill, "the sense of sin and guilt is real in modern life." Promoting Burkhart's "healthy" theology complicated the existing "disease" of mankind and rendered the "central event in the Christian drama, the Incarnation," powerless. In other words, offering redemption through psychology, sociology, and adjustment, as Burkhart seemed to do, only compounded the problem. It was not that these modern approaches to individual and social ills were bad in and of themselves, but they were designed for "readjustment, not rebirth." Furthermore, they too often reinforced the illusion of the perfect life, whereas "Jesus, the moral exemplar," mocked the notion of a perfect life and instead promised a new life through salvation.[68]

The Correspondence column of the *Christian Century* filled with reactions to the Burkhart-Averill debate. Overall, pastors responded favorably to Burkhart's position. Averill had his share of supporters, as well, and those who criticized him focused mainly on what they judged to be the combative tone of his article. Some extreme views also appeared in the correspondence to the *Century*; one staunchly liberal writer argued that humans could eventually achieve harmony throughout the world, while a skeptic questioned whether Burkhart was actually a Christian. Another pastor, however, represented the general position of most respondents. He challenged Averill's insistence that sin weighed so heavily on modern man but doubted Burkhart's optimism about human goodness. He argued instead that "a sense of sin and guilt is not the worst thing that can come upon one; the all too prevalent lack of it is far more disastrous."[69]

As the debate between liberal and neo-orthodox theologians and pastors continued, *Newsweek* spotlighted the problem of the human condition in its Christmas issue of 1957. Readers were greeted with a cover entirely blank, save for a verse from Luke's Gospel: "And the angel said unto them, Fear not." The corresponding article opened with a laundry list of national problems. Americans suffered "feelings of fear and anxiety" and were "perplexed and unsettled" by international and domestic uncertainties, though some were "apathetic in the face of great events." The article may have been inspired in part by the Soviet Union's successful launch of *Sputnik* earlier that year, an event that had embarrassed Americans and challenged their sense of international supremacy. The piece, however, made no mention of the Soviet triumph and seemed more concerned with the theological disposition of its readers. It warned that "Christianity offers no easy cure for the evil of the world, nor any rapid antidote for fear. Its concern is with eternity, not with panaceas." If American believers heeded this warning, they might experience the "most sober, most profound, and perhaps the most rewarding" holiday season in the nation's history.

The balance of the article featured the testimonies of leading national and international Christian thinkers concerning the collective fear and anxiety felt throughout the world. After dismissing Pealeism as inadequate, the author quoted Niebuhr at length. In these times, the church's duty, while perhaps "heavier now," had not changed: "It should teach that men always have a dignity beyond nature, but that they are also miserable creatures." What saved humanity from itself was "faith that God has given a meaning to existence no matter what comes." Niebuhr's statement introduced several equally foreboding, yet prophetic, comments from such church leaders as Ralph W. Sockman, the popular American radio minister; Walter Robert Mathews, the dean of St. Paul's Cathedral in London; and Karl Barth, the world-renowned European theologian.

Paul Tillich also numbered among the esteemed commentators. He interpreted the Gospel passage bluntly: "I've heard too much sentimental nonsense about Christmas and the easing of fear. . . . Anxiety is a state of man." To withstand the unceasingly anxious situation of man, Tillich prescribed the courage of faith: "the courage of the human being who feels all the riddles and all the meaninglessness of life, and who, nevertheless, is able to say 'yes' to life."[70] The article concluded with three additional variations on the theme of Christian fortitude, driving home its thesis that Christianity offered no "easy cure" for the tragedies of human life and community.

Unlike the mainstream periodicals, the majority of Protestant denominational magazines were not often embroiled in the national conversation about captive or theological trends. Reporting in these periodicals favored the internal news of the journals' respective denominations. There was, however, no shortage of options. Protestant denominational and independent publications dominated the nearly fourteen hundred religious periodicals in circulation after the war. Some of these had large readerships. *Presbyterian Life*, for instance, delivered more than eight hundred thousand issues to churches and private homes, while the Methodist Church's *Midmonth Magazine for Methodist Families* had seven hundred thousand subscribers. Of the nondenominational Protestant periodicals, the *Christian Herald* had the largest circulation, with four hundred thousand subscribers.[71] But the *Herald* read much like a denominational magazine: its articles were narrow in scope and rarely ventured into theological battlegrounds.

When national church issues and matters of theology did arise, these periodicals usually referenced the three most influential Protestant magazines of the day: the *Christian Century*, *Christianity Today*, and *Christianity and Crisis*. The *Christian Herald*, for example, although it was older and more captive in tone—and had twice the circulation of *Christianity Today*—often deferred to the authority of its more sophisticated evangelical counterpart. The editors of many other denominational magazines followed suit, frequently reprinting articles carried first in one of the three flagship magazines. Consequently, the three distinct conduits of the theological revival—the liberal *Christian Century*, the evangelical *Christianity Today*, and the neo-orthodox *Christianity and Crisis*—shaped theological issues for a readership that ranged far beyond those who actually subscribed to the magazines.[72]

The audiences who subscribed to Christian periodicals bought religious-themed books as well. Sales of religious nonfiction spiked after the war, creating a lucrative publishing niche. Both captive and theological titles rolled off the presses, many becoming best sellers.

Books such as Liebman's *Peace of Mind* (1946) and Peale's *Guide to Confident Living* (1948) had helped jumpstart the growth of religious book publishing in the postwar era. The success of the burgeoning Protestant self-help genre encouraged two scholars, Louis Schneider and Sanford Dornbusch, to undertake a full-length study of such literature. Schneider and Dornbusch argued that whereas most popular religious writers after 1940 were gloomy and put great emphasis on forgiveness of sin, the inspirational writers generally stressed themes of happiness, emotional security, and pragmatism and furthered the "instrumentalization of God." Peale, of course, received much attention in the book, while Billy Graham, tellingly, was not included. His work, though quite popular, was evidently not sufficiently "inspirational" for Schneider and Dornbusch. Still, the authors concluded that with few exceptions, "the theological content" of popular religious books was "very thin." This was an unsurprising conclusion: according to Schneider and Dornbusch, theological works were not really "part of popular religious culture."[73]

At first blush, the study seemed to confirm the general captivity of popular Christian literature at midcentury. Yet the exceptions among the writers considered in the book—most notably Harry Emerson Fosdick and Bishop Fulton Sheen—were tremendously significant. Both Fosdick and Sheen offered a decidedly un-captive message in their books and, in Sheen's case, through his enormously popular television show, *Life Is Worth Living*.

Even television, the box synonymous with escapist programming for suburban families, had become a conduit of the theological revival. Between *Life Is Worth Living*, his best-selling *Peace of Soul* (1948), and his radio show, *Catholic Hour*, Sheen rivaled Peale in popularity from the Catholic side of the street. His Catholicism was, however, no barrier to countless Protestants. Believers of all stripes contributed to the success of Sheen's television show, which ran opposite Milton Berle's *Texaco Comedy Hour* and *The Frank Sinatra Show*. To the bewilderment of many in the television business, Sheen often drew larger audiences than either Berle or Sinatra on Tuesday nights. But Sheen's Catholicism prevented him from embracing anything like Peale's optimism about human nature. Although scholars have correctly portrayed Sheen as an anticommunist crusader, the former neo-Thomist philosophy professor as often stressed the crises of sin and meaninglessness on his program. He also approvingly quoted Reinhold Niebuhr on *Catholic Hour*, another indication of his leanings away from the captive camp.[74]

And like Niebuhr, Graham, and Tillich, Sheen made his own appearance on the cover of *Time* magazine in 1952, offering a window into both his popularity and his theology. The theme of the article was similar in tone to those of his Protestant counterparts. The cover caption read "No Easter without Good Friday," which meant, as Sheen explained in the article, that "modern man" seemed caught in a "Good Friday age." In the spiritual darkness, man has looked for peace in the wrong places, either within the self or within "scientific and political cure-alls," and found only disillusionment. Sheen inveighed against those seeking an easy route to Christian salvation by ignoring the event of Good Friday, declaring that

Christ without the crucifixion, "without His nails," is no saving answer. There was, remarked Sheen, "no pleasure without pain, no Easter without Good Friday."[75]

Apart from the exceptional Sheen and Fosdick, Schneider and Dornbusch judged too hastily the theological content of the popular religious book market. The surge of interest in religious books and the advent of the paperback industry spawned several major imprints devoted expressly to theologically themed texts. In the midfifties, Meridian Publishing created Living Age Books; Harper Brothers launched Torchlight, and the YMCA's Association Press started Reflection Books. Executives at Meridian considered calling their new venture "Reformation Books" before settling on "Living Age."

The standout among Living Age's first half dozen titles was *Primitive Christianity* (1956) by the world-renowned German theologian Rudolf Bultmann. Torchlight published reprints of New Testament scholar Edgar J. Goodspeed's *Life of Jesus* (1950) and Søren Kierkegaard's *Purity of Heart* (1956).[77] James Rietmulder, the director Reflection Books, sought Reinhold Niebuhr's judgment regarding the imprint's first list of titles. Conceived as a "popular Protestant line," the books were intended for "average church-goers." The company, Rietmulder continued, intended to provide special display racks for churches as part of a "determined effort and program" to bring "the material to the layman."[77]

Niebuhr was no stranger to such projects, having served as consulting editor to yet another religious imprint, Doubleday's Christian Faith Series. Doubleday quickly drew on Niebuhr's considerable theological expertise regarding sin, publishing under his watchful eye E. Cherbonnier's *Hardness of Heart: A Contemporary Interpretation of the Doctrine of Sin* (1955).

Theological books targeting the layman came from other publishing houses as well. Cambridge University Press, for example, offered theologian John Seldon Whale's *Protestant Tradition* in 1955. According to a *Newsweek* review, Whale's history of Protestantism had virtually solved the problem of "theologian-layman communication." Whale's survey included a synopsis of the contemporary theological scene in which he argued that "the most urgent issue of our time" was "man's estrangement from his fellowmen." *Newsweek* gave a sample of Whale's "reasoned and readable" prose in which he expanded on this most "urgent issue": "Serious people in the twentieth century have found themselves forced to reckon with the paradox . . . that man is evil as well as good, contemptible as well as admirable . . . The pilgrim making his way to the celestial city is also a wolf to his brother man. . . . [T]he experience of the twentieth century leaves little room for the sentimental optimism which supposes that sinful man can rediscover within the actual system of his civilization the saving power which he needs."[78] Whale's paradox, "that man is evil as well as good, contemptible as well as admirable," was in essence a definition of original sin, one all the more convincing, as he suggested, in the harrowing context of the twentieth century.

Whale and others, however, hardly compared to British author C. S. Lewis in influence upon America's theological revival. If the titles published by the major religious imprints of midcentury exposed Protestants to important aspects of Christian theology, C. S. Lewis popularized theology itself. Although Lewis's fans numbered in the millions, his work was not universally embraced. Critics charged Lewis, by training a scholar of medieval English literature, with having only an amateur's grasp of theology and the Scriptures. To be sure, as a reviewer for the *Atlantic Monthly* quipped, Lewis wrote "as a layman writing to laymen." Yet Lewis's writings were a rare mix of sophistication and simplicity that bridged, as the *Atlantic* reviewer noted, "the gap between low-brows and high-brows." And his popularity endured, despite his refusal to "sweeten Christianity" at the expense of such doctrines as original sin. On the contrary, according to the same *Atlantic* review, "original Sin occupies a prominent position in Lewis's theology."[79]

The most noted midcentury critics of American Christianity shared Lewis's resistance to its saccharine version. The exacting works of Will Herberg, A. Roy Eckardt, Martin Marty, Peter Berger, and Gibson Winter revitalized the prophetic tradition of the Jewish and Christian faiths.[80] At their most critical, these thinkers excoriated the state of American belief, targeting Protestantism in particular. Herberg, the most influential of this circle, characterized the faith of Americans as "very often a religiousness without religion, a religiousness with almost any kind of content or none, a way of sociability or 'belonging' rather than a way of reorienting life to God."[81] Eckardt, Marty, Berger, and Winter challenged the authenticity of postwar piety with equal sharpness.

Yet each author cautioned that such analyses did not describe the whole Judeo-Christian community. They argued that popular religious trends, while a serious concern, had not completely overtaken, as Berger put it, "the classical Christian emphasis on transcendence and judgment." Likewise, Herberg noted pockets of Protestantism undergoing a "theological renaissance."[82]

Among the works by these authors, Herberg's *Protestant, Catholic, Jew* was and still is the most influential of the critical titles of midcentury. Yet Herberg's portrayal of the postwar revival was confusing, even contradictory at times. His standard thesis asserted that the "operative faith" of the American people was "by every realistic criterion the American Way of Life," a phrase that remains the preferred shorthand for descriptions of postwar religiosity. But Herberg's expanded thesis—rarely explored in histories of the period—was more complex. Many Americans, in fact, distinguished between their Christian faith and the American Way of Life. Herberg identified three groups "resistive" to the "American Way of Life as religion." They included: "immigrant-ethnic" churches—selected Lutheran, Reformed, and Catholic communities—that still "cherish their traditional creeds and confessions," the "not large but increasing" orthodox, neo-orthodox, and liberal groups with "explicit and conscious theological concern, and finally the "numerous and influential" holiness, Pentecostal, and millenarian movements in America. "All of these cases," Herberg continued, were "hold outs against the sweep of religious Americanism." He concluded by severely qualifying his thesis to the point of undermining it: "For the great mass of the American people the American Way of Life is not avowed as a super-faith above and embracing the historic religions." While the American Way of Life united Americans in a "'common faith,'" it made no "pretensions to override or supplant the recognized religions, to which it assigns a place of great eminence and honor in the American scheme of things." In the end, Herberg both conflated and distinguished the American Way of Life and the historic faiths, yet simultaneously accorded preeminence to both of them in shaping American consciousness.[83]

The problem with Herberg and his fellow critics, in other words, was their failure to pursue the complexities of the religious revivals that they noted but ultimately dismissed in favor of sweeping judgments about the superficiality of American piety. The prophetic attitude of this cohort also betrays the vitality of the midcentury religious scene. If these damning indictments of American religiosity are taken at face value, how does one explain the audiences amenable to their criticisms? Herberg's book, for example, was a best seller. Hudnut-Beumler, the author of *Looking for God in the Suburbs*, argues that the sales of Herberg's, Winter's, and Berger's books "indicated that their authors were not just prophets crying in the wilderness, but also prophets speaking for a people. . . . The jeremiads succeeded most, therefore, in moving these religious and cultural issues to a central place of concern in American society."[84]

In January 1960, historian Eric Goldman bade the 1950s a bitter good-bye. Calling the climate of the late fifties "the dullest and dreariest in all our history," he hoped that the ensuing decade would break away from "old ideas." Goldman included "false piety and religiosity" in the list of things he desperately wished Americans would leave behind.[85] Goldman misread the complex nature of 1950s religiosity, and his wish for religious change was slow in coming.

Although the 1960s ushered in "Death of God" theology, liberation theology, and religious experimentalism,[86] these shifts within Protestantism occurred largely after 1965. Until then, Niebuhr, Tillich, and Graham remained the deans of the church. Because of their work throughout the postwar era, the issue of sin remained prominent in Protestant culture in the sixties. Other voices followed their lead. Even Norman Vincent Peale focused attention on sin, publishing *Sin, Sex, and Self-Control* in 1965.[87] The conservative evangelical wing of Protestantism never failed to emphasize the doctrine of sin, as some of its liberal counterparts had. Although evangelicals tended to discuss sin legalistically, a contributor to *Christianity Today* noted in 1962 that "thanks to the dialectical [neo-orthodox] theologians, sin in the singular, and with a capital 'S,'" had recaptured theological and religious attention.[88] Such a shift in concern, while perhaps not universal within evangelicalism, was nonetheless momentous, and all the more so given the evangelical acknowledgement of the theological contribution of neo-orthodoxy.

In the early sixties, mass-market magazines such as *Look, Reader's Digest,* and *Time* featured articles identifying this renewed concern with "sin in the singular." In 1963, senior *Look* editor J. Robert Moskin conducted a three-month investigation into the state of America's "moral code." In his subsequent article, "Morality USA," he vacillated between alarmist warnings about America's moral decline and careful analysis of such issues as racism and wealth and poverty. On the one hand, Moskin paraded "the beatnik, the racist, the wild kid, the price-rigging executive, the pregnant high-school girl, the dope addict, the vandal, the bribed athlete, the uncared for aged, and the criminal" as evidence that America had lost its moral compass. On the other hand, Moskin challenged America to do better with regard to race and money. Most of this discussion focused on the latter, and Moskin concluded that "many Americans worship money." Having asked, "Can We Mix Morals and Profits?" Moskin failed to rigorously pursue this tough question, but his identification of money as a form of idolatry reflected the influence of the wider conversation about sin in the postwar years. In fact, Moskin had sought Tillich's views on the problem and had printed the scholar's contention that the churches' responsibility in a "well-to-do society" was "to undercut the 'false security'" created by wealth.[89]

In *Reader's Digest*, the elderly and chastened liberal churchman Harry Emerson Fosdick warned Americans away from another form of false security: "easygoing optimism." "Thoroughgoing pessimism," however, was equally problematic, so Fosdick implored his readers to adopt a realistic sense of Christian hope. World events had taught humanity a hard lesson, rendering unfettered optimism "silly." To illustrate his point, he used the example of atomic power. After quoting J. Robert Oppenheimer's famous remark, "The physicist has known sin," Fosdick continued: "Our whole society knows the tragic sin of misusing a gift which is inherently promising and good."[90]

As Fosdick had, *Time* drew attention to the paradox of sin with a cover story on Karl Barth, regarded by many as the most influential theologian of the twentieth century. The Swiss-born Barth did for Europe what Niebuhr and Tillich had done for America: he recovered the importance of the doctrine of sin in Christianity. In particular, the article noted, Barth reasserted sixteenth-century reformer Martin Luther's famous description of humanity, *simul justus et peccator* (simultaneously righteous and sinful).[91]

Martin Luther King Jr., like his forebear and namesake, understood his own reform efforts in the context of sin. Not coincidentally, King counted both Niebuhr and Tillich as crucial influences over his confrontation with and exposure of what he understood to be the sin of segregation.[92] Indeed, the palpably religious nature of the civil rights movement as a whole challenged American Christians to confront what *Look* headlined as "Our Churches' Sin against the Negro."[93] Editors at *Christianity Today* echoed those at *Look*. After fire hoses and attack dogs were used against protesters in Birmingham, Alabama, in 1963, an editorial in the evangelical magazine concluded that such events unequivocally demonstrated the "deep evil in the human heart." Yet although the actions of Birmingham officials deserved moral condemnation, Southerners were not to be singled out as "special sinners." The evil of the human heart was universal, and the editors made their point vividly: "Any man not blinded by twisted prejudice could see that Nazi Germans were not special sinners, for morally nothing distinguishes anti-Semitism from Birmingham's racism. . . . He who looked hard at the social ugliness in Birmingham saw not special sinners who fight for state's rights but trample on human rights; he saw the human nature we all share. He saw a time to weep, to repent, to remember—'inasmuch as ye have done it unto these ye have done it unto me.' "[94]

Whether American Christians adopted the editors' democratic sense of sin and evil was another matter. In 1965, senior editor T. George Harris of Look suggested that Protestants, particularly young evangelicals and liberals, were leaving "legalistic definitions of sin to the old folks" in favor of "risky, self-critical religion." This group of Protestants was yet a "minority," but Harris wondered what upheavals these "radicals" might instigate within the church. In anticipation of the "unexpected things" to come from this dedicated corps of believers, Harris ended the piece with an ominous, if somewhat melodramatic, prediction: "We may yet find out why the prudent Romans fed their lions on Christian meat."[95]

Harris's forecast of radical religious change was accurate in one sense. Change did come, just not quite to his speculations. Still, signs of the religious and cultural realignments that would shape the next theological era had begun to cluster around the middle of the decade. The most conspicuous marker of such change appeared on the cover of Time on 8 April 1966. The cover read simply: "Is God Dead?" The article showcased the work of the so-called Death of God theologians—Harvey Cox, Gabriel Vahanian, William Hamilton, Paul Van Buren, and Thomas Altizer—who expanded upon German theologian Dietrich Bonhoeffer's ideas about "religionless Christianity."[96] A lesser-known scholar, Philip Rieff, announced not the death of God but God's transformation into a psychologist in The Triumph of the Therapeutic (1966). By the late 1960s, interest in non-Western religions had surged, especially within the countercultural movement. Finally, feminist, black, and Latino liberation theological movements developed and intensified after the midsixties.[97]

Yet these changes were not total. In the first place, few Americans attended God's funeral. If God was not yet dead for most Americans, neither was he a psychologist or a hippie.[98] The various strains of liberation theology, while significant, arguably had their greatest impact—in this country anyway—within the halls of academe.

These religious shifts, however circumscribed, were not immediate, and the theological revival continued well into the 1960s. Though Niebuhr had slowed considerably by the early 1960s, he remained a commanding presence within the culture. *McCall's* featured him in a lengthy retrospective of his career in 1966. That same year, he published his last focused discussion of sin, *Man's Nature and His Communities*. His opposition to the Vietnam War, moreover, raised his old prophetic indignation and brought him once again into the center of public life.[99] In fact, his only competition for the title of America's leading theologian was Tillich. The German émigré flourished in the 1960s, right up to his death in October of 1965. He published in popular as well as academic media and continued to crisscross the country on lecture tours that exposed him to all manner of believers and seekers. Graham's massive evangelistic efforts continued to draw record audiences. Nothing quite compared to his eighteen-week triumph in New York City in 1957, but attendance at his 1962 Chicago crusade totaled 700,000. Chicago, though, outshined New York on one count: 116,000 people crowded into Soldier Field for the closing service, breaking Graham's previous record of 100,000 set at Yankee Stadium in 1957.[100]

CHAPTER 2

A Curious Trinity

The Prophet, the Evangelist, and the Theologian

Despite their shared leadership of postwar Protestantism, Niebuhr, Graham, and Tillich had little in common on a personal or intellectual level. Separated by age, geography, and theological disposition, these men came from and operated in quite different worlds. Niebuhr, the prophet, led the American neo-orthodox movement; Graham, the evangelist, stood at the helm of neo-evangelicalism; and Tillich, the theologian, reinvigorated American Christian thought with his Continental theology. Consequently, they spoke in different accents to very different constituencies of Protestants.[1]

In spite of these disparities, Niebuhr, Graham, and Tillich shared a common theological principle: behind every sinful act was the indisputable, universal condition of original sin. In one sense, their emphasis of the doctrine of original sin was to be expected. As Christian ministers, they were steeped in the biblical laments offered by the prophets, the psalmists, and the apostles regarding the shortcomings, injustices, and tragedies of individual and communal life. Niebuhr's, Graham's, and Tillich's visions of sin had deeper historical roots as well. As academics, Tillich and Niebuhr shared a familiarity with the doctrinal history of original sin from its initial formulation by Augustine through its subsequent interpretations by such major thinkers as Luther, Calvin, and Pascal. As products of American culture, Niebuhr and Graham, unlike the German émigré Tillich, had been shaped by the palpable influence of the doctrine of original sin in American culture from the seventeenth century onward.[2]

Beginning with the colonial settlements, the Reformed and later Evangelical views of the sinful nature of humanity dominated much of American intellectual and cultural life. Especially in colonial New England, political and clerical leaders like John Winthrop, John Cotton, and Increase and Cotton Mather had governed and preached in full recognition of what they understood to be the depraved condition of humanity. Even Winthrop's famous "city on a hill" declaration of 1630—a phrase that has been used (mostly misused) time and again in American politics—was uttered with the pervasive reality of sin in mind. To be a "city on a hill," according to Winthrop, required strict obedience to the covenant that God had established with the Puritans; yet Winthrop and his audience of Puritans knew just how disobedient humans could be and thus just how precarious and burdensome such a covenant was.[3]

In the next century, the doctrine of original sin remained a crucial aspect of the theology—including that of John Wesley—that inspired the colonial revivals of the 1730s and 1740s. George Whitefield, Jonathan Edwards, and William and Gilbert Tennent, to name the best-known leaders of what is sometimes called the "First Great Awakening," shared a common belief in the ruination of the human spirit, and they preached accordingly. The most famous sermon from this period is Edwards's "Sinners in the Hands of an Angry God" (1741). Although many readers mistake this sermon for the epitome of hellfire and damnation and fail to recognize its context or its greater emphasis on the grace of God, there is no mistaking Edwards's insistence on the sinful condition of humans. Later in his career, Edwards continued to stress the doctrine, publishing in 1758 *The Great Christian Doctrine of Original Sin Defended*.[4] The founders of the American Republic shared Edwards's suspicion of human nature, in spirit if not in its doctrinal particulars, and they constructed a government with that weakness in mind. James Madison, the principal author of the Constitution, deeply mistrusted the ability of individuals and groups to wield their influence and power justly.[5]

The series of revivals that swept through the American frontier and western New York prior to the Civil War, though marked by syncretism, Arminianism,[6] and even denials of original sin by the prolific revivalist Charles G. Finney, nevertheless introduced vast numbers of Americans to the God of judgment as well as the God of mercy. As Lewis Saum, author of *The Popular Mood of Pre–Civil War America*, observes, antebellum Christians possessed a "severely qualified" optimism about the prospects of humanity: "They seemed rarely, if ever, to confuse providence with progress."[7] That sober attitude, however, changed for some Americans in the late nineteenth and early twentieth centuries. The acceptance of Darwin's theory of evolution and the technological advances of modernization substantially curbed—but did not eliminate—the importance of original sin in human nature among a group of liberal Christians known as "modernists." For these modernist-liberals, Darwin's theory affirmed the forward march of humanity: if life had originated in a cesspool and over thousands of years evolved into an advanced race of human beings, progress was inherent in the world. This evolutionary notion of progress, linked with a belief in the immanence of God and the bright horizons of a modernizing nation, assured these modernists that Americans and their civilization were, however slowly and imperfectly, leaving sin behind and advancing toward righteousness.[8]

Yet the doctrine of original sin was far from marginalized in Protestant discourse during these decades. The modernists were but one of two dominant expressions of liberal Christianity. The other important group—the evangelical liberals—was less optimistic than its modernist counterpart about the possibility of historical progress outrunning individual and social sin. The social gospeler Walter Rauschenbusch and America's favorite radio preacher, Harry Emerson Fosdick, for example, repeatedly identified sin as the origin of unjust social and economic conditions in the United States in the 1910s and 1920s.[9] From the other side of the theological spectrum, the conservative, evangelical-fundamentalist wing of Protestantism, led in those years by revivalists Dwight Moody and Billy Sunday and the academic J. Gresham Machen, continually stressed the principle that sin was one of the paramount issues of the era. This robust sense of sin, moreover, underpinned the newly articulated and increasingly popular end-times theory known as dispensational premillennialism. For dispensationalists like Moody and Sunday—though not Machen—and a growing number of their evangelical-fundamentalist constituents, the moral decline of America and its citizens was an essential precursor to the Second Coming of Jesus Christ.[10]

These immediate and historic contestations over human nature shaped Reinhold Niebuhr's intellectual development. Niebuhr was born June 21, 1892, in Wright City, Missouri. The son of Gustav Niebuhr, a pastor in the small German Evangelical Synod, he grew up in his father's churches in Missouri and Illinois. At an early age, he decided to follow his father into the pulpit, studying for the ministry at Elmhurst College in Illinois and then at Eden Theological Seminary in Missouri. In the spring of 1913, Niebuhr had graduation from Eden in sight, and he was making plans to attend Yale Divinity School, when his father died unexpectedly. The death forced Niebuhr home to serve the grieving congregation on an interim basis until a full-time replacement could be found. The twenty-year-old Niebuhr shepherded the congregation through the crisis as best he could, breaking from his duties only once, for his graduation from Eden in June. Upon completion of what must have been heart-wrenching work, Niebuhr departed for Yale in the fall of that year, as his father and he had originally planned.[11]

Niebuhr's theological education—both at his father's knee and at Elmhurst, Eden, and Yale—took place at the height of theological liberalism's influence. Niebuhr's training, then, prepared him for a pastoral career largely in step with the tenets of that tradition. His moderately liberal father, his education at Eden, and his mentor at Yale, D.C. Macintosh, offered no serious challenges to this reigning theological paradigm. With regard to sin, Niebuhr's views aligned with those of the evangelical liberals, but he was not yet convinced that man's story was not a success story.

After finishing his master's of divinity at Yale in 1915, Niebuhr received a call to Bethel Evangelical Church in Detroit, Michigan, that interrupted this liberal theological trajectory. Thirteen years in the pastorate in the burgeoning city of Detroit gradually distanced Niebuhr from his liberal roots. The reasons for his change of heart were many and diverse. One perhaps surprising factor was the degree of sympathy he had developed for the fundamentalist emphasis on sin, if not for the movement's other doctrines. In a somewhat favorable review of Billy Sunday's 1916 revival in Detroit, Niebuhr commended the evangelist's emphasis on sin and on a God of both judgment and mercy as a "wholesome antidote against the 'tender-mindedness' of modern Christianity."[12] Niebuhr's diary from those years, published in 1929 as *Leaves from the Notebook of a Tamed Cynic*, documents with self-critical honesty several other factors in his emerging theological reformulation. Niebuhr wrote, among other things, of what he could see only as the sinful pettiness of parishioners and preachers alike, the complexities of good and evil revealed through the horrors of World War I, the temptations of American consumerism, and the un-Christian character of modern industrialism (Niebuhr had aggressively criticized Henry Ford's business practices in the mid-1920s). In each of these situations, he found liberal ideas about the power of individual and corporate sin wanting.[13]

Niebuhr's interest in the concept of sin intensified after his arrival at Union Theological Seminary in New York City in 1928. His continued reevaluation of liberal thought was, in part, a byproduct of his own sense of professional inadequacy. His appointment as associate professor of Christian ethics and philosophy of religion filled him with trepidation. His lack of a doctoral degree set him apart from his colleagues at Union, and he doubted his command of the fields he was charged with teaching. Later in his career, he recalled the discomfort of his first decade as a teacher, his sense of "being a fraud who pretended to a larger and more comprehensive knowledge than I possessed." He met these challenges by diligently immersing himself in the works of such historic Christian thinkers as Blaise Pascal, Søren Kierkegaard, Miguel de Unamuno, and Jonathan Edwards. He also studied the works of his contemporaries, including Karl Barth, Emil Brunner, Nikolay Berdyayev, and the Jewish rabbi Martin Buber. His reading of Augustine—the father of the doctrine of original sin—was perhaps the decisive factor in his turn away from the ultimately, even if chastened, progressive assumptions of evangelical liberalism.[14]

Niebuhr forcefully announced his changing theological vision in his landmark *Moral Man and Immoral Society* (1932). He disturbed the liberal theological community by arguing that political and social groups were innately and irredeemably immoral because of the powerful self-interest that colored their actions. The individual "moral man," he further argued, while less corrupt than human collectivities, could hardly boast of his virtue. Liberal reviewers objected loudly, decrying the book's "defeatism" and "pessimism."[15] Yale theologian H. Richard Niebuhr, the younger and more conservative of the brothers Niebuhr, was not so sure of the depth of Reinhold's pessimism about the human condition. He suggested to Reinhold that the book was "still too romantic about human nature" and that his older brother was still a "liberal" overall.[16] H. Richard had a point. Although Reinhold clearly doubted the morality of social groups and stopped well short of praising the "moral man,"[17] he had yet to articulate a comprehensive doctrine of sin. Still, most liberals of the day agreed, Niebuhr had departed their camp.

Billy Graham was a mere fourteen years old when Niebuhr published *Moral Man.* Consequently, he experienced little of the modernist-fundamentalist controversy or the liberal theological infighting that defined Niebuhr's early career. But Graham was a child of Moody, Sunday, and their many followers, whose staunch resistance to modernist views of sin and salvation had survived within the fundamentalist subculture after the infamous Scopes trial of 1925.

Like so many of his contemporaries in the Bible Belt, Graham was also deeply influenced by the thriving Christian culture of the South. At the age of sixteen, while attending a tent revival, Graham recommitted himself to Christ at the behest of the legendary evangelist Mordecai Ham. The conversion experience prompted the adolescent Graham to consider entering the ministry. In preparation for this career, Graham headed for Tennessee to study at the ultraconservative Bob Jones College. The choice was a disaster. Graham left the college after one semester because of poor grades and clashes with Jones's strident vision of Christianity. His departure from the college signaled his dissatisfaction with extreme fundamentalism, a discontent that marked his later career.[18]

Graham, however, was undeterred. After his disappointment in Tennessee, he attended the Florida Bible Institute (FBI) in Tampa. The FBI was a mecca of evangelical revivalism. In addition to the regular faculty, a constant stream of major revivalists from the glory days of Moody and Sunday served as visiting instructors. Graham carefully watched and listened to these warhorses of a bygone evangelical era, sorting through their preaching styles as he aspired to one of his own. Before long, he was putting this pulpit knowledge to work, damning sin and calling for repentance on street corners, at area churches and revivals, and on local radio. Upon graduation from the Florida Bible Institute in 1940 at the age of twenty-two, he packed his evangelical bags for Wheaton College in Wheaton, Illinois—the most respected and intellectually rigorous of the conservative Christian colleges.[19]

Wheaton broadened the scope of Graham's evangelicalism. The FBI may have been a fertile training ground for preachers in the South, but an Illinois audience, especially one more academically inclined, was a different constituency. Graham adjusted rapidly. Curbing though never abandoning the dramatic preaching style he had learned in the South, Graham was soon in demand both on and off campus. After one such foray to a small Baptist church in suburban Chicago, the congregation offered him their pastorate upon his graduation from Wheaton. Graham accepted and in 1944 began service to the one and only fixed congregation of his long ministerial career.[20]

It was neither American liberalism nor its fundamentalist opposition that shaped Paul Tillich's theology, but the decidedly non-American traditions of German theology. Tillich was born in 1886 in the small village of Starzeddel in Brandenburg. Raised Lutheran by his staid pastor-father and more expressive but equally firm mother, Tillich recalled a happy if somewhat serious childhood. The household was clearly an intellectual one, and expectations for the obviously bright Tillich were high. He noted later in life that at the age of eight he first "wrestled with the idea of the

Infinite." Whatever the truth of this charming anecdote, Tillich did indeed "wrestle with the idea of the Infinite" from the time of his confirmation in the Lutheran faith at age fifteen to his later years of anxiety about the worth of his theological project. While he was still an adolescent, the issues of doubt, guilt, and sin joined the problem of the Infinite on his list of worries. At age seventeen, the loss of his mother to cancer added another layer of intensity to his personal and intellectual development.[21]

Tillich's studies progressed unabated, despite his youthful theological consternation and the premature death of his mother. He was classically educated in the *Gymnasium* system of Germany before deciding on the ministry in 1904 and commencing theological studies at the University of Berlin. The three-year program allowed students to pursue courses at other German universities, and so Tillich also enrolled at the University of Tübingen and the University of Halle. In 1907, he returned to Berlin to prepare for his ordination examinations and to begin work on his licentiate in theology—the highest academic degree awarded in the field. Waylaid in 1908 by several months of service as a pastoral assistant to a rural congregation near Berlin, Tillich nevertheless progressed toward his degree, studying the thought of nineteenth-century philosopher Friedrich Schelling, the subject of his dissertation for the licentiate. Between 1909 and 1912, in a whirlwind of academic activity, Tillich attended a preaching college; completed his dissertation under the auspices of the University of Halle; wrote a second dissertation on Shelling for a doctorate in philosophy (awarded by the University of Breslau); and stood for his final examination for the licentiate, again at the University of Halle. At the age of twenty-five, Tillich was qualified to lecture in both theology and philosophy at the university level.[22]

Throughout Tillich's academic training, there reigned in Germany what most Americans would understand as liberal religious thought. In fact, American religious liberalism drew heavily from the teachings of leading German theologians. The faculties at divinity schools and seminaries, such as Harvard, Yale, Union, and the University of Chicago, were filled with professors who had studied in Germany. Consequently, the works of German liberals, such as Albert Ritschl, Adolf von Harnack, Wilhelm Hermann, and Ernst Troeltsch, dominated the reading lists of seminarians at these institutions.[23] Tillich, then, trained among liberals—his teachers included Harnack and Troeltsch—at Berlin, Halle, and Tübingen. But unlike American liberalism, Tillich's education was steeped in the German emphasis on systematic theology, classical Lutheranism, and ecclesiology, aspects of the Continental tradition all but lost by those who had imported it to the United States in the late nineteenth and early twentieth centuries.

Despite his immersion in the liberal theological world of early twentieth-century Germany, Tillich became dissatisfied with its optimism on the questions of sin and social progress. He had first questioned the dominant liberal perspective on the basis of his reading of Søren Kierkegaard in 1905 and 1906. Questions about the validity of the liberal tradition continued to gnaw at him throughout his course of study, and they intensified in 1908, when he served in the pastorate and was exposed to the same challenges that Niebuhr had encountered among the churched.[24]

Tillich's final break with liberal theology on the issues of sin and evil came abruptly, with the onset of World War I. The war literally blew apart any fidelity he still harbored toward liberalism's optimistic notions of human goodness. As a volunteer chaplain on the front lines—where he won the Iron Cross and survived several ferocious battles, including those at Verdun, Amiens, and Aisne-Marne—Tillich witnessed firsthand the ugliness and horror of war. As his biographers, Wilhelm and Marion Pauck, described, "Tillich became a grave-digger as well as [a] pastor."[25] The experience of war shattered conventional concepts of God for him, as they did for thousands of other Germans and Europeans, and convinced him of the fundamental ambiguity of the human spirit—the simultaneous radical goodness and evil of humanity.

With these new ideas in tow, Tillich returned to the University of Berlin after the war as a *Privatdozent* (lecturer). As Germans struggled to rebuild their cities and towns after the devastation of World War I, Tillich took on a rebuilding project of his own, attempting to reconstruct theology in the wake of the seeming godlessness of the war. His cultural-religious project combined elements of his Christian heritage, German romantic idealism—particularly the thought of the early seventeenth-century Christian mystic Jakob Böhme and, of course, that of Schelling—and the intellectual movements of existentialism, psychoanalysis, Marxism, and expressionist art that flourished amid the chaos and desperation of postwar Germany. Though familiar with all these traditions, except expressionism, before the war, Tillich incorporated insights from them into his theology more explicitly in the 1920s. He attempted to harness the "prophetic" quality of each school's opposition to the prewar liberal-capitalist ethos of Germany, which had emphasized control, order, and self-sufficiency, for his own criticisms of early twentieth-century liberal theology. For Tillich, these intellectual and artistic schools of thought helped reanimate the "unconditioned" character of God—reminiscent of the transcendent God of Luther and Calvin—amid the finite disorder of both individual and social life.[26]

Tillich's adventurous theological exploration was matched by his political and personal explorations, and all of it encouraged by the situation in postwar Germany. Deep-seated animosity toward the old regime made Weimar Germany and especially its capital city, Berlin, the site of "experimentation, not only in the arts but in all spheres of life: government, science, [and] sexual mores." Tillich reveled in the newness of it all and soon lived in two worlds: the academic and the bohemian. While maintaining his scholarly credentials, he preferred the company of artists, actors, journalists, and writers, embracing what he called their "non-bourgeois" outlook. He began professing religious socialism and helped form a small group and a journal dedicated to linking the political and the religious. The intensity of his interest in politics, however, diminished when he departed from Berlin in 1925 for the University of Marburg.[27]

The move was one of professional advancement. Eager for promotion beyond the rank of Privatdozent, Tillich accepted an associate professorship in theology at Marburg. He continued to develop his broad theological vision there, engaging his colleague Martin Heidegger in a curious form of indirect disputation.[28] Tillich left Marburg in 1925 after less than a year, again to further his academic career, becoming a professor of philosophy at the Dresden Institute of Technology. Although he enjoyed the rank of full professor, Dresden was not yet an accredited university, and Tillich missed teaching in his true discipline, theology. To keep his hand in both university life and his preferred academic field, Tillich moonlighted as an adjunct professor at the University of Leipzig, beginning in 1927. Two years later, he departed from Dresden and Leipzig to accept a prized chair in philosophy at the University of Frankfurt. Tillich, now forty-three, had arrived, academically speaking. He enjoyed the prestige of a full professorship at a respected university. His chair paid well, and it allowed him the freedom to teach what he wanted in the way he wanted. Tillich thrived in his new position: students adored him; his book *The Religious Situation* (1925) continued to receive accolades; and he became a widely admired and sought-after lecturer in Germany.[29]

Only five years later, Tillich moved again, this time involuntarily, arriving in the United States as a refugee from Nazi Germany in 1933. As an early opponent of the Nazi regime, Tillich was among the first non-Jewish professors dismissed by the new government. Shortly thereafter, jobless and crestfallen, Tillich received an offer—orchestrated in part by Reinhold Niebuhr—to teach at Union Theological Seminary. Niebuhr had never met Tillich, but he had long admired the German theologian's work (H. Richard Niebuhr had translated *The Religious Situation* into English in 1932). The one-year contract paid modestly—the faculty at Union had agreed to 5 percent pay reductions to fund Tillich's salary—but the offer included a spacious apartment. Torn between his desire to stay in Germany and his concern for the safety of his family, Tillich reluctantly accepted his new post at Union. At age forty-seven, and with extremely limited English, Tillich began his theological career anew. It would take him more than a decade to equal and ultimately surpass the stature he had attained in Germany.[30]

✤ These marked differences in the early lives and thought of Niebuhr, Graham, and Tillich continued after World War II. Niebuhr still led American neo-orthodoxy, and he gained a reputation as the nation's "establishment theologian."[31] Closely linked to the elite religious institutions of mainstream Protestantism and to postwar American liberalism as well (his earlier affinities for Marxism and socialism having faded), Niebuhr appealed to a broad constituency that included secular intellectuals, some of whom became "atheists for Niebuhr."[32] Virtually overnight, Graham became the undisputed leader of neo-evangelicalism, a movement determined to cast off the elements of fundamentalism tainted by sectarianism and bigotry. Beginning in 1949 with his "Christ for Greater Los Angeles Crusade," Graham embarked on a tireless evangelical barnstorming tour, holding crusades in dozens of cities over the next decade. Tillich, meanwhile, was synthesizing elements of his Continental theological and philosophical training, as well as aspects of existentialism, psychology, and art, into his three-volume *Systematic Theology*. Although he shared some affinities with American neo-orthodoxy, Tillich was generally categorized as the nation's premier Protestant liberal—even ultraliberal— theologian. This simple classification, however, missed the ways in which Tillich significantly differed, in background and outlook, from the older style of American religious liberalism.

These dissimilarities of religious disposition and audience that characterized each of their pre- and postwar experiences have overshadowed their common emphasis of the doctrine of original sin. Despite these differences, a proper understanding of the unity of their thought on this one critical element redraws the conventional narratives of each of their careers and the larger cultural significance of their ministries. Not only does it focus attention on the centrality of the doctrine of original sin in their respective theologies, but it also unearths and brings to vivid light the power and disturbing force of the theological doctrine that underpinned their influence.

In one sense, Niebuhr's work had become closely associated with the concept of sin by the late 1940s. The publication of his magnum opus, *The Nature and Destiny of Man*, had left no doubt about his theological interest in the doctrine of original sin. Few contest the judgment that he belabored the point of humanity's corruption in that book. Yet, outside the circle of a few of his former theological students and colleagues, Niebuhr's theology of sin remains the least understood and least studied aspect of his work among scholars, especially historians.[33] Instead of treating Niebuhr's theology of sin as a concept grounded in his wholly Christian identity and his pastoral dedication to disseminating the Christian message, scholars have often dealt with it in cursory and, in some cases, reductive ways.[34]

His theology is typically viewed as being at the service of his politics and cultural criticism rather than as the underlying motivation for these activities. For some, Niebuhr was a cold war liberal who articulated a realistic or pessimistic perspective of American social and political life that encouraged complacency. In these analyses, Niebuhr plays the part of an apologist, albeit a chastened one, for American democracy, anticommunism, and the status quo and thus appears as one of many midcentury consensus intellectuals.[35] For others, his use of the discourse of sin to criticize the Protestant revival also appears commonplace—yet another elite voice decrying the superficiality of the piety of ordinary believers after the war.[36] To be sure, Niebuhr questioned and even dismissed the captive revival's legitimacy, calling it not a revival but a "revival of interest" in religion and an exhibition of faith not in a transcendent God but in faith itself. In either case, his doctrine of sin has not received sustained attention from historians. The postwar Niebuhr, then, functions as a gadfly whose pronouncements about sin placed him within the broad contours of cold war liberalism and intellectual skepticism about the purported Fourth Great Awakening.

These limited understandings of Niebuhr's thought have distorted his singular contribution to and position within midcentury American culture. The concept of sin was not merely a cover for maintaining the social and political status quo, nor was it simply a useful concept for blasting the enthusiasms of the Protestant revival. For Niebuhr, it was an endlessly rich doctrine that he deployed as a means of criticizing both conservative and progressive attitudes as well as their solutions to the problems of individual and corporate life. He employed the doctrine to cut through what he perceived as the undue conceit and righteousness emanating from both the right and the left, in the hope that a deep awareness of such false pride would advance the cause of justice in human life. In other words, the doctrine's negative evaluation of human nature mapped the surest path toward a positive, though still imperfect, social, political, and economic structure.

More important, and more often forgotten, is Niebuhr's emphasis of the doctrine of original sin in his role as a Christian pastor. Though his congregation was the public at large rather than a particular parish, as it had once been, he labored to spread the good news of reconciliation. When commissioned in 1954 by *This Week* magazine, a Sunday newspaper magazine with a readership of 11 million, to select the most important passage of scripture, Niebuhr chose Ephesians 4:32: "And be ye kind one to another, tender-hearted, forgiving one another, even as God for Christ's sake hath forgiven you." He explained to *This Week*'s readers that the verse contained the whole message of the Christian faith. The essential point of Christianity, Niebuhr observed, was that "we are asked to forgive one another." But in order to forgive, humans had to admit that "we are ourselves sinners, and that we have been forgiven." For Niebuhr, without an acknowledgment of the universality and inescapability of sin, Christianity—and by extension his deeply Christian criticism—had no center of gravity.[37]

Billy Graham, like Niebuhr, ministered to a national congregation. Although he had been a rising star in evangelical circles in the 1940s through his Youth for Christ work, Graham gained true national prominence in 1949 with his "Christ for Greater Los Angeles" crusade. By its conclusion, Graham had preached to three hundred fifty thousand people in the City of Angels and won six thousand "decisions for Christ" during the revival. Graham followed the Los Angeles event with a grinding schedule, holding crusades in a dozen cities for each of the next two years. His travels drew frequent coverage from local newspapers and from such national magazines as *Life*, *Look*, *Time*, and *Newsweek*. He soon reached tens of millions of Americans through his radio program, *Hour of Decision*, begun in 1950, and through his syndicated newspaper column, My Answer, that followed two years later. Within two years of its inception,

Graham's radio hour had squashed the competition: more than seven hundred stations in the United States carried his program, more than any other commercial or noncommercial broadcast show of the time. The press dubbed him the "Protestant Pope" in recognition of his growing fame, and he quickly became a mainstay on the "most admired men" Gallup polls of the 1950s. One other measure of his prominence within the culture was the fact that correspondents needed to provide only his name and the city of Minneapolis, Minnesota (the location of the Billy Graham Evangelistic Association headquarters), for letters to reach him. The only other figure to whom normal postal requirements did not apply was the president of the United States.[38]

Graham's swift rise to Protestant stardom met with a variety of responses. To many believers, he was the moral leader of the country. To others, he was an inspiring evangelist, but one who oversimplified the Christian Gospel. To fundamentalists, he was an apostate who had forsaken true Christianity for mainstream popularity. To his critics, he was a symbol of the cultural captivity of the Christian gospel.

With little exception, however, the Graham known to historians is the one presented by those critics. From the patently hostile articles in the *Nation* and the *Christian Century*[39] in the midfifties to the biased neo-orthodox accounts in Martin Marty's *New Shape of American Religion* and A. Roy Eckardt's *Surge of Piety in America* (1958), Graham's ministry is depicted as, at best, a simple—or even a simpleton's—version of the Gospel, and one captive to the American way of life.[40] In recent studies, scholars have more or less repeated the gibes and stereotypes of their predecessors, placing Graham under the rubric of cultural captivity. Within this framework, he is usually cast in one of two ways: either erroneously lumped together with figures like Norman Vincent Peale as an expositor of Protestant uplift or viewed as lagging a few paces behind Peale on the march toward Christian communion with American culture and celebration of the nation's power and virtue.[41]

Graham's emphasis on sin frustrates attempts to categorize his ministry so generically. Despite his seeming simplicity, biblical literalism, and frequently intense moralizing about behavioral sins, Graham shared with Niebuhr and Tillich the classical Protestant belief in original sin. His moralism—even at its most petty—was never separate from this conceptualization of original sin as the fundamental cause of such corruptions of the self. Graham's explanation of human wrongdoing was straightforward and popular, but rarely superficial.[42]

Graham could be imbalanced, however, in his emphasis of particular sins over original sin. This tendency did not arise from any lack of conviction or grasp of sin as a causal agent but reflected his role as an evangelist rather than a theologian. Graham never claimed any theological expertise, and while his theology evolved throughout his career, he was in the business of saving sinners, not that of explaining the theological origin of sins.[43] He never abandoned, however, his conviction that the particular sins (plural) that he preached about were a manifestation of sin (singular). "The heart and core of my preaching," Graham told *Newsweek* in 1955, "is a call to repentance of sin and a turning by faith to Jesus Christ as Savior." As a result, his work of diagnosing humanity's condition and identifying its greatest need never ceased; for as Graham saw it, "The story of history is the story of sin."[44] But his ministry targeted the chief expressions of original sin, such as pride, unbelief, and what Graham called "lawlessness" and "decadence"—the wanton indulgence in alcohol, sex, and material comfort.[45]

Reassessing Niebuhr and Graham in terms of their core belief in sin recasts the nature of their own public relationship. Not only did they argue from a common theological anchor, but they also often appeared side by side in news accounts of the postwar religious situation. Their opinions on the revival were often juxtaposed in popular periodicals, as in *McCall's* and *Newsweek* in 1955.[46] That same year, *Reader's Digest* printed Graham's and Niebuhr's reflections on the prospect of world peace. Both were hopeful, but not optimistic; both cited the corruption of human nature as the biggest obstacle to any lasting peace.[47] To one graduate student at the University of Washington, the reason for their pairing in such articles was obvious. As he observed in his 1960 master's thesis, "There is an outstanding similarity in the theologies of these two men and that is their belief in the doctrine of Original Sin and its effects on human beings." Yet, he continued, Niebuhr and Graham interpreted sin differently. Niebuhr focused on both collective and individual sin, while Graham focused on individual sin alone.[48] Niebuhr, to be sure, concerned himself with individual sin. His problem with Graham was the latter's extreme "pietistic individualism" and seeming ignorance of the complex web of social sin that inevitably ensnared Christians.

These concerns about Graham's theology of sin so preoccupied Niebuhr in the midfifties that he penned several articles critical of Graham. He launched his fusillade in March 1956, as preparations mounted for Graham's New York City crusade scheduled for 1957. Writing in anticipation of the crusade for *Christianity and Crisis*—the journal he had founded in 1941—Niebuhr declared: "We dread the prospect." Though he agreed with Graham that New York City was a modern-day "Babylon" whose "'sins'" invited condemnation, he doubted Graham's ability to "discern the real sins of such a Babylon." Niebuhr worried that Graham's pietism would "accentuate every prejudice which the modern 'enlightened,' but morally sensitive, man may have against religion."[49]

The *Christianity and Crisis* editorial was Niebuhr's harshest critique of Graham, and it has unfortunately colored later views of their whole relationship. Historian Mark Silk has characterized this piece as the first assault of Niebuhr's two-year "guerrilla action" against Graham. Silk's view is typical of the dominant understanding of Niebuhr and Graham's relationship: that it was marked only by antagonism and critique.[50] That was part of the relationship, but it was also richly complicated by moments of charity and respect. Indeed, besides his *Christianity and Crisis* editorial and a patently hostile article published in *Life* during the New York City crusade, in which he famously characterized Graham's evangelical message as a "bargain."[51] Niebuhr's other assessments of Graham in the midfifties were far from unsympathetic. Although not devoid of trenchant criticism, these articles illuminate Niebuhr's consistent praise of Graham's sincerity, integrity, and aspects of his evangelism. More important, they express Niebuhr's hope that Graham might realize his potential as a prophetic leader within American Protestantism.[52]

Niebuhr exhibited both of these tendencies—the critical and the complimentary—in *Pious and Secular America* (1958), which concluded and in many ways summarized his assessment of Graham's ministry. He admitted, "It is a thankless task to criticize Graham, for he is such an honest and sincere, rhetorically skilled protagonist of this faith." Graham was also "infinitely superior to the other popular versions of the Christian, or at least Protestant, message," and he "preserved something of the biblical sense of a Divine judgment and mercy before which all human strivings and ambitions are convicted of guilt and reduced to their proper proportions." Finally, Niebuhr observed, "he genuinely helps those who are engulfed in personal moral confusion or in the sense of the meaninglessness of their existence."[53] These were hardly ringing endorsements of Graham, and Niebuhr leavened them with his usual rigorous objections to Graham's pietism. But Niebuhr rarely separated such sharp criticism from his measured appreciation of Graham. Outside of the two aforementioned articles, one of which he later retracted in the *Christian Century*,[54]

Niebuhr admitted in *Pious and Secular* and in other places that Graham's ministry was "infinitely superior" to other forms of popular Protestantism and that it helped individuals in crisis.

For his part, Graham openly acknowledged his respect for Niebuhr and even counted him among his theological influences. In 1957, he credited Niebuhr in the *Saturday Evening Post* for pushing him to broaden the scope of his ministry: "When Dr. Niebuhr makes his criticisms about me, I study them, for I have respect for them. I think he has helped me to apply Christianity to the social problems we face and has helped me to comprehend what those problems are." In 1958, Graham again surprised the Protestant world, noting that he had read "nearly everything Mr. Niebuhr has written." Graham apparently meant what he said. As late as the 1980s, Graham claimed, "Look, I need some more Reinhold Niebuhrs in my life. I would say Reinhold Niebuhr was a great contributor to me. He helped me work through some of my problems."[55]

Niebuhr's influence was especially evident in Graham's treatment of racial discrimination. Although Graham had boldly spoken against racial inequality as early as 1952 and desegregated his 1953 crusade in Chattanooga, Tennessee, he had, for the most part, proceeded cautiously on the question of race. For example, it was only after the U.S. Supreme Court issued its decision in *Brown v. Board of Education of Topeka, Kansas* (1954) that he insisted on open seating for whites and blacks at all his crusades.[56] In his 1956 article "A Proposal to Billy Graham," Niebuhr challenged him to reverse his gradualism and, as a Christian, to pursue a "whole-souled effort to give the Negro neighbor his full due as man and brother." Graham responded a few weeks later in *Life* with a six-page indictment of racism and segregation, answering Niebuhr's concerns in the article point by point, though he never mentioned Niebuhr's name in the article.[57] Graham confirmed Niebuhr's role in shaping his firmer position on race in the 1970s, recalling to his biographer, John Pollock, "He [Niebuhr] influenced me, and I began to take a stronger stand."[58]

Despite this responsiveness to Niebuhr's critique, Graham ultimately frustrated Niebuhr's hopes. Niebuhr never fully accepted the evangelist's ministry, yet he could not fully dismiss Graham in the 1950s.[59] To do so would have been to deny the genuine merits of Graham's ministry— namely, his integrity and his unflagging message of individual repentance. It was this latter emphasis, despite his criticism of Graham's "pietistic individualism," that prevented Niebuhr from issuing a total indictment of the evangelist. After all, since the 1940s, Niebuhr had been laboring to demonstrate the complexity and universality of individual sin. To be sure, he also had focused attention on the sin of institutions and even nations. But he admitted in his *Christian Century* retraction that corporate sin had its origin in "the residual egotism of even the best people," and thus acknowledged the validity of Graham's evangelical theology.[60]

✠ If it is surprising that Niebuhr and Graham had a guarded respect for one another, it is more surprising that Paul Tillich had any appreciation at all for the evangelist. The German theologian drew from a vast reservoir of erudition, and his ruffled appearance and monotone presentation made him the polar opposite of the evangelist, who combined colorful suits— pistachio green was not too bold for the southerner—with an equally colorful, folksy preaching style. Unfortunately, the record of Tillich's estimation of Graham is thin. But what does exist suggests that Tillich, like Niebuhr, considered Graham an authentic representative of the Gospel, despite what he called Graham's "primitive theological fundamentalism."[61]

In 1954, Graham visited Union Theological Seminary, and Tillich attended Graham's forty-five-minute talk in the school's chapel. A former Union student later recalled in the *New Yorker* that while Graham spoke, Tillich stood by with tears rolling down his face, muttering under his breath. Tillich probably disagreed with much that Graham said that day, though he remembered the occasion differently and less dramatically than the student. He rated Graham's presentation of the Gospel "as good as any average sermon" and remarked, "He's a serious man, although I question his method, I'm open to argument." And although he considered Graham's method of conversion "primitive and superstitious," he granted that "Graham at least desires to bring people to the 'ultimate concern'" (Tillich's term for faith).[62] While Graham and Tillich had almost nothing to do with one another personally, it is noteworthy that both sought to bring people to faith—or "ultimate concern"—in God. This shared evangelistic concern thus drove both to make their audiences aware of the universality of the condition of sin without which understanding, they agreed, no genuine faith could arise.

If Tillich shared an emphasis on the doctrine of original sin and a pastoral inclination with Niebuhr and Graham, he also shared with them the Protestant spotlight. Few intellectuals, before or since, have enjoyed the popularity that Tillich achieved in the decades after World War II. Mixing academic prestige—after his term at Union, he held professorships at Harvard University and the University of Chicago—with an uncanny ability to communicate with wide audiences, Tillich became, as one former colleague remarked, "a wonderful phenomenon."[63] Indeed, phenomenon, if not oxymoron, aptly described Tillich's place in American culture. After his death in 1965, one denominational magazine noted his "popular works of philosophical theology"—a phrase unthinkable, by most accounts, in American Protestant culture at midcentury.[64]

Tillich's theology, as profound and difficult as it seemed to some, was indeed highly popular, and it popped up in a wide array of cultural milieus. The Supreme Court confronted his concept of God in a decision in favor of a conscientious objector. Countless invitations to speak at churches and universities in North America, England, Europe, and Japan filled his calendar years in advance and sent him traveling virtually every weekend of the academic year. Additionally, he attracted the attention of such diverse and popular periodicals as *Time*, *Vogue*, and *Playboy*. An editor of this last publication hoped that Tillich might speak to—interestingly enough—questions of morality, ethics, and the nature of man's existence. After Tillich's death, this singular renown prompted Niebuhr to remark simply: "Paul Tillich was a giant among us."[65]

Tillich's emphasis on the doctrine of original sin has been overlooked, much like the stances of Niebuhr and Graham. His concern with the doctrine has been overshadowed by two primary factors: his reputation as an extremely liberal theologian and his reputation for sexual irresponsibility. On the one hand, his substitution of terms like "alienation," "separation," and "estrangement" for "sin" seemed to confirm his break with the historical doctrine. As crowds flocked to hear him lecture about human estrangement from the "Ground of Being" (God) and the "New Being" (Jesus Christ) and still more hoped for the "courage to be," it was easy to wonder whether his audiences had been captivated by a seductive, liberal, quasi-Christian guru. Even the liberal theologian Nels Ferré referred to Tillich in 1955 as the most "dangerous theologian alive," while the *Christian Century* and *Union Seminary Quarterly Review*—two Tillich-friendly publications—carried stories in the early sixties about his "borderline atheism" and wondered about his "compatibility with the Gospel."[66] Not surprisingly, a reviewer for the evangelical *Christianity Today* argued that Tillich's *Systematic Theology* occasionally "drops into the pantheism of Hegel and Schleiermacher."[67]

On the other hand, revelations of Tillich's freewheeling sexual life seriously tarnished his standing in some circles and only added to the controversy over his stature and significance within modern Christian thought. Hannah Tillich exposed her husband's sexual practices, unpublicized during his lifetime, in her 1973 memoir, *From Time to Time*. The book candidly detailed the affairs of both partners—the results of an open marriage—as well as Tillich's interest in pornography. Naturally, these disclosures undermined for many Tillich's credibility as a theologian who took sin seriously. For a few others, it actually added to his appeal as an avatar of sexual liberation.[68] In either case, since the publication of *From Time to Time*, rumors and campus legends about Tillich's personal life have multiplied and can still be heard in the halls of Union, Harvard, and the University of Chicago.

These accounts of Tillich's sexual practices, however, have been considerably embellished by titillating anecdotes and urban legends. That Tillich was guilty of inappropriate sexual indulgence and felt his own guilt is certain.[69] Beyond those facts, the precise nature and extent of his affairs, interest in pornography, and by some accounts, sadism, remain unknown.[70] Still, there are facts enough, and they cannot be avoided; but perhaps they can be constructively understood in the context of Tillich's own theology of sin.

Rollo May's *Paulus: Reminiscences of a Friendship* (1973) offers one helpful lens for an evaluation of Tillich's sexual life. Unfortunately, May takes a rather euphemistic view of his longtime friend's actions. He insists, for instance, that Tillich practiced "sensual," not sexual, seduction and enjoyed only "good pornography." Yet amid these absurdities, May also asks his reader to view Tillich's failings in the context of the stark reality of human nature and to contemplate the "impossible," that is, "to admit that we all possess these "daimonic" [demonic] tendencies.[71] May's observation allows Tillich his humanity in all its fallibility—the very thing that the theologian pressed Christians to acknowledge and accept throughout his career. More important, May dares readers, as Tillich did, to reflect on their own condition, their own war within. In other words, Christians might view Tillich's actions from the standpoint of the doctrine of original sin, and non-Christians might consider them from the perspective of the hypocrisy and contradiction that pervades human life. Through either lens, Tillich's failings and obsessions can be seen as understandable, even if they are not excusable. Moreover, they should not be grounds for dismissing his theology of sin but rather should constitute an occasion for considering its interpretive power.

Despite Tillich's theological liberalism and his promiscuity, the idea of universal, inescapable human corruption was no less profound, no less true, and no less biblical for him than it was for Reinhold Niebuhr and Billy Graham. He employed the term "estrangement" to clarify the meaning and force of the doctrine of original sin, while making it more comprehensible and palatable to a modern age. Convinced that sin underlay human anxiety, despair, and evil, Tillich nevertheless feared that the traditional language surrounding original sin, burdened by abundant misinterpretations and confusion, was in danger of irrelevance. For example, belief in the literal story of Adam and Eve and the notion that their transgression was biologically inherited by each successive generation was preposterous in the eyes of higher biblical criticism and modern science. But although Tillich disputed its literal historicity and unsophisticated understandings of its transmission to all humanity from the seed of Adam, he argued that the myth of the fall was replayed in every human life and in every human act. For Tillich, just as the mythological Adam and Eve asserted their independence from God, all humans without exception had done the same. This predicament, like the one that faced "Adam," convinced Tillich of the universal character of estrangement (original sin).[72]

Tillich's articulation of the entrapment of humanity in original sin was actually simply another version of the classic concept of the bondage of the will. Human freedom, for him, was inextricably linked to and limited by the condition of original sin:"Sin is a universal fact before it becomes an individual act, or more precisely, sin as an individual act actualizes the universal fact of estrangement. As an individual act, sin is a matter of freedom, responsibility, and personal guilt. But this freedom is imbedded in the universal destiny of estrangement in such a way that in every free act the destiny of estrangement is involved and, vice versa, that the destiny of estrangement is actualized by all free acts. Therefore, it is impossible to separate sin as fact from sin as act."[73]

And despite his more frequent and presumably more "modern" use of the term "estrangement," Tillich never eliminated the word "sin" from his vocabulary. Late in his life, he offered a brief but profound summary of his wrestling match with the word: "Therefore, even Christian teachers, including myself, shy away from the use of the word sin. We know how many distorted images it can produce. We try to avoid it, or to substitute another word for it. But it has a strange quality. It always returns. We cannot escape it. It is as insistent as it is ugly. And so it would be more honest—and this I say to myself—to face it and ask what it really is."[74] Tillich's semantic play, then, was not liberalism or syncretistic religion run amok. Without question, he believed completely in the concept of original sin and labored tirelessly to reintroduce it through new language precisely because he thought it so central to Christianity.[75]

✣ From one point of view, Billy Graham, Reinhold Niebuhr, and Paul Tillich make for a curious trinity. Graham's sawdust-trail evangelicalism was quite different in its tone and cultural timbre from Niebuhr's and Tillich's refined theology and their station in academia. Niebuhr and Tillich were not without their differences as well. Niebuhr especially resisted Tillich's philosophical ontology and was less interested in the wide framework of knowledge—especially art—that Tillich brought to bear on his theology.[76]

Still, when the doctrine of sin is given its proper place as a fundamental element in the thought of each, the differences can be seen as superficial, not essential. Niebuhr's prophetic neo-orthodoxy, Graham's powerful neo-evangelicalism, and Tillich's sophisticated Continental theology all pointed in the same direction: the doctrine of original sin. While their theologies of sin cannot be synthesized, neither can they be easily separated or seen as anything but central to their respective ministries.

CHAPTER 3

Original Sin

"The Only Empirically Verifiable Doctrine of the Christian Faith"

Toward the end of his life, Reinhold Niebuhr took up his pen once more in an effort to summarize his immense body of work, a task that eventuated in the publication of *Man's Nature and His Communities* in 1965. He undertook the project in part to discuss how his opinion had changed after a lifetime of considering man[1] and community. His opinion, however, had not changed much with regard to original sin; he approvingly quoted the following from the London *Times Literary Supplement*: "The doctrine of original sin is the only empirically verifiable doctrine of the Christian faith."[2] Graham and Tillich would have been equally appreciative of the *Times*'s statement. Indeed, for all three, the long history of humanity's inhumanity supported the truth of original sin. For them, the record of human discord, while tragic, was not surprising, having arisen from a common origin. The myriad evils of the world and of history—small and large—emerged from a fundamental disharmony within human beings. In short, particular evils or sins were but expressions of original sin.

Beyond this shared conviction of the empirical truth of the doctrine of original sin, their interpretations of it both diverged and converged. To be sure, their understandings of the Genesis account of Adam and Eve, their philosophies of man, and their explanations of the chief symptoms of original sin—unbelief, pride, and desire—differed in several ways. Yet their differences on these points, apart from Graham's biblical literalism concerning Genesis, were more in degree than in kind. In other words, on the issue of sin, these men occupied some common theological ground, which included the view that the Christian faith made little sense without a robust interpretation of original sin.[3]

The biblical emphasis in Niebuhr's, Graham's, and Tillich's views of original sin centered quite predictably on the Genesis story of Adam and

Eve. Niebuhr, as an ethicist with a theological avocation, interpreted Genesis allegorically, understanding the biblical account of the first sin as a profound myth that revealed the truth about humanity's sinful condition. Graham approached the problem of sin from a literal reading of Genesis. For him, as for Augustine in the fifth century, sin was a matter of birthright, inherited by each successive generation as a consequence of Adam and Eve's first sin.[4] Tillich, like Niebuhr, read Genesis as a myth of great consequence, and, as the most sophisticated thinker of the three, he provided a more systematic theological analysis of sin than either Niebuhr or Graham.

✣ Neither the record of history nor the biblical account of sin, however, extinguished Niebuhr's, Graham's, or Tillich's belief in human goodness. Sin may have ruled the mind and heart, but it did not rule absolutely. While all humans were touched by the condition of original sin and thus existed in a sinful state of being, the situation was not one of total depravity. Humans, they argued, were created in the image of God (*imago dei*)—a notion supported by both scripture and theological tradition. Accordingly, humans were endowed with goodness and freedom, but original sin distorted that fundamental goodness; moreover, the blame for that distortion lay with humans, not with God. Consequently, both the Bible and Christian tradition offered a picture of humanity as simultaneously good and wicked, free and bound, sainted and sinful.[5]

This concept of man—a creature simultaneously good and evil—was crucial to each thinker's explanation of sin's operation in the life of the individual. Indeed, for Niebuhr and Tillich, the paradoxical nature of humanity—what they termed "finite freedom"—was the locus of and occasion for particular sins. Graham offered no such definition or careful analysis of the double nature of the human situation. But even he, as his theology matured, began to present the occasion of human sin as a function of this paradox of the human spirit.

In their conceptualization of finite freedom, Niebuhr and Tillich drew heavily from the nineteenth-century existentialist philosopher Søren Kierkegaard. They revived Kierkegaard's analysis of the "dizziness," "dread," and "angst" that humans experienced because of their double nature. Like their Danish predecessor, Niebuhr and Tillich asserted that humans were overwhelmed and shaken by the finite limits of human freedom—ultimately expressed in human mortality—and yet the seemingly infinite possibilities of human freedom. Finite freedom, then, was simply a technical way of describing the fundamentally enigmatic and ambiguous nature of human existence.

Niebuhr's and Tillich's updated Kierkegaardian diagnosis of the human predicament had a direct bearing on their explanation of sin. The profound anxiety provoked by the condition of finite freedom was the wellspring for particular sins. Humans, they reasoned, attempted to escape the ambiguity of the human situation by emphasizing either freedom or finitude. In other words, humans, unable to bear their own ambiguity— what Niebuhr and Tillich both stressed as the defining characteristic of life—overestimated or underestimated their worth, their freedom, or their finitude. Thus, humans fled in one direction or the other and in their false sense of freedom or, conversely, finitude, committed the principal sins of unbelief, pride, and concupiscence.[6]

Although both thinkers owed intellectual debts to Kierkegaard, Tillich possessed a deeper knowledge of the melancholy Dane's thought and of the general trajectory of existentialist philosophy than did Niebuhr. One of Tillich's doctorates was in philosophy, after all. The problem of human goodness and evil, of human essence and existence, had preoccupied philosophy since the time of Plato. Tillich, too, was invested in this perennial question but unsatisfied by either the essentialist or the existential emphasis alone. For instance, he resisted G. W. F. Hegel's notion of "perfect essentialism," the idea that the world and humanity were marching toward a realization of goodness and thereby toward a closer unity with the infinite. Accordingly, he appreciated existentialist critics of Hegel, including, of course, Kierkegaard, as well as Friedrich Schelling— whose work had been the subject of Tillich's dissertation—Karl Marx, and Friedrich Nietzsche. These thinkers collectively rejected Hegel's notion of essentialism. Instead, they argued that the existential predicament corrupted any such realization of human progress and unity with the divine. For Tillich, these objections recalled Augustine's clear distinction between essence and existence, a distinction drawn by the early church father because of the reality of original sin.[7]

Tillich used the myth of the Fall to explain his own ideas about essence and existence. "Adam," as the symbol of essential man, existed in a kind of limbo, as one who possessed freedom, but a freedom not yet "actualized." In other words, in the state of "essence," an unrealized stage of human development, "Adam" experienced his finite freedom in harmony. In a state of existence, however, finite freedom was distorted, producing profound anxiety and creating the conditions for sin to flourish.[8] Thus, in

Genesis, when the serpent presented "Adam" with a choice, "Adam's" freedom was awakened, something Tillich described as a "dangerous situation." The danger corresponded to the "double threat" of finite freedom: the limits and freedoms of human existence. Therefore, conscious of his situation, "Adam" experienced "the anxiety of losing himself by not actualizing himself and his potentialities and the anxiety of losing himself by actualizing himself and his potentialities."[9]

Niebuhr absorbed much of Tillich's existentialist thought when the German émigré arrived at Union Theological Seminary in 1933. As Tillich began his tenure there, he and Niebuhr naturally gravitated toward one another. Not only had Niebuhr secured Tillich's position at Union, but Niebuhr also spoke fluent German, a great boon in light of Tillich's extremely limited English. The pair conversed regularly in the 1930s, often exchanging ideas as they strolled through Riverside Park.[10]

Tillich's existentialist influence is easily discernible in Niebuhr's publications from the midthirties. Despite his pathbreaking focus on the sin of collectivities in *Moral Man and Immoral Society* (1932), Niebuhr had described the workings of sin without analyzing the concept in depth and had preserved the possibility of a "moral man."[11] In subsequent works, he provided a more thorough examination of sin and shed his optimism about the moral character of humanity. This shift began in the two books that followed *Moral Man*, *Reflections on the End of an Era* (1934) and *An Interpretation of Christian Ethics* (1935). In both books, Niebuhr's debt to Tillich was obvious—something he acknowledged in the preface to *An Interpretation of Christian Ethics*. In fact, in *An Interpretation*, Niebuhr undertook his first systematic explanation of sin, and throughout he relied on Tillich's thought. He borrowed liberally from his friend's definition of finite freedom and his mythological view of the Fall. Niebuhr's appropriation of Tillich's ideas combined with his own developing theology to produce a somewhat inchoate picture of sin. Still, these texts of the mid-1930s improved upon his earlier discussion of the subject.[12]

Niebuhr's existentialist turn and his repudiation of the "moral man" were unmistakable in his two-volume study *The Nature and Destiny of Man* (1941, 1943).[13] Niebuhr had mastered the concept of finite freedom and made it his own, brilliantly analyzing its centrality phenomenon of sin. Niebuhr drew the reader into his provocative investigation of the human situation from the opening sentence of *Nature and Destiny*: "Man has always been his own most vexing problem."[14] Niebuhr had concluded—

via Tillich and Kierkegaard—that man was a problem to himself because man possessed finite freedom.

He clarified the concept of finite freedom through the use of several complementary categories. Man, for Niebuhr, existed at the juncture of time and eternity, nature and spirit, weakness and greatness. Man endured the bondage of time, but human imagination, memory, and foresight lifted man out of the strictures of time, enabling him to "touch the fringes of the eternal." Man as spirit had "purposes and ends beyond the limits of physical existence," though as a being of nature, man, even by faith, could "not resolve the mystery" of life beyond nature. As a creature of weakness, man suffered the fragility of the body and the frailties of reason, but the resiliency of the human body and the creative use of reason illustrated his greatness.[15]

All of these categories illuminated a single truth for Niebuhr: humans were radically free and radically dependent beings. Man was "both strong and weak, both free and bound, both blind and far-seeing." Despite man's freedom, he still existed as an animal among other animals. He ate, slept, defecated, and died like other organisms. Yet he was not only an animal, for he was conscious that he was an animal and thus able to contemplate his own mortality. In seeming exasperation, but not without a touch of humor, Niebuhr later summarized his whole doctrine of man, quipping in a 1955 sermon, "What a contradiction—to be the judge of all things and yet to be a worm of the earth."[16]

In a minimal way, Graham also viewed humans as creatures finite yet free. To be sure, Graham's analysis contained little theological depth in comparison to Tillich's and Niebuhr's discussions of the concept. Nevertheless, Graham placed human freedom and goodness in the context of the limiting power of sin. He did so, however, inconsistently. Caught between his Presbyterian roots and his Southern Baptist evangelical theology, he expressed sin alternately as a condition of depravity and as a condition to be surmounted during the Christian life.[17] In both instances, he departed from the ambiguity of human nature of which Tillich and Niebuhr were so convinced.

Yet by 1965, in *World Aflame*, Graham was offering a more developed conceptualization of the problem. The book was the closest approximation of theology that Graham had ever produced. In contrast to *Peace with God* (1953), *The Seven Deadly Sins* (1955), and Graham's many sermons of the postwar era, *World Aflame* went beyond his usual descriptive approach to concepts like sin and freedom and provided reflections on their meaning. Graham's references to Kierkegaard, Barth, Pascal, and, surprisingly, to thinkers such as Nietzsche, Sartre, and Camus were another indication of his theological turn. While Graham's limited discussion of these figures indicated a degree of intellectual name-dropping, it was clear that his thought had developed. He spoke of man's "self-consciousness" as a clue to "man's freedom," noting that "the animal does not objectify itself." Graham also described the "paradox" of man: "On the one side there is futility, degradation, and sin; on the other side, there is goodness, kindness, gentleness, and love." The existence of these capacities did not eliminate the fact that "sin has been passed on to us from our first parents," but it did establish that humans "are also sinners by choice."[18] Graham's attention to the paradoxical nature of the human situation—the coexistence of goodness and sin—brought his thought a step closer to that of Niebuhr and Tillich.

In sum, all three believed that sin was inevitable, but not essential. They resisted the doctrine of total depravity, regarding man ambiguously, as a creature created in God's image, yet alienated from that divine image in existence. For Niebuhr and Tillich, the paradox of finite freedom generated profound and discomforting anxiety within humans which tempted them to sin. In fact, anxiety, as Niebuhr asserted, was "the internal precondition of sin."[19] In the Age of Anxiety, it was little wonder that Niebuhr's and Tillich's analyses proved germane to the lives of countless Protestants. Graham never developed a doctrine of humanity parallel in depth to that of Niebuhr and Tillich, but he nevertheless had a sense of the paradox of man, and he, too, cast it in terms of sin. Despite the differences between Tillich's and Niebuhr's interpretations of sin's inevitability on the one hand and Graham's on the other, they nevertheless collectively viewed sin as the central problem of existence. Within this fundamental accord, moreover, their explanations and analyses of particular sins closely paralleled one another.

✦ Niebuhr, Graham, and Tillich exhibited significant theological affinity in their respective descriptions of the chief expressions of original sin— unbelief, pride, and concupiscence (unlimited desire). For all three, these fundamental symptoms of original sin overlapped with and reinforced one another, but the first expression of original sin was always the rejection of God (unbelief), followed by an assertion of the self as its own "god" (pride) and a final turn toward the things of this world (unlimited desire). This is not to suggest that their considerations of these symptoms of original sin were identical. Niebuhr analyzed these expressions of sin less systematically than his colleague Tillich, and he devoted the majority of his attention to the sin of pride. Graham was significantly less sophisticated than either Niebuhr or Tillich in his discussion of these sins, but he compensated for his lack of erudition with the forcefulness of his conviction of their pervasiveness in human life. Tillich, for his part, probed the depths of each of these variant forms of sin and offered the most compassionate understanding of how psychologically damaging these symptoms were to believers and nonbelievers alike.

Unbelief received less attention than pride and desire in each man's explanation of sin. Niebuhr and Graham most often addressed the problem of sin in the language of pride. As Niebuhr averred, pride was man's first or "primal sin." Tillich, however, asserted that unbelief preceded pride. Logically, humans had to first turn away from God before pride emerged, although pride encouraged that initial turn from God.[20] Lacking Tillich's theological precision, Niebuhr and Graham neglected the logical order of unbelief, pride, and desire. But for both Niebuhr and Graham, pride implied unbelief in its expression of the same idea: the sinful denial of the sovereignty of God.[21] The important point for Niebuhr and Graham, as well as for Tillich—his careful theological reasoning notwithstanding—was not the proper sequence of sinful expression but the fact that undue human self-assertion in unbelief, pride, or desire reduced the primacy of God.

Niebuhr's focus on the sin of pride led him to provide the most vigorous and sustained analysis of it. In fact, criticism of his theology has long questioned the dominance of pride in his thought to the exclusion of other forms of sin and even to the exclusion of grace. Niebuhr did indeed stress the sin of pride above all others, contending that "man's self-glorification" summarized the "whole biblical doctrine of sin." He credited the Pauline-Augustinian tradition—in which he included Pascal, Luther, and Calvin—for this theological emphasis.[22] Niebuhr's rearticulation of pride in the modern age, however, related directly to his view of grace. Without a thorough diagnosis of sin, the potency of the antidote was lost.

Niebuhr organized his description of the sin of pride around three interrelated categories: pride of power, pride of knowledge, and pride of virtue. The pride of power, for Niebuhr, had two principal expressions. The first was "the pride which does not recognize human weakness," and the second, "the pride which seeks power in order to overcome or obscure a recognized weakness." In his analysis, "established and respected individuals" suffered principally from the first type of pride, while those "less secure" suffered from the latter type. Though a distinction could be made between them, the two forms of pride overlapped: for Niebuhr, insecurity was basic to human existence. The temptation of every individual—irrespective of social position—to "make himself doubly secure" and to "prove his significance" demonstrated the universality of human insecurity: "The fact is that the proudest monarch and the most secure oligarch is driven to assert himself beyond measure partly by a sense of insecurity."[23] Ultimately, the pride of power was man's attempt "to make himself God." Both the assumption of power and the pursuit of power denied the fact that final security and power rested with God.[24]

The pride of knowledge mirrored the pride of power. Just as man in his sin of pride pretended to be more secure than he was, Niebuhr maintained, knowledge pretended "to be more true" than was the case. Drawing on Marx, Niebuhr argued that all knowledge suffered from an "ideological taint." Knowledge was finite, perhaps "good from a particular perspective," but "it pretend[ed] to be final and ultimate knowledge." This "ignorance of ignorance," or unwillingness to admit the contingent and prejudiced character of all knowledge, was made more devious by the continual presence of "a known or partly known taint of interest." But pride of knowledge refused to acknowledge the taint, either by ignoring "the finiteness of the human mind" or by denying the contingent and self-interested character of all knowledge.[25]

Niebuhr considered the pride of virtue as the most serious of the prideful offenses. The Bible clearly admonished "the righteous in comparison with 'publicans and sinners.'" Yet man consistently boasted of his goodness, making "virtue the very vehicle of sin." Like the other two forms of pride, self-righteousness made a claim to finality, in effect mistaking human standards "for God's standards." As Niebuhr explained, "Moral pride is the pretension of finite man that his highly conditioned virtue is the final righteousness and that his very relative moral standards are absolute." The moralist—to extend Niebuhr's earlier reasoning—pretended to be more than he was. And this moral pretension, "the unwillingness of the sinner to be regarded as a sinner," was, as Luther suggested, "the final form of sin." The stakes of moral pride were extremely high: "The sinner who justifies himself does not know God as judge and does not need God as Saviour."[26] To Niebuhr's mind, a deficient analysis and awareness of the sin of pride threatened the very center of Christianity.

Moral pride often led to the "quintessential" sin: spiritual pride. Niebuhr's prophetic indignation reached its height in his discussion of this "ultimate sin." Spiritual pride was the folly of the religious, in which the "self-deification" implicit in moral pride became explicit. The gap between God and man disappeared, and claims to holiness emerged either by affirmation or negation. Affirmative spiritual pride equated "partial standards and relative attainments of human righteousness with Godly righteousness." Niebuhr illustrated his point with an indictment of the Christian church itself: "Religion is not simply as is generally supposed an inherently virtuous human quest for God. It is merely a final battleground between God and man's self-esteem." Negative spiritual pride, in contrast, amounted to self-righteous contrition. Humility, Niebuhr recognized, could easily become another form of vanity. Excessive self-deprecation was often a cry for attention or an invitation for praise. "Even the recognition in the sight of God that he is a sinner," wrote Niebuhr, "can be used as a vehicle of that very sin."[27] The comical irony of Christian practice was that Christians—whether righteously or despairingly—all too frequently committed this most egregious manifestation of sin.

Like Niebuhr, Graham highlighted pride as humanity's first sin. "Modern man," like Lucifer and Adam before him, was unwilling to admit that God was God and that man was man.[28] It wounded human pride to acknowledge something greater than the self, and so, Graham asserted, "we try to limit God as we are limited."[29] This limitation of God had multiple expressions, but operated principally through four broad categories of sinful pride: social, material, intellectual, and spiritual.[30] Those who valued their power, money, talents, and wisdom above God suffered from social, material, and intellectual pride. For Graham, these were gifts from God, and parading them about in self-congratulation was an affront to God's blessing.

Graham issued his severest warnings against spiritual pride, the "most repugnant" of the four categories. Spiritual pride refashioned God after the wants and needs of humans. Liberal Christianity suffered most from this propensity, according to Graham, in its conception of God as a palatable, "soft-hearted God" devoid of wrath, anger, and judgment.[31] Graham, however, saved his strongest critique for the self-righteous, be they liberals or not. Individuals who thought "themselves to be pure and all others impure" and who judged themselves worthy not by the good that they did but by the sins they avoided were "guilty of spiritual pride." Nothing raised the ire of Graham more than the "self-sufficient" Christian. His entire ministry resisted such arrogance. Only the humble and repentant sinner could receive salvation in Christ, and the self-satisfied believer only mocked God's sacrifice of Jesus on the cross.[32]

Graham's view of pride in particular and his view of sin in general drew first and foremost from the Bible. Unlike Niebuhr, he considered other thinkers and intellectual traditions only sparingly in his discussion of sin, and when he did so, his treatments were intellectually inadequate. For example, in his discussion of the human situation in *World Aflame*, he littered the pages with references to Shakespeare, Pascal, Kierkegaard, Freud, Jung, Sartre, Fromm, and Barth as support for his views on sin, but he offered no substantive commentary on their thought. Even biblical nuance on the issue of sin did not often enter his preaching. He relied most often on the conservative evangelical interpretation of the story of Adam and Eve to explain sin's origins and to illustrate its continued presence in humanity. Although Graham's view of sin did evolve—becoming more complicated and even somewhat existential—the change was minor. Graham's message of sin and salvation stayed constant and relatively simple from the 1950s onward.[33]

Still, Graham's articulation of the sin of pride paralleled Niebuhr's, at least in form, if not precisely in content. Graham's pride of intellect correlated to Niebuhr's pride of knowledge; material and social pride could easily fall under Niebuhr's pride of power; and both men presented spiritual pride as the worst form of all. The similarities may have been more than happenstance. Since the 1950s, Graham had admitted his admiration for and reading of Niebuhr's theology.[34] Graham may also have consulted Edward John Carnell's *Theology of Reinhold Niebuhr* (1950). Carnell was a rising theological talent within the neo-evangelical world and later served as president of Fuller Theological Seminary. Whether Graham benefited from Carnell's critically poignant but respectful treatment of Niebuhr is unknown, but he clearly had an interest in and some points of agreement with the views of his counterpart. Still, Graham's moralism often overshadowed whatever "Niebuhrian" strain may have existed in his thought. Despite the usual polarization of Niebuhr and Graham, both then and now, the similarity of their thought on the point of pride brings them, at least in this one way, closer together.

Tillich preferred the term "hubris" to "pride," but the basic contours of his articulation of the former matched Niebuhr's and Graham's definition of the latter. Hubris was the human aspiration to be equal with God. As Tillich wrote, "Hubris is the self-elevation of man into the sphere of the divine." Humans, in other words, claimed an unwarranted dignity and finality for themselves. In hubris, the individual practiced a radical self-centeredness, making himself "the center of himself and his world." These expressions of hubris boiled down to one thing: man's refusal to acknowledge his finitude. Though mortal, insecure, and anxious, man acted as if he was not limited in these ways. But, according to Tillich, echoing Niebuhr's view of negative spiritual pride, even if an individual was "ready to acknowledge them [his finite characteristics], he makes another instrument of hubris out of his readiness." Although Tillich began his discussion of particular sins with unbelief, he considered hubris to be man's primal sin, as Niebuhr and Graham had. Hubris, he explained, "is sin in its total form, namely, the other side of unbelief or man's turning away from the divine center to which he belongs." As a consequence, Tillich observed, "[man] attributes infinite significance to his finite cultural creations, making idols of them, elevating them," and finally substituting them for God.[35]

Tillich summarized his views of hubris with what he called the "Protestant Principle." Recalling Luther's initial break with the Catholic Church, Tillich argued, "The first word Protestantism has to say is the word of protest." The principle reclaimed Luther's objections to the righteous claims that religious individuals or groups assigned to their works, morality, doctrine, and, worst of all, sanctity. Tillich broadened Luther's original protest and applied it to the secular sphere as well as to the religious. For Tillich, secular individuals could be just as self-righteous in their solipsistic elevation of their achievements, morality, and ideology. In short, the Protestant Principle always affirmed the "absoluteness of the absolute" over "anything finite" that was given ultimacy by religious or secular traditions.[36]

The first word of Protestantism, then, was also the word of original sin in Tillich's thought.[37] By definition, the concept of original sin denied the undue elevation of humankind at the expense of the "divinity of the divine." This prophetic protest revealed itself consistently in Tillich's published books, articles, sermons, and in his public addresses, though it was not the last word on Protestantism for him. The protest was the "corrective not the constitutive" of Protestant belief. The last word was the love, mercy, and forgiveness of God through Jesus Christ, and this word rippled throughout the work of Tillich, as well.[38] Yet the last word, Tillich argued, echoing Niebuhr and Graham, had no meaning without the first.

Tillich distinguished his analysis of hubris from Niebuhr's and Graham's by his more thorough development of the negative form of pride—the pride of self-hatred and despair. Tillich was acutely aware of the inability of humans to accept that God truly forgave sinners. Without the courage to acknowledge God's acceptance—a frequent refrain in his writings, most famously in his sermon "You Are Accepted"—Christians languished in guilt over their estrangement. As a function of pride, this inability to accept God's forgiveness and, by extension, the inability to forgive the self denied the sovereignty of God. Individuals thus suffered from an inverted perfectionism. The melancholic Christian—provided that the melancholy was not clinical depression—was just as arrogant as the self-righteous Christian. Both betrayed a belief in human perfectibility. The righteous Christian expressed perfectionism positively, believing falsely in the sure improvement of human character through virtuous living. The melancholic Christian, in contrast, expressed perfectionism negatively, despairing in his unworthiness, as if there were any other condition of humanity before God. The negative form of pride destroyed the individual from within, according to Tillich, heightening experiences of loneliness, meaninglessness, emptiness, and depression.

Tillich's theological assessment of negative pride benefited from his knowledge of psychology and existentialism. Self-loathing and the seeming arbitrary character of modern life were themes developed in each discipline and made known to countless Americans through their growing purchase within the postwar culture. For Tillich, both fields became unwitting partners in the articulation of negative pride and thus were also revelatory of "the ultimate conflict which underlies all other conflicts:" original sin.[39]

Niebuhr, Graham, and Tillich understood desire, like pride, as a symptom of original sin. But within their common view of original sin, each interpreted desire differently. First, each employed different terminology in his evaluation of desire. Niebuhr preferred "sensuality," while Graham spoke of "worldliness," and Tillich favored the technical theological term "concupiscence." Still, certain parallels were evident, particularly between Graham and Tillich, who discussed desire at greater length than did Niebuhr.

Sensuality figured less prominently than pride in Niebuhr's analysis of sin because he understood sensuality as a derivative of pride. He defined it as "the self's undue identification with and devotion to particular impulses and desires within itself." And, in accord with Graham and Tillich, he resisted the association of sensuality exclusively with sexual license.

Sex was but one expression of sensuality, along with "gluttony, extravagance, drunkenness and abandonment to various forms of physical desire."[40] Such activities were not inherently sinful, but wanton indulgence in them and in other "creaturely and mutable values" was. Such behavior was, at root, yet another form of pride, a conclusion he rooted in Augustine's view of sensuality as both "a further sin" and a "punishment for the more primary sin of pride."[41] In other words, if the self loved itself more than God, then the self would show "inordinate love" for all the passions of the self and the pleasures of the world. But such extravagance and gratification were forms of escape, as well. Niebuhr used the example of drunkenness to illustrate his point. According to him, an individual might get drunk out of pride and the concomitant feeling of self-importance, but the individual also knew that the action and the feelings of importance were motivated by a false sense of self. The individual, then, would drink also to escape that unpleasant self-awareness. "Thus," Niebuhr concluded, "drunkenness is merely a vivid form of the logic of sin which every heart reveals: Anxiety tempts the self to sin [e.g., excessive drinking]; the sin [drunkenness] increases the insecurity which it was intended to alleviate until some escape [again excessive drinking] from the whole tension of life is sought."[42] This vicious, self-perpetuating cycle illustrated how deeply sin penetrated human existence.

The signature aspect of Graham's ministry was his passionate warnings against the desire for worldly pleasures. For him, Americans, including Christians, had too easily placed their faith in everything but God. As Graham asserted, Americans preferred the "altars of appetite and desire" to the wisdom of God.[43] Graham never provided a formal theological explanation of the flight into worldly values, but at times his descriptions of such behavior mirrored those of Niebuhr and Tillich. According to Graham, there was a void in those who lacked a personal relationship with Jesus Christ, and it drove them to "search for something" that might give life meaning, peace, and happiness. This search sent humans in all directions. Some claimed emancipation from the search through an overvaluation of success, wealth, sex, power, knowledge, or leisure, while others lost themselves in such pursuits in an effort to escape from the burden of finding peace. In either case, the outcome was the same: emptiness and misery.[44]

Graham, though at times an apologist for the American way of life, nevertheless shared with Niebuhr and Tillich a suspicion of capitalism. Underneath Graham's moralism and occasional triumphalism ran a strong critique of consumer capitalism, which, he contended, accelerated the sin of desire. In the 1950s, he argued that in comparison with other peoples of the globe, Americans suffered the greatest dissatisfaction because of their obsession with worldly pleasures and modern conveniences. Despite boasting the highest standard of living, the United States also boasted the "highest per capita boredom." It was colloquial, to be sure, but sincere and fortified by Graham's questioning whether "the American way of life . . . made us happy?" He answered with an unhesitating no, declaring, "We are a nation of empty people."[45] Graham emphasized his point again in the mid-1960s. In a reversal of the "Kitchen Debate"—then vice-president Richard Nixon and Soviet premier Nikita Khrushchev's heated exchange in 1959 over the virtues of Soviet and American household appliances—Graham argued that "the worst human beings" came out of the civilization that produced the best in things material.[46]

Graham's warnings about the ultimate futility of worldly pursuits often led to less thoughtful declarations about the poor present state of American morality. Charges that Graham was a moralist, if not a prude, have some merit. His sermons and books from the 1950s and 1960s contain frequent and exaggerated diatribes against vice, especially sex and alcohol. Time and again, he warned that immorality would be the undoing of western civilization, once thundering that the decadent "moral binge" of midcentury superseded even the excesses of pagan Rome.[47] In particular, sex—"America's greatest sin,"—threatened "the very structure of our society!" Evidence of licentiousness was everywhere. The "outward signs of inward impurity" included "the shifty eye" and the "lewd stare." Sloth endangered American civilization, as well. "On its account," Graham wildly asserted, "lives have been lost, cities have been ravaged by fire, and homes have been broken. It has kept the hobo from a life of respectability, the prostitute from living a life of purity, and the thief from being honest."[48] These vague, alarmist comments made Graham an easy target for his critics—Niebuhr and Tillich among them.

It is not that Graham's warnings about these behaviors were entirely unfounded or atypical of the postwar period. Especially with regard to sex, his attitudes largely reflected those of his contemporaries, something the heated controversy over the Kinsey studies of human sexuality makes plain. Still, his charged and frequent denunciations of sex, sloth, and drink left the impression that these were the main or even the only effects of original sin. Consequently, his emphasis on these individual sins sometimes masked his deeper concern with original sin, the source of these and many other sins.

Despite this moralistic tendency, Graham's evangelism defies attempts to classify his work as merely a gospel of good behavior. Graham insisted throughout his career that "right living" had nothing to do with salvation. Christians could not "worship, or moralize [their] way to God."[49] According to Graham, humans experienced good and evil mixed together in the soul. So deep was this condition that sin accompanied even seemingly harmless human action. Graham argued, "Sin is not always flagrant and open transgression. It is often the perversion and distortion of natural, normal desires and appetites."[50] He explained that love easily became lust and that self-respect degenerated into "godless ambition." In short, Graham did not indict worldly pleasures as such, but the flagrant abuse of pleasure, a subtlety lost amid his moral jeremiads and the prejudices of his critics. Sex, for example, was not sinful in itself, but the misuse of sex was. In these moments, Graham's resistance to moral righteousness and his awareness of sin's covert operation in humanity approached a degree of similarity with Niebuhr's and Tillich's discussion of sensuality and concupiscence. He also echoed their thought in his contention that much of American religiosity was yet another form of escape. He likened it to a form of "addiction," a "shot in the arm" that gave temporary "conscience relief" on Sunday mornings.[51] Graham, then, was neither a simple moralist nor a prophet. His ministry bounced between these two poles, and both his critics and his supporters, it would seem, listened for the Graham they wanted to hear.

While Niebuhr devoted more attention to pride than to sensuality and Graham mixed the prophetic and the moralistic, Tillich's contribution was to redefine the term "concupiscence" for theology and make it relevant for the modern age. In contrast to reductive definitions that associated it only with sexual lust, Tillich defined concupiscence as a general lust: "the unlimited desire to draw the whole of reality into one's self." The key for Tillich was the phrase "unlimited desire." Concupiscence was the unconstrained desire for and indulgence in all variations of human experience, including, most commonly, knowledge, food, sex, power, wealth, or religion. These pursuits were not in themselves matters of concupiscence, but as objects of unlimited devotion, they became "symptoms of concupiscence."[52] Christians, however, had lost this broader definition of concupiscence, and Tillich credited philosophers, writers, artists, and psychologists with helping Christianity rediscover its meaning. These nontheological disciplines were filled with illuminating portrayals of insatiable human striving for stimulation, possession, and experience that ultimately begat dissatisfaction and self-destruction.[53]

Tillich found concupiscence to be a concept particularly useful for illuminating what he understood to be the situation of the anxious, empty citizen of modern American capitalist society. Concupiscence was the estranged (sinful) and therefore idolatrous search to fill the void left by an individual's turn away from God (unbelief) and toward the self (hubris). Because estrangement presupposed connection to the divine—Tillich reasoned that individuals could not be estranged from God without having at one time been in union with God—concupiscence was a distorted attempt at reunion and fulfillment. Instead of finding this peace in God, however, man concupiscently sought fulfillment in and through the world.[54] Capitalist culture epitomized concupiscence in its unceasing quest for things " 'better and better, bigger and bigger, more and more.' " In other words, capitalism's endless promotion of choice and experience facilitated the pursuit of better and bigger and the desire to "cram the whole world into one's own mouth."[55]

This panoply of consumer options and lifestyles, observed Tillich, was not an end in itself. The ambitious, striving individual in capitalist America inevitably suffered from an ennui that propelled him or her ever deeper into the abyss of empty achievements and activities.[56] Concupiscence, then, described the human effort to achieve satisfaction or wholeness through the things of the finite world—a violation of the Protestant Principle. But because this insatiable desire for stimulation, possession, and experience had no real aim beyond continued pleasure, according to Tillich, it could never be satisfied. Thus, persons, things, and places became little more than objects to be used, "swallowed up," and tossed aside.[57]

While Niebuhr, Graham, and Tillich spoke out of distinct theological and rhetorical traditions, they shared an understanding of the nature of sin and its operation in human life. In their scrutiny of individual and corporate existence, Niebuhr's prophetic criticism, Graham's evangelical denunciations, and Tillich's theological philosophizing pointed toward the problem of original sin and its symptoms: unbelief, pride, and desire. Although Niebuhr and Tillich avoided Graham's moralistic condemnations of drink and sex, and Graham in turn never probed the depth and ambiguity of human sin to the extent of his learned counterparts, they argued from the common locus of traditional Christianity, and thus their thought cohered in a fundamental way even if it diverged superficially.

✦ If Niebuhr's, Graham's, and Tillich's convictions about and analyses of the doctrine of original sin fundamentally aligned, their differences were drawn most sharply in their articulation of the Christian answer to the problem of sin. First and foremost, although each thinker stressed that the power of sin was revealed in and vanquished by the crucifixion of Jesus Christ, Graham believed in the literal resurrection of Jesus Christ. Niebuhr and Tillich did not. Graham, moreover, preached substitutionary atonement, the idea that God punished Christ instead of humanity for the sin of the world. Finally, Graham had greater confidence in the process of Christian sanctification—the progressive but fitful realization of holiness in the life of a Christian. Niebuhr and Tillich, in contrast, understood both the atonement and sanctification dialectically. They emphasized that the tension and burden of sin continued in Christian life, and they regarded with dubiety any claim of final character transformation.

These differences in interpretation had consequences for their respective views of the "benefits" of Christian life. Graham held that the redeemed would lead lives of increased fulfillment, happiness, peace, joy, and righteousness. Sin would continue to bedevil Christians, but they would, in effect, become better people. Jesus's death on the cross literally "cross[ed] out—cancel[ed] forever—sin's power." It was just that simple. Prior to faith, unbelievers were filled with sin; but upon the new birth in Christ, the saved experienced total victory over sin and experienced a definite change in their nature.[58] This was Graham's evangelical appeal to the unconverted, and it was a position that invited much criticism, including Niebuhr's characterization of it as a "bargain."[59]

While Niebuhr may have judged him too harshly, Graham's folksy rhetoric and poor analogies occasionally confused his own strongly developed doctrine of sin. At times, his optimism about Christian sanctification almost trivialized the power of sin in the believer's experience: "As the Christ-nature unfolds in your life, you will find that the old strivings, the old envyings, are more easily conquered."[60] And even when he managed to maintain the dialectic of sin and salvation in Christian life, he could, in the same breath, offer breezy slogans that trivialized this complexity. His discussion of justification in *Peace with God* is a case in point. Although he argued that justification was an "act of God whereby He declares an ungodly man to be perfect while he is still ungodly," he prefaced this insight somewhat cheaply, writing, "By being justified is meant 'just-as-if-I'd' never sinned."[61]

Yet Graham's simplicity served a purpose beyond placating price-conscious Protestants with a "bargain" faith, as Niebuhr and others had argued. He stressed the basic tenets of Christianity—especially Christ's saving death and resurrection—to plainly communicate the Gospel and to combat the false expectations that often accompanied faith. Accordingly, Graham often preached a sermon titled "Facts, Faith, and Feeling." The sermon urged his audiences to have faith in the facts of Jesus's life and ministry and to avoid confusing faith with feeling. Belief was not "some electric sensation" or a series of "spiritual thrills" or a function of intellectual commitment—a contention shared by Niebuhr and Tillich, it should be said, lest Graham be summarily labeled an anti-intellectual. Faith trusted the "finished work of Christ on the Cross," nothing more and nothing less.[62] Graham warned that feelings of either spiritual elation or despair were not to be trusted as indicators of faith. His focus on the basic facts of Christianity, then, had as much to do with the spiritual and emotional health of believers as it did with simple reassurances about peace with God.

Niebuhr and Tillich were also concerned with certainty, though they did not share Graham's literal interpretation of the "facts." While the cross was the indubitable gesture of the grace of God toward humanity, Niebuhr and Tillich guarded against substitutionary interpretations of the event. The cross, Niebuhr argued, did not simply begin "tragically but end triumphantly."[63] For Niebuhr and Tillich, the ubiquity of sin gave life an inescapably ambiguous quality. There was nothing only good or only bad. Such one-sided perspectives led to false conclusions that good or evil easily outmaneuvered the other in history and in the individual Christian life.

True to form, Niebuhr and Tillich discussed the cross paradoxically. The sacrifice of Jesus revealed the essence of God's relationship with humanity. It was colored by the simultaneous judgment and mercy of God; at the cross God said both a "no" and a "yes" to humankind. The "no" of the cross was its indictment of humans as sinners; Christians stood before the cross in need of forgiveness. The "yes" was God's participation through Jesus Christ in human sin and evil, bearing it for the sake of humanity. But in contrast to substitutionary models of atonement, such as Graham's, here the reconciling act of God was not so procedural. For Niebuhr and Tillich, Jesus did not simply satisfy the wrath of God as a propitiative sacrifice so that humans might be saved. That view rendered God a calculating God, one who judged first and loved second. For Niebuhr and Tillich, the justice and mercy of God were mutually involved. The experience of forgiveness illustrated this plainly. God's forgiveness was both a humiliating judgment—to be forgiven exposed the depth of one's sin—and a gift of uncompromising love in spite of that sin.[64]

Like Graham, Niebuhr and Tillich viewed justification as a wholly unmerited healing. But in their interpretation, the gift functioned in spite of human sin, not as a wipe-the-slate-clean erasure of sins. In short, Graham's view of sanctification was too complete. In the eyes of Niebuhr and Tillich, humans remained in an ambiguous position, even after conversion. Human sin was "overcome by divine mercy," wrote Niebuhr, "though man remains a sinner."[65] In other words, the divine gift of grace was unambiguous, but humans, despite their reception of the God's grace, continued to live in ambiguity. Niebuhr and Tillich balked, furthermore, at equating redemption with human happiness and peace, as Graham occasionally did. Graham contended that the Christian, though never immune from the sin and temptations of the world, could announce confidently: "I know where I've come from, I know why I'm here, I know where I'm going—and I have peace in my heart."[66] Niebuhr and Tillich effectively reversed Graham's optimism about Christian equanimity. No one knew for certain where they came from, why they were here, or where they were going, but they could trust in the promise of forgiveness.

Niebuhr and Tillich, then, had a more circumscribed view of the regeneration of humanity through Christ. For them, sin was conquered, as Niebuhr put it, "in principle but not in fact." The Christian was free from the power of sin, but not finally free from sin in existence. At best, Tillich explained, humans experienced a "New Creation" in the world and in themselves "here and there . . . and now and then."[67] Niebuhr summarized the point carefully in volume two of *Nature and Destiny*: "Yet whatever 'newness of life' flows from the experience of repentance and faith is, when governed by true Christian faith, conscious of a continued incompleteness and a certain persistence of the strategy of sin. For this reason the peace which follows conversion is never purely the contentment of achievement. It is always, in part, the peace which comes from the knowledge of forgiveness."[68] Tillich voiced this same opinion concisely in his famous reformulation of the doctrine of justification. He implored Christians to "accept their acceptance" in spite of their being "unacceptable." In a single phrase, Tillich communicated the simultaneous judgment and mercy of God: God judged humans as unacceptable sinners and yet as saints deserving acceptance.

Ironically, then, Graham's doctrine of atonement had more in common with the progressive, liberal theology of the early twentieth century. Conversely, Niebuhr and Tillich's insistence on the fragmentary and ambiguous nature of redemption in existence pushed them further to the right theologically.

✠ Niebuhr's, Graham's, and Tillich's articulations of the doctrine of original sin placed them at the vanguard of American culture in the postwar era. The concept of universal sinfulness resonated with Americans who had lived through the lean Depression years, the realities of World War II and Korea, and the lurking nightmare of potential atomic holocaust. They were the American equivalent of the cultural havoc wrought by the trauma of World War I in continental Europe, and they had left the nation shaken.

The postwar context, then, was ready-made for the rearticulation of the doctrine of original sin. Americans from all walks of life—from the intellectual "atheists for Niebuhr" to the average believer in the local Protestant parish—identified with the concept. Historian Donald Meyer referred to the latter group in a 1955 article as "pre-liberal, Bible reading Americans," the sort referred to in this study as "lay theologians."

According to Meyer, an expert on social gospel and neo-orthodox thought, these pre-liberals intensely believed in sin and the tragic situation of humankind. He further argued that Graham was their prophetic leader and portrayed him as no less a "realist" than Reinhold Niebuhr. In fact, he chided the "post-liberal tragedists" (read Niebuhr and Tillich) and their sophisticated audience that "pines for tragedy; [but] unable to body it out, settles for irony; and complains that the folk will accept roles for neither." Meyer speculated that the "tragedists" chastised Graham because they were embarrassed "at finding a kind of parody of [their] own tragic illusions." But for Meyer, Graham was no parody: "He conforms to the mood of the post-liberal disillusionment, and indeed, in the range of his attack upon false idols, ranks with the most vigorous of the realists."[69]

Although Meyer meant to defend Graham and to distinguish him from Niebuhr and, by implication, from Tillich, he actually made a strong case for yoking them together. Graham was but one among the "most vigorous of the realists," a group that included, of course, Niebuhr and Tillich. And it was precisely their realism about and common emphasis on sin that gave each of these very different men the power to speak to the anxieties of postwar Protestants. The doctrine enabled each of them—though they employed various interpretations—to strike a common chord with an audience of lay theologians who listened to their lectures and sermons and carefully read their books and articles. By addressing sin, and perhaps only by addressing sin, these prominent figures tapped into a vast subterranean current of popular religiosity attuned to a traditional Christian doctrine.

Graham's thought transferred most easily to the popular media. His "theology" was already in popular form. Judged by their prolific output and publication in popular periodicals, Niebuhr and Tillich had less difficulty than might be expected in translating their theology into an accessible form. As former pastors, they knew that technical theological language would not play well among the majority of Protestants. In fact, Tillich insisted that ministers refrain from using his theology irresponsibly. He was concerned that the theological idiom of myth and symbol and his own creative terminology could be easily misrepresented by pastors communicating these ideas to their congregations.[70]

Niebuhr and Tillich did not, however, dumb down their theology. Their substantial analysis of the human predicament appeared in their articles and sermons with less abstraction and formal language. Yet both thinkers had faith that ordinary Americans contemplated the big questions of life, including the question of human nature, simply by virtue of being human.[71] As Christian theologians, they asserted a doctrine of man that they contended fit the experience of all humans. Thus, Tillich, usually regarded as the more cerebral and esoteric of the two, believed that ideas about the nature of existence were democratic. All humans had the capacity to explore what he thought to be the painful depths of the soul:

Our attempt to avoid the road which leads to such a depth of suffering and our use of pretexts to avoid it are natural. One of the methods, and a very superficial one, is the assertion that deep things are sophisticated things, unintelligible to an uneducated mind. But the mark of real depth is its simplicity. If you should say, 'This is too profound for me; I cannot grasp it,' you are self-deceptive. For you ought to know that nothing of real importance is too profound for anyone. It is not because it is too profound, but rather because it is too uncomfortable, that you shy away from the truth. Let us not confuse the sophisticated things with the deep things of life.[72]

Tillich—as well as Niebuhr and Graham—identified the doctrine of original sin as the deepest and most mysterious, yet simplest, doctrine of the church. All three men understood humans as clearly divided against themselves and alienated from God. They asserted, furthermore, that human grappling with that condition was the essence of the Christian life. For those lay theologians who responded to and engaged with the theology of each thinker, sin's "simplicity" was not too much for them to grasp.

Part Two

CHAPTER 4

Reinhold Niebuhr, America's Prophet-Pastor

In March 1961, the valedictorian of Andalusia High School in Andalusia, Alabama, wrote Reinhold Niebuhr for advice on her upcoming commencement speech. With his customary generosity and humility, Niebuhr replied that he was honored by her request for help with her speech. He demurred, writing, "I doubt if one can give any guidance which has not been given by now." But he continued and suggested a topic: "I can only say we live in an era which has great promise and great peril."[1]

That a young girl from a small town in Alabama appealed to Niebuhr for guidance demonstrates the extent of his cultural presence at midcentury. Despite Niebuhr's impeccable credentials as a public intellectual—his thought appeared in virtually every major media outlet of the day—scholars have yet to trace his influence outside of intellectual or elite circles. Richard Fox, author of the most comprehensive Niebuhr biography, only alludes to exchanges like the valedictorian example in his study. At the outset of his book, Fox describes Niebuhr as one "totally without ostentation, constitutionally unable to condescend" and calls him a "pure democrat in personal relations" who answered his many "unknown correspondents in the heartland." But this man of the people is absent from the remainder of Fox's text. Other studies of Niebuhr mention his vast audience of everyday Protestants, but they, too, leave this most important facet of his career unexamined and ultimately reflect only his influence on the upper echelon of society.[2]

On the face of it, there is good reason for this separation of Niebuhr from the masses. After all, in 1928 he had left his ministry at Bethel Evangelical Church in Detroit for Union, the nation's premier seminary. As his career advanced, moreover, he routinely associated with other academic superstars and political dignitaries.

Yet despite his departure from parish ministry for academe, Niebuhr retained an interest in and a fundamental respect for lay believers. He

communicated his deep regard for the laity to generations of students at Union by telling two stories about his days at Bethel. One of these was the story of a young boy who had challenged Niebuhr in a Sunday school class. The lesson for the day was the Sermon on the Mount and Jesus's command that his followers "turn the other cheek" if struck by another. The boy interrupted the lesson and told Niebuhr of his work at a local newspaper and its importance to his family's livelihood since the premature death of his father. He explained that daily fights occurred among the newsboys for the most lucrative corner for hawking papers. The boy then asked Niebuhr how he could possibly "turn the other cheek" instead of fighting for the best corner so that he might better provide for his poor family.[3] Niebuhr would finish the story by recalling how, at the time, he had no sufficient answer for the boy. Niebuhr confessed that this experience had taught him a lesson about the naïveté and inadequacy of simplistic Christian piety in the face of such a tragic, sinful world.

The second story was about a humbling encounter with a dying woman from his Bethel congregation. As a preface to the story, Niebuhr related how this woman had made "good use of the school of life and pain." She had, he recollected, "raised a large family under great difficulties" and thus had gained the reverence of both her children and the larger community. Niebuhr numbered among her admirers, and he explained why. As she faced her death, he observed in her an "inner serenity" and "quiet courage" that left him in awe. At the end of the story, he paid this woman a high compliment even as he noted his own sinfulness, admitting that he visited her for "selfish reasons" because he left her bedside "with a more radiant faith" of his own, which in turn increased his "confidence in both man and God."[4]

The dying woman, no doubt, served as a partial inspiration for the "peasant mother" archetype that Niebuhr sometimes invoked in his teaching and writing to express his great respect for members of the laity. He described the peasant mother to his biographer June Bingham as a symbol of "many a simple mother whom I have known, who cares for her brood and achieves a very great serenity in the enterprise, which escapes more sophisticated people." However nostalgic, romanticized, and—as Bingham contended—hyperbolic this picture of the peasant mother may have been, Niebuhr took the idea seriously enough to include it in *The Self and Dramas of History* (1955), and he supported his opinion of the peasant mother with scripture: "I thank thee, Father, that Thou hast withheld these things from the wise and prudent and revealed them unto babes" (Mt 11:25).[5] He used this archetype, to be sure, as a useful rhetorical tool—even a foil—for exposing the excesses of puffed-up clerical and cultural elites. Yet these formative parish experiences and the peasant mother trope clearly indicate that Niebuhr—despite his trenchant criticism of much of midcentury Protestant expression—possessed a genuine appreciation for the wisdom of everyday Protestants.

Another typical and equally understandable rationale for separating Niebuhr's thought from that of everyday Protestants is the idea that for most people, his writings were either too difficult or too gloomy or both. This view is universally repeated in recent accounts of Niebuhr's work, and it is often apparent—though less pervasively—in reviews of his work at midcentury. For example, reviewers of his collection of sermons, *Discerning the Signs of the Times* (1946), had problems identifying the book's audience. One reviewer noted in *Time*, "Intellectual Theologian Niebuhr is no man for the masses," pointing out that the professor even confused his best students at Union. From this perspective, Niebuhr appeared to be no man for anyone. Other reviews of *Discerning the Signs of the Times* in the *New York Times* and in various Christian periodicals characterized the book as somewhat less of an impenetrable intellectual fortress, but all of them cautioned prospective readers, especially the laity, not to expect an easy time with Niebuhr's sermons.[6]

The problem with all these impressions of Niebuhr as "no man for the masses" is that they are unsupported by hard evidence. A lifelong Niebuhr reader and self-described "ordinary fellow" offered a more accurate assessment of the theologian's career. Writing from Atlanta, Georgia, this layman sent a sympathy letter to Ursula Niebuhr after the death of Reinhold in 1971. He wrote that her husband had been his "hero" through the decades and that he had shared Niebuhr's work frequently with his friends, also presumably ordinary fellows. He closed with the hope that Ursula would be consoled by the knowledge of the "influence Dr. Niebuhr had on the 'high and mighty' and on the masses, too!"[7] This letter, the letter from the valedictorian in Alabama, and the letters from the many other heretofore "unknown correspondents" that follow suggest an appreciative laity unaware that Niebuhr was off-limits to them.

Narrow views regarding Niebuhr's audience have also led to a narrow understanding of Niebuhr himself. Niebuhr is normally cast as a prophet of Christian Realism who thundered against nationalist and religious self-righteousness. But this predominant view of Niebuhr obscures the fact that he was also essentially a pastor.[8] His reply to his Alabama correspondent illustrates perfectly this dual role. The grim yet hopeful theme he suggested for her address was as much a prophetic commentary about human nature as it was an observation about the dangerous cold war years of the early sixties. For him, any historical era was one of promise and peril: any given period reflected the ambiguous, sinful natures of the human actors who made history. The pastor in Niebuhr is also evident in his unassuming consideration of the needs of an anonymous teenage girl.

As a prophet-pastor, Niebuhr reached untold numbers of American Protestants. This national congregation was deeply touched by him, moreover, because they had access to their minister in three ways: through his preaching, his teaching of future pastors, and his prolific writing. Indeed, after arriving at Union Theological Seminary, he became something of a modern-day circuit rider, preaching upward of forty weekends each year in the 1930s and 1940s. When he was not on the road, he taught at Union and ministered to the future pastors that he trained there. Meanwhile, he authored nineteen books and published hundreds of articles for a broad range of periodicals, in which he criticized the Protestant revival of mid-century yet, ironically, contributed to its substance. The central and common feature of this three-pronged ministry was his conceptualization of sin. It provided the foundation for his view of the "great promise and great peril" of all human life, a perspective that stirred his many followers to think about their place in the world and their relationship to God.

✣ Niebuhr always understood his calling as a pastoral one. In fact, he repeatedly denied that he was a theologian or a scholar, claiming instead that he was most at home in the pulpit. Late in his career, while counseling a friend who had doubts about his own qualifications for a job at Union Theological Seminary, Niebuhr remarked, "I'm not a scholar, really. I am basically a preacher."[9] And preach he did, first for thirteen years at Bethel and subsequently as an itinerant minister crisscrossing the country to address eager audiences at universities, churches, and forums such as the Chicago Sunday Evening Club.[10] This exhausting regimen, he later told June Bingham, was what he believed had caused the strokes that he suffered in 1952 at the age of sixty, noting that the demanding schedule "did me in more than any other factor."[11]

Despite Niebuhr's rigorous preaching schedule, there exists only a limited record of these events. But two things are clear from what has survived. First, he spoke most often at university-sponsored events. Second, though he rarely preached from a prepared text, his themes were consistent and, as a contemporary noted, "comparatively few."[12] The nature of sin, of course, topped his short list of subjects. The repetition served a purpose; the many layers of human sin, he believed, continually unfolded in human existence, and the issue of sin was therefore an inexhaustible one. In fact, Niebuhr seemed always to be preaching about sin. Outside his formal engagements—the number of which dropped off significantly in the 1950s after his illness—his pulpit was his pen. In this way, he preached to empires and nations and to pastors and parishioners. Indeed, whether he addressed the crisis of the cold war, racism, economic inequity, or American piety, he delivered a consistent homiletic message about sin and salvation.[13]

Niebuhr's discussion of sin usually related in some way to his objections to what he considered the two basic "faiths" of modernity: the perfectibility of man and the notion of a progressive, redemptive history.[14] For Niebuhr believed that if these false answers could be recognized as the idolatries that they were, a renewal and transformation of human life and society was possible. Yet he also believed that genuine repentance eluded the majority of individuals and definitely eluded racial, class, and national groups. Thus, he preached the word of sin out of pastoral concern, hoping to drive believers and communities to contrition.[15] In other words, Niebuhr could speak of renewal for individuals and society only because he could speak so powerfully and profoundly of sin.[16]

The evidence regarding Niebuhr's reception by his audiences suggests that he made lasting impressions on them. A now-legendary incident during his delivery of the prestigious Gifford lectures at the University of Edinburgh in 1939 symbolizes Niebuhr's intensity as a speaker and his ability to hold an audience in the palm of his hand. As the story goes, Niebuhr lectured right through a Nazi air raid, pausing only briefly at the "interruption" caused by bombs falling on Edinburgh, Scotland. A less dramatic report of his command of the pulpit came from a Boston laywoman who heard Niebuhr preach in the early 1930s. "There is no one quite like you" she wrote, "for originality of thought and gift of expression." Niebuhr's unusual talent so moved her that she admitted further, "Though I do not approve of applause at our services, I confess that I was so carried away by your words that I joined with the rest for the first time ever!" Ten years later, a group of teachers, also from Boston, became equally enthusiastic about Niebuhr's preaching, so much so that they formed the "The Niebuhr Club."[17] These and other listeners were perhaps caught up in the authoritative and charismatic presence of Niebuhr. But Niebuhr himself guarded against excessive histrionics while preaching because of his own disdain for exhibitionist preachers.[18]

Yet those impressed by Niebuhr's captivating style also appreciated the content of his sermons. An elderly woman from Chicago, who heard him twice on a single Sunday, recorded her fascination at witnessing the torrent of words coming from Niebuhr's mouth, which she likened to "swift arrows darting through the air" that nevertheless "hit the mark each time, and leave a bloody spot." Her admiration of Niebuhr's skill had as much to do with the clarity and potency of his ideas—hence the reference to "a bloody spot"—as it did with his scintillating presentation.[19] Others in the 1930s and 1940s spoke of his clarity as well as his courageous message and ability to articulate things that they had thought about but had difficulty expressing.[20] Even those Protestants challenged by the complexity of his sermons reported that after hearing Niebuhr preach they had come to a better understanding of themselves as human beings.[21]

Niebuhr's sermons could also penetrate the armor of skeptics and atheists. The "ruthlessness and clearsightedness" of his sermons prompted one skeptical New Yorker to take along two of his atheist friends to hear Niebuhr preach. Niebuhr's critique of the pride of the human will and the "necessity of placing [the] individual will under the Ultimate Will—or God's Will" left all three "deeply shaken" but wanting more. The skeptic noted in his letter that all three eagerly awaited the next opportunity to hear him preach and even suggested a follow-up sermon topic: "the nature of God's will." Apparently, the effect of Niebuhr's words had once again left a "bloody spot." Another New Yorker summarized the gripping yet sustaining impact that his proclamations had on those who heard him: "Thanks for the courage you have given one who sincerely desires to follow Christ but has not found it easy."[22]

Niebuhr continued to preach to everyday Protestants even after his poor health limited his actual pulpit appearances. For example, two women struggling with feelings of guilt concerning their relationships with men and their sexual desires wrote him heartfelt letters seeking his counsel. While an interest in preserving a degree of anonymity certainly informed the decision of each to consult Niebuhr, both expressed an awareness of and a respect for his reputation as an honest Christian thinker. He replied to both correspondents, but to one of the pair, a woman from California who had bluntly asked for his view of premarital sex, Niebuhr wrote what amounted to a brief sermon on sex and sin.[23] The unmarried twenty-eight-year-old woman had written of her doubts about finding a marriage partner because her independence and high standards of "intelligence and ethics" limited her options. Despite her professions of strong spiritual commitment and selectivity, she told Niebuhr that her sex drive was overriding these considerations. Since sex was, in her opinion, an "enriching facet" of religious life, she could not see how premarital sex "within trustworthy friendships" would "flout that religion." Yet she also understood that sex apart from marriage was a sin in the Christian tradition and socially taboo. This quandary troubled her greatly, and her analysis of it demonstrated an affinity for—if not a familiarity with—Niebuhr's suspicion of both individual and religious self-deception. "Should I trust my own reasoning in this matter which I know is likely to be highly colored?" Or, she wrote, "should I trust the Church's reasoning which I feel may not be the final truth?" She had sought Niebuhr's advice on the matter, therefore, because she anticipated that the answer of her own church would be one of judgment and one not necessarily "from God."[24]

Niebuhr answered her carefully and agreed that the "conventional religious answer might be reactionary and thoughtless." But he still affirmed the Christian tradition's prohibition against premarital sex because he believed it to be in accord with the "true facts of human nature" and therefore "not arbitrary." Sexual activity, he warned, deeply affected the human spirit. Consequently, sex without mutual respect was "bound to hurt one or the other partners." He explained, furthermore, that the possibility of emotional injury was greater for the woman. Males, he said, were "much more tempted to waive the convention [against premarital sex] in order to get sexual satisfaction." He also cautioned his correspondent of the consequences of such action, noting that it affected the chances of future marriage for women far more than it did those for men, but he also assured her that premarital sex was not a "mortal sin."[25]

Niebuhr's reply to the young woman must have confirmed for her at least that he was indeed an honest clergyman. In a rather prurient age, Niebuhr had advised the woman without specific prescription or judgment. Clearly, his first concern was not for the moral teaching of Christianity but for the emotional well-being of the woman. Although as an ordained minister he had upheld the Christian injunction against premarital sex, he could have done so with less pastoral grace than he did.

✥ Those Protestants who did not have the privilege of direct contact with Niebuhr's preaching nevertheless benefited from it through his mentoring and teaching of future pastors. In his thirty-two years of work at Union, Niebuhr trained at least two generations of seminarians, many of whom graduated as Niebuhrian disciples and carried his Christian Realism with them into churches throughout America. Early in Niebuhr's tenure at Union, a minister who had audited a course recorded his amazement at the immense "respect" and "affectionate regard" the students held for their teacher. This minister wrote to Niebuhr out of a concern about "whether you had any idea of the influence you exert, or the power you wield, in the lives of the younger generation of ministers and students." He hoped that Niebuhr realized how intensely his students revered him and what a "tremendous responsibility" he carried as one "helping many of us to see more clearly" in a "confused and troubled" world.[26]

Years later, Ronald Stone—Niebuhr's last teaching assistant and a professor of Christian ethics in his own right—studied just how important Niebuhr had been to the ministerial careers of those he taught. Stone canvassed hundreds of former students from every year of Niebuhr's career at Union and found that an overwhelming majority of Niebuhr's pupils treasured his expertise and generosity as a teacher. In particular, Stone's results indicated that Niebuhr's interpretations of sin, ambiguity, irony, justice, history, and love had left an indelible mark on his former students. These concepts, Stone wrote, "became part of who they were in their work."[27]

Niebuhr's influence on pastors outside the Union family, while less personal, is nevertheless apparent. By the 1950s, his theology was so widely known that at least one midwestern church (and likely many more) asked candidates interviewing for a pastoral vacancy for their opinions of Niebuhr's thought.[28] One Lutheran pastor, already established in a church, had definite opinions about the Union professor's work. In his letter to Niebuhr, he asked for advice about his development of a book project for the laity around the theme "immoral man and immoral society," clearly playing off the title of Niebuhr's 1932 classic, *Moral Man and Immoral Society*. There is no record of Niebuhr's reply, but by the 1940s, he also had come to doubt the existence of an unqualifiedly moral man.[29]

Niebuhr "taught" and mentored one young pastor as far away as Texas. This new pastor, who served two small Southern Presbyterian churches in what he described as the "drought-stricken wastes" of West Texas, thanked Niebuhr in his letter for the sustenance that his books had given him in his pastoral call. In fact, he explained, *The Nature and Destiny of Man* lay open on his desk, and he would soon resume reading it, adding that it had been an "enormously helpful" text, especially in helping him complete that week's sermon on "innocent suffering." The image captured in this letter is a powerful one: a lonely preacher stationed in the dusty plains of Texas, who not only found communion in the theology of the nation's leading Christian thinker some two thousand miles to the East but also passed Niebuhr's thought along to his congregations through his sermons. Niebuhr replied with his usual graciousness and no doubt fortified and thrilled his Texas "student" when he commented, "Of course it is always nice to make contact with kindred spirits."[30]

Another pastor and "kindred spirit" recorded an equally powerful story of Niebuhr's long-distance teaching and mentoring. After collapsing from overwork as a newspaperman, this Methodist had "demanded *The Nature and Destiny of Man*" from his hospital bed and subsequently found himself at Drew Seminary. As he prepared for the ministry, the importance of Niebuhr's theology to his studies became so acute that he transferred to Union to "find out," he said, "how you were saying these words" that he had first encountered in books. He feared they were spoken in arrogance. His first class with Niebuhr convinced him, to his great relief, that the man he had admired in print was even better in person. Niebuhr taught, he wrote, in "a spirit of love and charity." The pastor documented his moving theological journey for Niebuhr simply to inform his former professor of the "unseen ministry you perform daily via your writings."[31]

Niebuhr's *Leaves from the Notebook of a Tamed Cynic* was another crucial piece of his "unseen ministry" to pastors. *Leaves* was a compilation of Niebuhr's diary from his years as a pastor at Bethel; published in 1929, it was a favorite among clergy from that day forward. The honesty with which Niebuhr exposed his own pettiness and self-suspicion, as well as his recording of the pleasures—but more often the pitfalls—of parish work, comforted pastors who faced the same personal and professional issues in their ministries. Niebuhr's candor about his own faith and the eager reception of the book among clergy are important reminders that pastors were and are searching Christians too.[32] Niebuhr understood this about himself and about the office of the ministry in general: ministers, from Niebuhr's perspective, were sinners like everybody else.

Niebuhr confronted this reality of the pastoral calling several times, but perhaps never more plainly than in the aptly titled address, "The Hazards and the Difficulties of the Christian Ministry." He first presented this essay to an audience of pastors at Union's Conference on the Ministry in 1953.[33] He began the talk with an obvious assertion: "The first difficulty to be really Christian is to have a vital Christian faith and maintain it." This difficulty, for all its obviousness, was no less painful, since obstacles to a "vital" and lasting faith surfaced in Christians immediately and often. One such roadblock to faith was Christianity's requirement of a trust that the mystery of existence had meaning, a trust that "God dwell[ed] in this mystery." Without this sense of mystery, he continued, the individual was "very far from the Christian faith." Christians, however, could deny mystery just as much as if not more than non-Christians. In fact, denials of divine mystery often came from the mouths of the most religious of Christians. Whether in the pulpit or the pew, these were Christians who denied God by affirming God so absolutely, something Niebuhr characterized as the "pretension of knowing more about God than anybody has a right to know, [of being] a pretender into the privacy of God."[34] Niebuhr warned pastors about this attitude—the sin of religious pride—because he understood them to be particularly tempted by it.

The final hazard of the Christian ministry, according to Niebuhr, was another form of denial. When Christians avoided and thus denied the fact that faith consisted of perpetual repentance, they committed the primal sins of unbelief and pride. At this point in his presentation, he provided a basic discussion of the workings of sin and grace in the Christian faith. He explained the problem of sin perhaps more simply than he ever had: "I think I am a good man. I pretend that I am a virtuous man, and a wise man, until I confront God in Christ, and then I know that I am in the wrong before him because of all these pretenses." The answer to this predicament, said Niebuhr, was Christ, who absolved the sinner in an ultimate sense, but not in any temporal sense. Although the believer became a "new creature" in Christ, the old, sinful self stubbornly remained and continued to assert itself. He told his audience of pastors that Christ, in fact, saved the Christian sinner on a daily basis. For Niebuhr, this vexing and paradoxical situation of the Christian marked the true stumbling block of faith: "Unless, on the one hand, we obey the biblical injunction to be like Christ, and on the other hand, know that we can never be like Christ, we have not mastered the difficulty of the Christian life."[35] The elementary lesson about the meaning of sin and salvation that Niebuhr gave to this audience of religious professionals who had studied the intricacies of theology for several years demonstrates the firmness of his belief that ministers needed this word as much as if not more than the laity.

Niebuhr's articulation of the sheer force of human sin assisted many like-minded pastors with their theology, their sermons, and their own personal Christian experiences. Of course, Niebuhr's blunt and uncompromising view of sin came in part from his keen sense of his own sinfulness, something that he had chronicled in his diary as a new pastor in Detroit and certainly something that informed his analysis of the condition in his writings, especially *The Nature and Destiny of Man*. He also confessed this self-knowledge late in his life to Bingham: "It's certainly not modesty which persuades me that my thought is not significant enough for recording, and that my personal life is certainly not. But I trust you even though you naturally can not know the secrets of the heart and will be too generous in your judgments."[36] It is no wonder, then, that ministers in contact with Niebuhr's thought preached a thoroughgoing doctrine of sin to their congregations, since it so thoroughly suffused their mentor's work. They also may have done so for the simple reason that, like Niebuhr, they were preaching to the "secrets" of their own hearts.

✠ The vast majority of Protestants and ministers never heard Niebuhr preach, nor did they have the opportunity to attend his classes. Yet many of them came to know of his analysis of sin through the astonishing output of his pen and through his unrivaled status as a public intellectual in the 1940s and 1950s. Bookstore owners and librarians, for example, cleared additional space on their shelves in the 1940s, as he added six new titles to his existing seven; they did so again in the 1950s, when he wrote five more. In these same decades, mainstream periodicals and newspapers reserved editorial space for him. The *Nation*, *Life*, *Fortune*, and the *New York Times*, to name a few, repeatedly sought articles and book reviews from him, and they generally covered his doings and sayings for an interested public.[37] From 1945 to 1948, the *Religious News Service* sent a weekly Niebuhr column over the wire to such newspapers as the *Boston Globe* and the *St. Louis Globe-Democrat* and to several leading denominational periodicals. Of course, Niebuhr continued to write for the *Christian Century* and for the two journals he had founded, *Christianity and Society* and *Christianity and Crisis*. While his books and articles landed most often in the hands of academics and everyday Protestants, even the State Department and the War Department used several of his volumes in conducting American diplomacy.[38] In addition to appearing in printed media, his powerful words were heard regularly over the airwaves on various radio shows. He also made an early appearance on television in 1948, headlining ABC's first *I Believe* program, which explored the connection of religion to "everyday living." The subject for the inaugural show was "How Far Should the Christian Make Security the Basic Motive of Life?"[39]

In the minds of some, including Richard Fox, this public presence made Niebuhr America's "official Establishment theologian." Fox, however, treats this title dubiously in his biography. For him, the Establishment Niebuhr is the complacent Niebuhr who traded his more radical socialist positions of the 1930s for a disappointing apologetic for American democracy in the cold war era.[40] Yet if Niebuhr was indeed America's Establishment theologian, then the Establishment and the many Americans who trusted in it at midcentury possessed a theological imagination that took the problem of sin quite seriously. This alternate Establishment hypothesis, in fact, looks quite plausible in the context of Niebuhr's 1948 appearance on the cover of *Time*; in the responses of everyday Protestants to his magnum opus, *The Nature and Destiny of Man*; and in light of his own complicated, ironic relationship to post–World War II Protestantism in general.

The bulk of the *Time* cover article—the "man's story is not a success story" issue—dealt with Niebuhr's doctrine of man and his explanation of how and why original sin tainted every aspect of man's existence. The article, authored by Whitaker Chambers, summarized why, for Niebuhr, "the tissue of history" was saturated with evil and "why at the height of man's perfection there is always the possibility of evil."[41]

For a small sample of *Time*'s readers—the magazine printed just eight letters—the weightiness of these ideas was less bothersome than what they considered Niebuhr's unintelligibility. Five of the eight respondents complained in this way, while the remaining three found his thought perfectly understandable and agreeable. That three readers concurred with Niebuhr's perspective is persuasive but not conclusive evidence of popular attitudes concerning sin. Similarly, little can be made of the fact that the five negative reactions were written by the most educated of the correspondents, though it at least hints at the difficulty in categorizing Niebuhr's audience as primarily an elite one. Two educated pastors, for example, protested the unclear nature of the piece, as did a presumably educated layman who, ironically, faulted Niebuhr for his "obfuscating theological phraseology."[42]

Beyond these rather inconclusive letters to the editors of *Time*, the relative silence of the rest of the magazine's readers may be the most important evidence concerning the reception of Niebuhr's "man's story is not a success story" cover. This silence, to be sure, could be interpreted in multiple ways. It could mean that subscribers did not read the piece or that if they did, they were not moved by its content. It could also mean that *Time*'s editors cut off debate by printing just eight letters in one subsequent edition, although the magazine's usual practice was to print letters for several weeks if enough readers wrote in. Or it is possible that the idea that "man's story was not a success story" was a common position in 1948, one not controversial enough to inspire too many letters from *Time*'s readers. The fact that the modest sales of Niebuhr's two-volume *Nature and Destiny of Man* doubled from forty to eighty per week after the 1948 cover story and that he received thoughtful letters from everyday Protestants who had read the book lends some credence to this last interpretation, as does Chambers's claim in the article that "any person of average patience can find out what he [Niebuhr] is saying in *The Nature and Destiny of Man*."[43]

Chambers may have overstated the case. In a review of the book in 1941, he had doubted that the "man in the pew" would read it, and then added, curiously but presciently, that congregations would "hear about it from the pulpit for years to come."[44] Chambers's comment anticipated Niebuhr's "unseen ministry" among pastors like the one from West Texas, even as it seemed to confirm the dominant impression of scholars that Niebuhr's readership was far more circumscribed. Richard Fox, for instance, called Niebuhr's opus "scarcely a 'popular' work" and one that "was no hit in the churches themselves." But he, like many others who assume that Niebuhr was cut off from the masses, marshals little concrete evidence for this view and simply asserts that the book was irrelevant to the churches because it was "too difficult," contained no real doctrine of the church, and offered no sustained discussion of salvation.[45]

Still, in one sense, Fox may be right that *Nature and Destiny* was "no hit" with the churches. Average sales of eighty copies per week marked the title as a respectable but not an overwhelming success if judged only by that criterion. But other indicators point to the conclusion that the book had a popular following and was indeed a hit with the churches. The National Conference of Christians and Jews, for instance, recommended *Nature and Destiny* for its national Religious Book Week program in 1944. In fact, the brochure for the program advertised *Nature and Destiny* as one among several titles selected with "the average reader" in mind.[46] Twelve years later, the book still commanded attention; a reviewer for the newly launched *Christianity Today* recommended several of Niebuhr's major works, including *Nature and Destiny*—despite his opinion that Niebuhr was not fully orthodox—and informed the publication's two hundred thousand readers that it was a "readily accessible" title. Such opinions of the book's readability and its importance to Protestant congregational life help explain why one rural Illinois parson, who spoke for many of his colleagues, ranked *Nature and Destiny* second only to the Bible for providing substance to his faith and to the sermons that he delivered in his country church.[47]

The 1964 release of the paperback editions of *Nature and Destiny* prompted similar reactions.[48] Although two decades had passed since its initial publication, Niebuhr's book remained relevant to a new generation of Protestants. From the 1940s through the 1960s, Niebuhr received short notes from lay readers who wrote expressing their appreciation as well as more detailed letters from the educated and uneducated alike. These Protestants were unfazed by the difficulty of the text. For instance, a reader from San Diego, California, admitted in his letter that he was "much challenged by this sort of intellectualism," but he also included an outline of the book that demonstrated a sound grasp of the content of *Nature and Destiny*. He added that the intellectualism of the text had strengthened his faith and noted that he tried to balance such intellectualism with a focus on Jesus in the Bible study classes that he taught. In his reply, Niebuhr affirmed the thrust of the layman's take on his book, since he also searched for a balance between his so-called intellectualism and the greater importance of Jesus Christ for the Protestant faith.[49]

Niebuhr's sophisticated analysis of the nature of man and sin inspired two other readers to write to him, each with a very different but equally significant reaction to the book. The first, a graduate student, observed that *Nature and Destiny* had, in his opinion, uncovered the central problem of Western civilization. He agreed with Niebuhr's warnings about the dangers of an underdeveloped view of human nature, blaming "the present catastrophe" of the modern world on its "false anthropology." According to this educated layman, the stakes of persisting in this error were high; the very sanity of the world depended upon its acceptance of a Niebuhrian perspective of the human situation.[50]

The second reader, a laywoman from New Jersey, had other ideas about the recovery of sanity in the world. She wrote, as she put it, as one without "authority" on matters of human nature who had pursued her interest in the subject through "countless letters" to those who were "in authority." Following this "passion," as she termed it, had led her to *Nature and Destiny*. She wrote of her belief in original sin, which she defined according to Augustine's view of man's inherited spiritual ill health, but she also offered her own definition. She wrote that "man cannot know God" because "he has something disturbing his personal relationship with God." She believed, however, that adjustments to one's diet and environment could help the individual "work to eliminate" the symptoms of sin. While her view was a little eccentric, this laywoman's admixture of nutrition and environmental factors with theology was still coherent. She went on to provide a sound, even sophisticated interpretation of the Garden of Eden story linking her concern for nutrition with the consumption of the forbidden fruit as an explanation for humanity's unhealthy eating habits. In all of this, including her desire to eliminate sinful action, she was entirely devoid of self-righteousness and made it clear that the process of elimination of sin was difficult and incomplete. These ideas about sin and sinlessness were part of her ultimate goal, which was, quoting Niebuhr, to "release [humanity] for the adventure of love."[51] This most unusual letter epitomizes the variety of response to

Nature and Destiny and demonstrates that lay theologians like this New Jersey woman thought seriously about sin. And the diversity of this correspondence sharply challenges any doubts about Niebuhr's influence with everyday Protestants, even when he was at his most difficult.

✥ As ordinary pastors and laypeople participated in the theological revival by paging through *Nature and Destiny* and writing their thoughts about it in letters to the esteemed professor, Niebuhr was busy evaluating the revival as a whole. In his analysis, Niebuhr found much to complain of and often referred to the phenomenon not as a "revival" per se but as the "revival of interest" in religion. As this revival of interest in religion advanced, so too did his skepticism of its legitimacy. At his most vitriolic, he dismissed the notion that Americans cared about a "God who can be known only through repentance." Instead, according to Niebuhr, Protestants had what he called a "faith in faith," a deference to a generic "God" that filled the void left after the Great Depression and two world wars had refuted American liberalism's faith in progress. Because of the spiritual emptiness of the "technical society" that remained after the failure of liberalism, in other words, religion had become attractive again to Americans. But, Niebuhr argued, this turn toward religion "had little to do with the Christian faith." "Our modern religiosity," he wrote, "expresses various forms of self-worship." Chief among these solipsistic Christian expressions, he said, was the religion of self-esteem proffered by Norman Vincent Peale and his "power of positive thinking." Judged by these facts, he bluntly concluded in 1955, "we can take no satisfaction in the pervading religiosity in our nation."[52]

This is the familiar, prophetic Niebuhr—the Niebuhr who was unrelenting in his criticism of America's "easy conscience" about sacred and secular issues, as well as its tendency to confuse the one with the other. The familiar Niebuhr, however, has become too familiar. With few exceptions, scholars have accepted his prophetic critique of the revival at face value. Rarely have historians acknowledged that Niebuhr's most damning comments about postwar Protestantism were also his most irresponsible. As a consequence, statements of his appreciation for certain aspects of the revival have been overshadowed by fulminations against other aspects.[53]

One conspicuous measure of Niebuhr's more charitable assessment of midcentury Protestantism was his defense of the faith of President Eisenhower. Ike's presidential piety has become a symbol of the superficiality of belief in the 1950s in large part because of one famous comment: "Our form of government has no sense unless it is founded in a deeply felt religious faith, and I don't care what it is." Yet in two different articles from the midfifties, Niebuhr suggested that Eisenhower was a sincere believer, even if he had less respect for the president's public assertions about Christianity. In one of these articles, though, he had credited Eisenhower for his eloquence at one of the well-publicized "prayer breakfasts" held in the capital—praise all the more surprising since these occasions are usually accounted as further evidence of Christianity's captivity in the era.[54]

Niebuhr provided a much stronger affirmation of midcentury Protestantism as part of a 1955 *Newsweek* feature on appreciation for "theology and the Gospel" in America. In the article, he noted the transition away from what he called "the sentimental if-theology" of American Protestantism. "If-theology," for Niebuhr, was the naively optimistic sort of faith that proclaimed, "If only everybody obeyed God's laws what a wonderful world this would be." To his mind, such utopianism and misjudgment of human nature was "being replaced by a hardheaded practicality that is long overdue."[55]

Niebuhr's lengthier, more substantive assessments of the revival were less sure about the demise of "if-theology" within American Protestantism. But even these more incisive articles retained a subtle hopefulness about the possibilities present in this return to religion. The *New York Times Magazine* published the first of these appraisals in 1950. Although Niebuhr viewed the resurgence of piety ambivalently, he cautioned against hasty judgments of its authenticity. The new interest in religion had many layers, he said, and both its supporters and critics tended to interpret it based on their own commitments, sympathies, and assumptions. The critics, therefore, emphasized the escapism of the revival, while the enthusiasts boasted only of the sincerity of the revival. Niebuhr, in contrast, saw evidence of both escapism and sincerity. In 1950, just as the revival was beginning to take hold, he favored the "sincerity" interpretation and noted the "serenity" possible within the revival. While he granted that some aspects of the new religiosity were "hysterical" reactions to the crisis of the times and that other aspects of it were sincere but "irrelevant" to the complexity of the age, he voiced the belief that something more profound might also be at work. He concluded the article with this hopeful view of the potential for a revival aware of the "depth and height of our human existence," of its "mystery and meaning" and of the "renewals of life which are possible if destructions and frustrations are appropriated with contrition rather than bitterness." Such a faith, he thought, "could contribute to the 'healing of the nations.' "[56]

His perspective had not changed substantially when he published his second major evaluation of the revival in the *New Republic* in 1955. The title of the article, "Varieties of Religious Revival," suggested the same multidimensional view of the phenomenon that he had articulated in 1950. He came down much harder on the "hysterical" forms of faith, which he identified with the peace-and-success gospel of Norman Vincent Peale and others. Billy Graham represented the sincere but irrelevant expression of Protestantism, and Niebuhr registered his aversion to what he called Graham's "simple religious moralism"—although, as he would maintain in his later articles on Graham, the evangelist was "certainly superior to the success cults."

Yet beneath the "dangerous" contribution of Peale and the "dubious" contribution of Graham lay a "genuine revival."[57] Niebuhr associated this genuine revival mostly with the "increased sympathy for faith among 'intellectuals.' " But he also wrote, condescendingly yet tellingly, that it had touched "the simple and the credulous," as well. And although he allocated more space in the article to his assault on mainstream Protestant expression, he indicated that the genuine revival of which he wrote had been preserved in "many churches." Niebuhr's conceptualization of the genuine revival was both brief and a bit vague. His impression that a genuine revival had occurred in "many churches," however, suggested that his hope in 1950 for a Christianity attuned to the "depth and height" and "mystery and meaning" of the human experience had been realized. In the remainder of his article, he encouraged the development of these "many churches," offering a theological road map that he believed to be crucial to their survival. These churches, he advised, had to continue to communicate the Gospel, what he termed "the age-old answer to the human problem." And that answer, for Niebuhr, was simple: only God could complete the otherwise fragmentary nature of human life. The task of these churches, then, was to hold fast to the "mystery and meaning of freedom, sin, and grace" as the wellspring of the religious life, while conceding that these mysteries remained irresolvable in the life of the believer. Niebuhr concluded his plan for the genuine church by arguing that it must recognize its own ambiguity. Indeed, only in the knowledge of its own incompleteness could it truly be the Christian church.[58]

A few *New Republic* readers responded positively to Niebuhr's evaluation of the revival, but not without criticism. Two of these wanted greater assurance that goodness existed outside of Niebuhr's conclusion that "evil seems so inextricably mixed with the good in the same man and the same culture." This hesitancy about Niebuhr's opinion of the nature of good and evil exposed the writers' liberal theological bias—unsurprising in readers of the *New Republic*—but they both acknowledged that the "great evils" of history had significantly challenged any easy faith in the triumph of the good. Another reader fully endorsed Niebuhr's complicated analysis of sin and evil in America. He had grown impatient with the many articles that said nothing more than "Retreat from sin, isn't it wonderful." Despite his affinity for Niebuhr's perspective, he judged Americans to be both more religious and less religious than Niebuhr allowed. For this correspondent, the Puritan legacy in America had guarded against uncritical faith in secular alternatives to Christianity, except that of the "religion" of capitalism. Faith in "material success," he wrote, "penetrates every highway and byway of our land," so much so that "success is the creed from the cradle to the grave."[59]

Paul Brinkman, a devoted fan who corresponded with Niebuhr for more than a year, raised similar questions about capitalism in his reaction to "Varieties of Religious Revival." "I, along with many others," he wrote, "have been wondering about this 'return to religion.'" He was not yet convinced of its "fruits," in part because he judged the revival to have neglected the "avarice which holds American people in thralldom." Brinkman's worries, however, went beyond the ethics of capitalism. In earlier letters, he had despaired over the whole state of the "modern world." From a Christian standpoint, Brinkman felt that "our modern world while it provides life for us actually kills us or commits suicide for us." The artificial and synthetic components of modern living did not allow humans to be truly human, as prescribed by the teachings of Jesus. Niebuhr's replies to Brinkman were direct and succinct, neither skirting the melancholic Brinkman's concerns nor answering them with his usual touch of pastoral grace. But Brinkman found them "helpful," writing, "It's a wonder you could take the time to reply to my queries!"[60]

Niebuhr's most favorable appraisal of the revival appeared in a Dutch periodical in 1956. He took the position that "at its worst," American religiosity mixed the Christian faith with faith in "The American Way of Life," which for him meant "faith in a free society and passion for good plumbing." The majority of the article, however, championed the "best" of American Protestantism. For Niebuhr, this list of bests included the strong tradition of "lay leadership and responsibility" and the "vitality" and "genuine communit[y]" of the congregations. These features, he continued, looked even better in comparison with the poor state of Christianity in Europe.[61]

Despite recognizing these virtues of the postwar revival, Niebuhr also argued that if America was the most religious of modern nations, it was also the most secular (an argument that he would reprise in his 1958 book *Pious and Secular America*). For at least the third time, he rehearsed his criticism of Norman Vincent Peale, who, he thought, epitomized the religious syncretism of the day by making "religious piety the servant of the desire for success." But he markedly changed his tone with respect to Billy Graham. Instead of again dismissing Graham as irrelevant, he explained that "the conservative revivalism under the leadership of Billy Graham has much more biblical foundations and defies, rather than serves, the ambition for worldly success."[62] This more forgiving view of the religious scene in America and of Billy Graham and his "conservative revivalism," in particular, may have been a defensive reaction against the European critics of American piety, but it also recalled Niebuhr's earlier impression that a "genuine revival" was taking place in 1950s America.

✤ Niebuhr's view of the American Protestant revival was mixed, although it must be said that he criticized it more than he complimented it. His critical apologetic, however, ultimately—and ironically—pushed the revival toward greater theological depth. In other words, his critique of postwar Protestantism and its widespread dissemination certainly perpetuated the enduring image of midcentury religious complacency, even as its popularity also successfully combated that same complacency.

The irony of Niebuhr's popularity in the midst of the captive revival was not lost on commentator William Lee Miller. Miller, a friend of Niebuhr's, published an article in the *Reporter* titled "The Irony of Reinhold Niebuhr." But Miller, in an otherwise laudatory review of Niebuhr's theology, gave the irony of Niebuhr's fame within the culture a negative turn. He argued that the regular coverage that Niebuhr received in the pages of Henry Luce's *Time* and *Life* magazines revealed the "ambiguities and paradoxes" of success. According to Miller, Niebuhr was a victim of "his own greatness," a thinker "admired but misunderstood, praised but not followed." Miller worried, moreover, that Niebuhr had been co-opted by a type of conservatism "which likes religion, and especially likes the doctrine of original sin."[63] Miller pressed the irony further, observing that

Time and *Life* promoted Luce's idyllic vision of America, precisely the attitude Niebuhr constantly attacked in his books and articles.[64]

While Miller had a point, he overstated both Niebuhr's appropriation by Luce and the irony of his success. In the first place, Luce, though described by one biographer as a "champion of God and free enterprise," had published one of Niebuhr's sharpest critiques of capitalism in *Fortune*, the businessman's weekly devotional.[65] In the 1942 article, Niebuhr called laissez-faire economics "a nice device for having your cake and eating it too . . . for it gave the assurance that 'each man seeking his own would serve the commonweal.' The only difficulty with the idea is that it is not true."[66] In fact, comments such as these eroded whatever congeniality might once have existed between Niebuhr and Luce. By the early 1960s, Niebuhr confirmed the deterioration of their relationship to Tillich, writing, "[Luce] does not approve of me at all."[67]

As it turned out, Niebuhr's success in America was not so ironic, even on Miller's terms. Niebuhr was, for him, "a product of American Christianity." Miller resisted both those who claimed that Niebuhr was something more, "a unique phenomenon" unrelated to American Protestantism, and those who claimed that he was something less, assuming, as the "atheists for Niebuhr" did, that his insights could be adopted without close attention to their derivation from Christianity. While Miller acknowledged that American Protestantism "did better than it intended in producing him," he insisted that Niebuhr could not be isolated from "the American Protestantism in which he was born, in which he grew up and was educated, and in which he . . . spent his whole life and career preaching and teaching."[68] Miller's point was well taken, even if he did not fully articulate its implications. Niebuhr was truly devoted to the American Protestant church, as his 1950 and 1955 appraisals of the revival indicate. In fact, Miller himself noted Niebuhr's dedication to the church by reproducing the theologian's comparison of it to Noah's Ark: "Despite the storm without and the smell within, [the church] points to a truth beyond its own stating of it."[69] The true irony of Niebuhr's position within the postwar context, then, is not Miller's negative irony but a positive irony that Miller and subsequent scholars have never really entertained. That is, if Niebuhr's critical thought was so widely distributed and appreciated—a fact that made him America's "Establishment theologian"— then Niebuhr must have constructively influenced the direction of Protestant expression at midcentury.

This positive irony is all too profound in light of how widely Niebuhr's theology circulated within the major popular periodicals of the day. Perhaps nowhere was this more evident than in *Life* magazine's Christmas issue of 1955. *Life* devoted the entire edition to Christianity and featured both the captive and theological revivals prominently. The principle article on the theological revival, "The World, the Flesh and the Devil," drew heavily from Niebuhr's theology, as well as from the thought of his brother H. Richard Niebuhr and his colleague Paul Tillich. The bulk of the article, however, relied more heavily on Reinhold's work than on that of the other two theologians. The editors reproduced his basic view of humanity, noting that he believed that "sinfulness is deep and universal in man," and Niebuhrian themes of sin and Godly transcendence framed the article's discussion of the temptation to sin and the false judgments and false redemptive schemes of non-Christian movements. For example, to the assurance of psychologists who stressed "salvation" by means of individual "wholeness, the integrated personality, and adjustment," the piece gave an utterly Niebuhrian response: "The true health of the Christian soul is not measured by a bovine 'adjustment' to life." Likewise, to the "world's promise of an attainable quasi-Eden," the article continued in a recognizable Niebuhrian tone, the Christian "must respond [to such promises] with an unqualified no." Finally, in a warning against the facile correlation of communism with Satan—though communism was referred to as "a form of Satan in action"—the article stated, just as Niebuhr would have, that Satan also lurked in the American penchant for national self-righteousness.[70]

Niebuhr's appearance in other popular media only added to the irony of his station within the culture. In these venues, as in *Life*'s Christmas issue, his work was both critical of American Protestantism and a constitutive component of it. For example, reprints of his sermons could be found in the multivolume set *America's Best Sermons* along with the work of other leading religious figures of the era. Similarly, the booming religious book market included introductory guides, such as *The Handbook of Christian Theology* (1958), that targeted a general audience. Niebuhr, not surprisingly, authored the short essay "Sin" for the volume. In fact, Arthur Cohen, an editor for Meridian, which published the text, informed Niebuhr that the book was "intended to meet the needs of serious Protestant readership."[71] In that same vein, William Hordern's *Layman's Guide to Protestant Theology* (1955) also disseminated Niebuhr's work to a broad audience of everyday Protestants. Hordern wrote his volume, in part, as a negative response to much of the piety of the 1950s; but he was also convinced that a hungry audience was seeking richer theological food and longed for such a book. He presented various theological positions in the book, from orthodoxy to liberalism (he favored the neo-orthodox stance), and he highlighted individual theologians, including Niebuhr. His discussion of Niebuhr's theology drew heavily from *Nature and Destiny*, supplying the layperson or the pastor with a firm grounding in the theology of sin.[72]

Another book, *The Search for America* (1959) by religious studies professor Huston Smith, introduced still more Americans to Niebuhr's thought. Smith's project had grown out of a public television series of the same name. The program had gathered together intellectual luminaries from the social sciences and humanities in an effort to study "American values" and to discern "who we are by asking what we would like to become." The comments of the contributors were originally broadcast over thirty-three television stations to several million viewers, and Smith judged that the "net effect" of the program had not been "soothing." He anticipated, therefore, that Americans would "draw little comfort from" the subsequent book. Niebuhr contributed two essays, one addressing the notion of progress and the other, morality. Both supported Smith's predictions about potential reader discomfort. Niebuhr argued in the first essay that progress as an article of faith deluded humankind into an unrealistic perception of the "congruity" of history. Progress was, at best, fragmentary and full of irony. He commented on the general malaise of the 1950s as an example, observing, "We have achieved an unprecedented standard of comfort, yet happiness eludes us." To drive home his point, he closed with one of his most famous passages, which had first appeared in *The Irony of American History* (1952). Before Americans became seduced by progress, he urged them to consider the following proposition: "Nothing worth doing is completed in our lifetime; therefore, we must be saved by hope. Nothing true or beautiful or good makes complete sense in any immediate context of history; therefore, we must be saved by faith. Nothing we do, however virtuous, can be accomplished alone; therefore, we are saved by love. No virtuous act is quite as virtuous from the standpoint of our friend or foe as from our standpoint. Therefore, we must be saved by the final form of love which is forgiveness." In the other essay, Niebuhr warned against easy assumptions about morality. He charged that the "evil and failure that permeate life and history at every level" made it impossible to understand existence as "in any obvious sense moral." The full weight and complexity of his thought about the distorted reality of the human condition, then, reached the American public in a variety of ways.[73]

Yet the abundant magazine coverage and the other popular media that circulated Niebuhr's thought paled in comparison to the special place that his Serenity Prayer occupied in the devotional lives of innumerable everyday Protestants in postwar America. The prayer, perhaps the most familiar in the United States after the Lord's Prayer, perfectly illustrates Niebuhr's prophetic and pastoral message in relation to the human situation. Though there is some doubt as to whether Niebuhr actually wrote the prayer—some credit St. Francis of Assisi as the original author—evidence gathered by Richard Fox and others has largely refuted the idea that he plagiarized it.[74] Over the years, the prayer has morphed into several variations, but Niebuhr favored the following version: "God, give us the serenity to accept what cannot be changed; Give us the courage to change what should be changed; Give us the wisdom to distinguish one from the other."[75]

Niebuhr's whole vision of a fallen humanity and a merciful God is present in this prayer. For him, the fundamental human predicament, characterized by the glories and the limitations of freedom and finitude, never changed, yet this elemental aspect of the human experience was the very thing that humans consistently rebelled against. Indeed, the universal refusal of human beings to accept "what cannot be changed" fertilized the already deeply rooted sin of pride—hence the opening plea of the prayer. In an early interpretation of the prayer, he stated the message of the prayer simply: "We are not God." Yet, from Niebuhr's perspective, little "Gods" are exactly what humans, in their prideful denial of human finitude, attempted to be.[76] Niebuhr's sense of human freedom, however, maintained that humans were not totally sinful and that they could still "change what should be changed." The final stanza of the prayer, though, returned to the theme of humility introduced in the first stanza. For the wisdom to navigate the dilemma of what could and could not be changed came from God, not from any human capacity. In sum, the Serenity Prayer reinforced not only Niebuhr's unwavering conviction of humanity's stubborn overestimation of its freedom to discern and direct its own destiny but also his equal conviction of God's great mercy and guidance for those contrite of heart.[77]

Masses of everyday American Protestants prayed these words on bended knee. Along with their cigarettes and chocolate bars, GIs received a copy of the prayer upon deployment overseas during World War II. Alcoholics recited it in their battle against addiction after Alcoholics Anonymous adopted it, with Niebuhr's blessing, as the organization's official prayer. Others encountered it in Christian devotionals and drugstore greeting cards. While many speakers of the prayer had no idea that Niebuhr had written it and may not have understood it as a commentary on human sin, few could have said it without a sense of its message regarding the obstinacy of the human will and the transcendence of God. Ultimately, then, the Serenity Prayer is the most prominent example of Niebuhr's ironic theological influence within midcentury Protestantism, even if his "congregants" in this case were mostly unaware of it.

✠ In addition to these examples of Niebuhr's imprint on the Protestant landscape at midcentury, more specific lay reactions to his work provide on-the-ground barometers of Protestant interest in and reception of his view of human nature. To be sure, not all Protestants who engaged with his thought embraced it. Since the 1930s, Protestants from both sides of the theological spectrum had objected to what they characterized as an overly pessimistic judgment of humanity. Some liberal Protestants, for example, wished that Niebuhr "would have a little more faith in man's potentialities." Conservative Protestants had less trouble with his powerful sense of sin than they did with what they thought was insufficient attention to Christ's triumph over sin and subsequent rebirth in righteousness. Still others, whose theological persuasions were not readily identifiable, accepted the ambiguity or, as one of them called it, "the moral gray" of the human situation and of history; but they balked, as the others did, at what they understood as Niebuhr's pessimistic fatalism. He clearly disturbed the equanimity of these Protestants and their optimism —drawn though it was from two separate theological traditions—about the human ability to be good. One layman, likely a theological liberal, expressed this sort of consternation with Niebuhr's view of human nature in a letter to Paul Tillich: "I really should gird my mental sword and do battle with Dr. Niebuhr, particularly about his original sin concepts," which the correspondent dismissed as "Teutonic morbidity." "But then," he continued, "in some respects I agree with him, which makes arguing more difficult."[78]

Some Christians, though far fewer, found Niebuhr too optimistic. A California man, for instance, objected to Niebuhr's emphasis on the grandeur rather than the misery of man. He doubted the existence of freedom of the will, and he and Niebuhr discussed the issue in some lively exchanges in 1956. He argued that Niebuhr conceptualized freedom too generously, and he claimed instead that "forces outside of the will" determined human action, "good or bad." In his answer to the Californian, Niebuhr defended human freedom, yet maintained that it was not an absolute freedom. This, he said, exemplified "why there can be no completely rational solution to the problem of determinism" (his own solution was the doctrine of responsibility despite inevitability).[79]

Finally, many Protestants simply valued his willingness to tackle the problem of sin directly. Some among this number wrote him brief but telling letters on the subject of human nature. One businessman, for example, read Niebuhr's "Cultural Crisis of Our Age" in the *Harvard Business Review* and commented on the theologian's impressive analysis of "self-interest" and "the hard facts of human nature and the world as it is." Far from the corridors of big business, a rural West Virginian wrote to Niebuhr of what he described as his own "amateur study" of the forces of good and evil, concluding as a good Niebuhrian disciple would, that pride bore the primary responsibility for the evil in the world.[80]

Occasionally Niebuhr received lengthier letters from Protestants who were pleased simply to share their views of the human condition with him. One of these, Stanley Tappan, of Connecticut, sought Niebuhr's counsel regarding the fallacy of those who distinguished between good and evil human beings. As he put it, "Is there a line drawn through the middle of all humanity, with all goody, goody, people on one side and bad people on the other side?" He argued that the issue was more complex. Since God had created all humans, God must have sanctioned both the "ugly, vicious and unjust" along with the "good and just." He illustrated his point by reasoning that both Albert Schweitzer and Adolf Hitler were "Godly" men because they were "both creatures of God." Although he did not genuinely believe that Hitler was a "Godly" man, he used the dictator as an example—albeit an extreme one—to highlight the degree to which humans relied upon "dogma, creeds, ritual, and authoritarian religion" to make swift judgments about human character without really considering the full implications of an omniscient God who was responsible for the human race. He asserted instead that "we are all Godly people, whether we be saint or sinner." Whether Niebuhr replied is unknown. It is reasonable to speculate that had he written back, he would have corrected some aspects of this man's theological outlook; but it seems just as likely that he also would have affirmed the dismay that this layman articulated about the easy divisions that humans employed to separate the "goody people" from the "bad people."[81]

Another lay theologian, who preferred to remain anonymous, had his own doubts about the goodness of humanity, though he had worked out his thoughts more carefully than had Tappan. Self-described as "a common-man," he considered Niebuhr a like-minded thinker. An avid reader, he had encountered what he called the "same story" of "how wonderful is man, the world, the universe" in many books. He agreed in theory with such estimations of humanity and the wider cosmos, but he had as yet found any single book that had proved "convincingly that man, the world, the universe is GOOD." It was *Moral Man and Immoral Society*, he said, that finally had told "the truth on every page." The truth of *Moral Man*, for him, was its confirmation of his own suspicion of "progress" and efforts to "reform man." Both activities struck this reader as products of a "vain imagination." Indeed, *Moral Man* had synthesized ideas from other writers who had fallen short of the full "truth." He freely quoted the "truths" that he had encountered in these other works. Favorite passages from other authors included Princeton philosopher Edwin Holt's contention "that self-interest is what controls men in the last analysis." He also reproduced some "truths" from *The Thoughtlessness of Modern Thought* (1934): "If people live longer, but live more miserably, is that progress?; We do not know where we are going, but we are on our way; the irrational conviction that the world is proceeding toward perfection."[82] To find these shards of "truth" fully expressed in *Moral Man* gave this correspondent not only a "conversation partner" in Niebuhr but also, it would seem, a sense of validation.

A final and dramatic example of Niebuhr's effect on the lives of Protestants came in the wake of his dismissal of Graham's approach to sin and salvation as a "bargain." Although Niebuhr was neither pastoral nor authentically prophetic in that *Life* magazine article, his criticism of Graham provoked more than 250 pastors and everyday Protestants to write to him, urging him to reconsider his opinion of the evangelist. To his credit, Niebuhr publicly responded to his critics in an issue of the *Christian Century*, even admitting that he had written the *Life* article in "a rash moment." His half-hearted apology turned defensive, however, as he answered the concerns of his correspondents. He euphemistically referred to the *Life* article as "mildly appreciative but also mildly critical" and insisted that his "chief point of criticism in the *Life* article was not Billy

Graham but official Protestantism, which gives support to his type of pietism."[83]

Alas, Niebuhr had confused his facts. Elsewhere he had offered more balanced treatments of Graham and distinguished the evangelist from "official Protestantism." But in *Life* he had clearly targeted Graham. In his response in the *Christian Century*, however, he refused to acknowledge that reality. Instead, he criticized his correspondents: "The reaction to these rather mild criticisms would prompt one to fear that American Protestantism has been engulfed by uncritical religiosity in the so-called revival of religion."[84] Had he actually engaged in "mild criticism," the letters of protest might have still flowed, but his criticisms were anything but mild.

From Niebuhr's summary of the correspondence, it seems clear that this sample of Protestants expressed more than an "uncritical religiosity." For instance, he registered particular disappointment at the letters from Lutherans who seemed to him unaware of Luther's "insistence that righteous men are still sinners." Yet there are two glaring problems with Niebuhr's analysis. First, these Lutherans were critical of Graham, something Niebuhr mentioned in his article. But they had directed their criticism at Graham's evangelistic method, not at the evangelist's view of sin as Niebuhr would have expected from good Lutherans. Second, Graham, though certainly more progressive in his view of Christian sanctification, never truly doubted that "righteous men are still sinners." In other words, Niebuhr's perception of the "uncritical religiosity" of his Lutheran correspondents was based on their failure to meet his expectations. Another problem with Niebuhr's assessment of the "uncritical religiosity" of his correspondents was his own admission that he had received a number of thoughtful letters. He mentioned that some of the "most moving letters" had come from those arguing from Scripture about the "diversity of gifts" within the church. As one writer put it, "Surely there ought to be room in the church for people like you and like Graham." Niebuhr may have been moved by this sentiment, but he warned that such logic would eventually turn the church into "an innocuous mutual admiration society."[85] Sadly, Niebuhr missed the significance of this view, apparently rather common among the many respondents. These Protestants were not willing to settle for only Graham's interpretation of sin and salvation or only Niebuhr's interpretation of sin and salvation. They saw virtue in both perspectives of the Christian faith.

If many of Niebuhr's correspondents were not entirely satisfied with his perspective of humanity, Floyd Brown, one of his most regular correspondents, was. Richard Fox came across the nondescript twenty-four-year-old Brown while conducting research for his biography of Niebuhr, and in the afterword of his book he expressed his admiration for Brown for deciding to "start a conversation about the nature and destiny of man" with the foremost expert on the subject.[86] Brown likely charmed Niebuhr as he did Fox. His letters paint a picture of a reflective lay theologian, exceptional perhaps in the extent and depth of his interest in Niebuhr, but typical in his wonderment at the meaning of his own life in relation to God. Brown, in fact, contemplated theological issues as a matter of course: "The other day while walking home I was thinking about theology and its aspects." The relationship between theological truth and faith occupied his attention that day, and he decided to consult Niebuhr on the problem. To Brown, theology was valuable, but it was not faith. Its truths were fragmentary and incomplete because, as Brown observed, "God is God, and he always has the last laugh." According to Brown, God directed his laughter not at the unsure, but at those "who think they know a 'great deal' about Him." Faith was faith as a consequence of its uncertain character, "because God is not merely truth." The point for Brown was that theologians, preachers, and lay believers should show proper respect for the "divine puzzle," humbly presenting their ideas before the transcendent God.

Brown's views of God, faith, and theology showed the mark of Niebuhr's influence, as did his belief in the universality of sin. He argued his case with a three-page exegesis of John 8:1–11 and asked for Niebuhr's opinion of his interpretation. The well-known verses describe Jesus's encounter with the Pharisees over the issue of adultery. The Pharisees confront Jesus with a female adulterer, reminding him that the law of Moses recommended stoning for her offense. For Brown, this passage summarized the essence of the Christian faith. As he understood it, the Pharisees represented all people, since every human judged others too easily in an effort to appear good and righteous, testing "God's wisdom with our own." Likewise, wrote Brown, "we are like the adultress not in physical function but in the spiritual sense, in the fact that all people are sinners." Jesus's intercession on behalf of the woman—"let him who is without sin cast the first stone"—and his subsequent admonition "to go and sin no more" led Brown again to conclude "that all are sinners" and "in need of God's grace, mercy, and forgiveness." What Brown demonstrated rather poignantly was that Niebuhr's theology of sin, for all its apparent complexity, was just that simple. And Brown and a host of other everyday lay theologians took that theology seriously in their practice of the Protestant faith.[87]

✠ At midcentury, the name Reinhold Niebuhr was practically a synonym for the doctrine of original sin. His preaching, his teaching, and his writing, as well as the many responses from the laity to each part of his ministry testify to that. His audience, moreover, was as varied as it was large. Appropriately, this diverse constituency fit Niebuhr's own analytical method. Whether he was considering the complexity of the individual as both sinner and saint or examining the complexities of the international rivalry between democracy and Marxism, the "answer" was never a matter of either/or. Likewise, followers of Niebuhr hardly fit an either/or scheme; they were an eclectic group of lay theologians drawn from the ranks of ordinary believers, unrestricted by class, education, or gender. As the editor of the national magazine of the Parent-Teacher Association commented, "No one knows better than you what kind of spiritual sustenance modern man hungers for, what kind of leadership he seeks from his church."[88] The food that Niebuhr provided to assuage these modern American hunger pangs was rich in complexity about the ambiguity of human nature—insights readily digested by some and chewed thoughtfully, at least, by others.

CHAPTER 5

Billy Graham, America's Evangelist

In the summer of 1950, Billy Graham received a wedding band in the mail. A man who identified himself only as a veteran of World War II had enclosed the ring as a "symbol of my broken marriage." In his letter, this former soldier explained that he had attended Graham's crusade in Boston earlier that year and had responded to the evangelist's call to accept Christ into his life. He had done so, he reported, in "an effort to save my marriage of 5 years," confessing he was "deep in sin." He asked Graham to hold the ring in trust until "with the Lord's help" he and his wife might "get together once more in God's love." The anonymous veteran had devised a clever plan to retrieve the ring if he and his wife reunited. He tore off the upper right-hand corner of the stationery on which he had written the letter, keeping the matching piece himself. If the marriage were saved, Graham would receive the missing corner "signifying regained happiness and love," at which point he was to send the ring back to the veteran. Sadly, the wedding band remained in the envelope fifty-four years after the heartbroken man had mailed it to Graham.[1]

Graham inspired similar confessions of sin in countless other mid-twentieth-century American Protestants. Yet Graham the confessor is mostly absent from scholarly chronicles of his ministry. Skeptics of Graham's ministry, both then and now, have explained his appeal for everyday Protestants not in terms of his message of sin and salvation but in terms of conformity and the emotional impact of his sermons—especially within the crusade atmosphere—and the emotionally turbulent cold war era. Fear, nostalgia, and excitement, no doubt, welled up in Graham's audiences—whether they heard him at a crusade or on the radio or read his books or advice column. But Graham and his team consciously sought to avoid gross manipulation of their audiences. Graham himself was skeptical of markedly emotional conversions and professions of faith. Accordingly, he preached, for the most part, without resorting to histrionic exhorta-

Billy Graham
(Hulton Archive/Getty Images)

tions. Indeed, Graham and his aides cultivated an atmosphere of respectful and restrained worship at the crusades, frowning upon applause and overt demonstrations of piety during the meetings.[2] Reporters, even the critical ones, who actually attended Graham's campaigns largely confirmed the absence of coercion and dramatics at the services.[3]

In all likelihood, then, something more than mere emotionalism and sublimated anxiety stirred the hearts of those Protestants who appreciated Graham and his message. The president of Princeton Theological Seminary, John A. Mackay, thought so. Writing in the wake of Graham's 1957 New York City crusade, he argued: "No amount of propaganda by high-powered advertising methods, no super organization, no degree of natural curiosity, no mass psychosis, is sufficient to account for the throngs that went to listen to a young man deliver a simple, straightforward religious message." Although such factors surely influenced the "throngs," Mackay's essential point is sound. At midcentury, Protestants came in droves to hear Graham preach. They responded to his message of sin and salvation, and they expressed how powerfully Graham affected their lives—and it was not all a function of something else.[4]

Graham was not simply revered, however. The millions of Protestants sympathetic to his ministry were also known to challenge him, especially in letters to his syndicated newspaper column, My Answer. Although among Protestants his supporters outnumbered his critics, many believers—both conservatives and liberals—strongly objected to Graham's evangelism. Graham's audience, then, was defined as much by Protestants concerned, whether positively or negatively, with his Gospel message as it was by those caught up in a generic interest in religion.

⁜ Graham's straightforward message of sin and salvation debuted before a national audience during his Los Angeles crusade in the fall of 1949. He opened the crusade at the "Canvas Cathedral"—so named for its reported distinction as the largest tent ever erected for a revival—with the sermon "We Need Revival." He began unflinchingly: "This city of wickedness and sin," Graham observed, had a choice between revival and renewal, on the one hand, or judgment, on the other.[5]

Although just thirty years old, Graham was already a fairly seasoned evangelist well-practiced at such large-scale condemnation of sin. Since the mid-1940s, he had preached to hundreds of thousands of teenagers at enormous Youth for Christ rallies and had led seven crusades with reasonable success. These audiences, moreover, generally adored the strikingly handsome, golden-haired evangelist, stuffing the collection plates with notes of thanksgiving for his ministry. Just one year earlier, in fact, he had delivered a version of "We Need Revival" to six thousand approving Georgians at his Augusta crusade.[6]

But Augusta, Georgia, was hardly Los Angeles. Graham had yet to conduct a crusade in such a large and diverse city; furthermore, the campaign was scheduled for three weeks, the longest to date. Graham organizers had taken precautions, however, to ensure some measure of success. Working under the name "Christ for Greater Los Angeles," Graham's team had helped establish prayer meetings a full eighteen months in advance of the crusade and, as would become routine in later crusades, had worked with local committees to publicize the event and whip up support for the revival among area churches. This careful and calculated planning paid off. By opening day, the Los Angeles Times reported that several hundred churches had joined with Youth for Christ and the Christian Business Men's Committee to sponsor the crusade.[7]

Despite all these efforts, attendance lagged during the first weeks of the event. Some among Graham's team blamed an unusual cold snap for the lackluster turnout. The merely respectable numbers meant that Graham had little reason to extend the campaign—the marker of a truly triumphant revival—and he and his team considered ending the crusade after its scheduled three weeks. In the midst of these deliberations about the crusade's fate, the weather warmed—a turn that Graham and his supporters thought providential—making the Canvas Cathedral a more hospitable venue for audiences to hear the Gospel. The break in the weather coincided with an equally fortuitous gesture by newspaper magnate William Randolph Hearst. In a now storied moment, Hearst purportedly instructed his many editors to "puff Graham." Accordingly, a gaggle of newsmen descended on the crusade, providing a much-needed publicity boost.[8]

This potent combination of sun and spin energized the crusade for five additional weeks. Empty seats were no longer a problem in the Canvas Cathedral. The massive tent filled to capacity each day—and twice on Sundays—with thousands more standing in the aisles and on the street outside. By the fifth week of the crusade, 160,000 people had attended services, and Graham had placed an advertisement in the *Daily News* of Los Angeles announcing, "Billy Graham's 5th Sin-Smashing Week!" The following week, not much had changed. Another advertisement in the *Daily News* noted Graham's "6th Great Sin-Smashing Week."[9] In the seventh and eighth weeks, "Christ for Greater Los Angeles" had become a national story, as major media outlets reported on the revival fires that had ignited out west. *Life* magazine, for example, observed simply but presciently: "A New Evangelist Arises."[10] When the sawdust settled, Graham had preached sixty-five sermons in seventy-two meetings—more than a year's worth of homilies for the average minister—to a total audience of approximately three hundred fifty thousand. Three thousand of that number converted, while another three thousand either "re-consecrated their lives" or came "back to Christ." And they did so penitently, "weeping forgiveness," according to the *Los Angeles Times*, "for their sins."[11]

As the advertisements had declared and as the *Times* had reported, the crowds who flocked to hear Graham preach got an earful of sin. Although the theme for the revival, "Christ for the Crisis," covered a lot of territory —the atomic crisis, the Red crisis, the crisis of the home, and the crisis of American morality, to name a few—the crisis that Graham emphasized most was the crisis of sin in Los Angeles, in particular, and in American life, in general.[12] Indeed, the root cause of these many problems, from international crisis to rampant immorality, was sin. This catchall diagnosis of the problems that Americans faced, despite Graham's evident moralizing throughout the crusade, signaled his fervent belief in the doctrine of original sin. The "first birth," Graham preached early on, "makes you a child of Adam and in sin." For Graham, this claim of sin upon all humanity required each and every person to be born again in Christ, and it was this pressing task that he undertook at Los Angeles.[13]

This sense of urgency—what the *Daily News* described as Graham's "whiplike vitality"—reflected his belief in the terrible destiny that awaited the unconverted. "Those who reject Christ," Graham warned in a typical sermon, "will be cast into the lake of fire and brimstone to spend eternity." In another sermon, titled simply "Judgment," Graham promised that Jesus would meet unrepentant sinners with "fire coming from His eyes" and a "sword coming from His mouth." Without question, such firebrand sermons induced fear in Graham's audiences. In fact, Graham ultimately employed a "swing shift" evangelist to counsel those who had awakened in the middle of the night—perhaps because of fitful dreams about a ghoulish Jesus—and returned to the revival site seeking forgiveness for their sins. But from Graham's perspective, the fearful converts had good reason to be afraid since there was no fate worse than that of the unredeemed.[14]

Near the end of the crusade, Graham reinforced his theme of sin and judgment when he preached Jonathan Edwards's sermon "Sinners in the Hands of an Angry God." According to biographer William Martin, an exhausted Graham preached "Sinners" simply because he had run out of sermons of his own. Yet surely the content of "Sinners" was in Graham's thoughts when he selected it for that fall day in 1949. Although it was a convenient text, both for its availability and for its renown within American culture, it was also a sermon compatible with Graham's evangelical mission to bring as many sinners as possible to Christ.[15] Graham twice stressed this very point as he introduced the sermon. In many ways, Graham could not have chosen a better text for the task. Accordingly, Graham, channeling Edwards, preached, "The wrath of God burns against them [sinners] . . . the pit is prepared, the fire is made ready, the furnace is now hot, ready to receive them; the flames do now rage and glow . . . and the pit has opened its mouth under them." Graham continued with more passages from Edwards's sermon, although he spliced in his own thoughts along the way and he ended the sermon well short of Edwards's original. At that point, Graham offered some words of comfort: "But Christ died on the cross, the Lord Jesus Christ can cleanse you from sin, and you can be assured of your salvation." And just before issuing the invitation for sinners to come forward and make a decision for Christ, he asked, "Wouldn't it be wonderful to walk out with peace in your heart, not worrying about the next step?" "Well," he added, "you can know that peace right now in an instant."[16]

Graham's ending, however, paralleled Edwards's original. The eighteenth-century evangelist also had spoken of the great mercy of Christ and the possibility of happiness and new life through Christ. Thus, Graham's delivery of "Sinners" was theologically suggestive and significant, even if it was motivated more immediately by exhaustion and necessity. Graham's essentially faithful recitation of the two-hundred-year-old sermon demonstrated a fundamental continuity with Edwards's theology of sin and judgment. Graham, like Edwards before him, had preached "Sinners" during a revival and hoped that it would "convict sinners" and drive them toward repentance.[17]

Precisely how many responded that night is unknown. Ruth Graham recalled later that the sermon did not go over well. But she may have misread the reaction. The audience likely was stunned after hearing Graham present, via Edwards, such a vivid discussion of the depth of human sin.[18]

✠ After Los Angeles, Graham embarked on a whirlwind crusading tour. For the next four years, he crisscrossed the country, evangelizing in every region of the United States, including stops in Boston, Columbia (South Carolina), Portland (Oregon), Minneapolis, Atlanta, Seattle, Pittsburgh, Albuquerque, and Detroit. This demanding schedule placed Graham in contention for United Airlines' "civilian traveler of the year," a designation he had received before. In addition to tens of thousands of air miles, the tour required efficient organization, advance planning, and money. Consequently, Graham and his team of supporters established the Billy Graham Evangelistic Association (BGEA)—Graham reluctantly agreed to the use of his name—in the summer of 1950. The BGEA not only facilitated Graham's itinerant ministry but also protected Graham from any hint of financial mismanagement. In a world where free-will offering baskets filled with donations large and small, the BGEA tracked every penny, paid Graham a generous but not unreasonable salary, and invited independent audits of its accounting practices.[19]

Most important, the BGEA released Graham to focus on the communication of the Gospel to the unconverted or uncommitted. Graham's approach to that work changed very little in these early crusades. He touched on many of the same topics that he had used at the breakout Los Angeles crusade: city after city was steeped in wickedness; the communists were Satan's minions; and drink, sex, gambling, crime, and juvenile delinquency threatened the social cohesion of America. But these troubling issues, as he had stressed in Los Angeles, were but manifestations of a single phenomenon: "Sin is found in back of every problem in the world." For Graham, the solution to these and other symptoms of sin began with individual rebirth in Christ.[20]

Many journalists who covered these crusades of the early fifties noted Graham's repetition of this essential message. During his 1950 tour of New England cities, a reporter wrote of Graham's consistent "gloom" about the prospects of humanity without God, but he observed that it was "counterbalanced by [Graham's] equally liberal outpouring of optimism concerning God's converts." A few years later, in Detroit, another reporter wrote that Graham gave "the same message every night, convicting his hearers of sin and telling them the way to salvation."[21]

Graham's gloominess occasionally sounded more prophetic than evangelistic in these early years. While his views positioned him well within the cold warrior mentality of the early 1950s, he was no simple apologist for American righteousness in the face of Godless communism. He reminded his audiences of the utter transcendence of God, insisting that God showed no special favor toward America or Americans. And more than once he suggested that perhaps the threat of communism was a judgment upon America's iniquities. In fact, Graham asked a Burlington, Vermont, audience in 1950, "Why should God not destroy America tonight?" and added, "God is no respector [sic] of nations." Over the next four years, as he gained experience—conducting thirty-three domestic and two international crusades—Graham continued to caution Americans against self-righteousness, but in more measured tones. At the end of 1954, for instance, Graham remarked: "Too many of us, I fear, feel that America is immune from God's judgment . . . This, of course, is not true. God actually has no international pets."[22]

Despite Graham's steadfast condemnation of the sins of individuals and of the nation as a whole, the people still came to hear him preach. And they came in great numbers; a staggering 10 million Americans attended his crusades between 1949 and 1954. These millions of Americans represented a broad demographic, from the rich and famous to the poor and uneducated. Even the notorious gangster Mickey Cohen became interested in Graham's work after his associate, wiretapper Jimmy Vaus, converted during the Los Angeles crusade. While Cohen never actually attended the crusade, he did meet privately with Graham—and the ever-discreet evangelist kept their conversation confidential.[23]

Cohen's later imprisonment at Alcatraz suggests that unlike Vaus, the mobster was not especially affected by Graham's message of repentance from sin. But what of the millions of less infamous Americans who listened to Graham's message? How did they understand sin in relation to their own lives? Because his crowds were predominately of the Christian persuasion—the crusades drew adherents of every major denomination in America—the idea of original sin was certainly not a new or foreign concept to them. Their understandings of sin, however, would have varied along a continuum defined at one end by those who would have emphasized "sin as act" as much as or more than "sin as fact" and at the other by those who would have reversed that emphasis. Graham, as a Presbyterian-turned-Baptist, fell into the former category. He combined a dominant moralist "sin as act" interpretation with a more prophetic "sin as fact" perspective.

Many if not most of Graham's audiences in the early 1950s shared the evangelist's sense of sin. Samples of letters gathered by the *Boston Post* in 1950 and by the *Detroit Times* in 1953 reveal a laity confessing to Graham that their cities were generally lost in sin and that specific problems, such as crime, sex, drink, and that 1950s obsession, teenage delinquency, had seriously damaged the moral fabric of America. Many of these correspondents, moreover, appeared to be recapitulating what they had heard in Graham's sermons. The views of sin that these Bostonians and Detroiters disclosed in their letters were also informed by the international fears of the day. The specter of communism and the looming threat of atomic warfare seemed to be evidence of a fundamentally disordered world.[24]

For Graham and his audiences, the doctrine of original sin may have been an ideologically "safe" genesis of that disordered world. The confusions and chaos of both individual life and global events perhaps seemed less confusing and less chaotic when identified with their common origin in sin. Individual confession of sin, furthermore, promised individuals salvation from eternal confusion and chaos. Such an analysis, however, tells only part of the story, and how much of that story it accounts for is debatable. Midcentury Protestants believed in the reality and power of sin. Some—including Graham—also believed, literally, in the figure of

Satan, the personification and source of sinful temptation and evil. While these beliefs were certainly influenced by the prevailing social and historical context of postwar America, they were not simply expedient covers for the anxieties provoked by such a context.

Two episodes from these crusades of the early fifties—one, again, from Boston in 1950 and the other from Pittsburgh in 1952—provide more specific examples of how everyday Protestants understood Graham's unequivocal emphasis on sin in his preaching. Following the Boston crusade, the editors of *Zion's Herald*, a national publication of the Methodist Church, printed a critical evaluation of the campaign. They censured Graham for his searing preaching that "dangl[ed] sinners over the pits of hell." The editors called instead for Methodists to awaken from their spiritual apathy without turning to the likes of the firebrand Graham. Readers of the *Herald* disagreed with that editorial position, and they peppered the magazine with letters supportive of Graham's work for the next four months. Graham, according to one correspondent, was a refreshing alternative to the "Methodist church that has turned into a sort of a club where mild preaching is still tolerated." The "dying" Methodist Church, this reader continued, needed Billy Graham to "recapture John Wesley's fire of evangelism."[25]

The protests of the *Herald*'s readers were similar to the argument made by one layman who felt compelled to defend Graham's preaching after the Episcopal bishop of Pittsburgh publicly criticized Graham in the local newspaper. The bishop had accused Graham of the sin of pride for the evangelist's blistering charge near the end of his campaign that despite the success of the Pittsburgh crusade, "the city has not repented . . . the great masses have rejected Christ." The layman wrote to the newspaper and explained, "Everyone should know that an evangelist is supposed to 'dish it out' as no local preacher or bishop has the nerve to do. An evangelist is not afraid of offending some paying member, nor does he get his glory from spreading salve and polishing apples."[26]

It seems that many of Graham's supporters expected and welcomed his "dish[ing] it out" to their cities. In other words, host communities understood Graham's shrill indictment of sin both as a reality and as a rhetorical tool designed to rouse congregations from their apathetic slumber induced by "mild preaching" and a clublike atmosphere. While it is true that such attitudes toward Graham and his message of sin suggest a degree of contrivance in both the evangelist's indictments of cities and his audience's enthusiastic reception of them, the Pittsburgh layman's final comment to the bishop that "most people need a jolt to awaken us to our needs" implies that he understood the contrivance as an aspect of Graham's evangelical-prophetic responsibility to communities of everyday Protestants.[27]

In contrast to the laity, pastors in crusade cities were generally less sure of Graham's prophetic importance to area churches. After the Seattle and Detroit crusades (1951 and 1953, respectively), the *Christian Century* printed the results of two surveys that found that a majority of the clergy in those cities was ambivalent at best about the value of Graham's campaigns. While the *Century's* liberal, somewhat anti-Graham bias was apparent in its reporting of the surveys, pastors were indeed ambivalent about Graham's ministry at midcentury. The ambivalence had several origins, including Graham's one-of-a-kind public ministry that no ordinary parish pastor could possibly match. For instance, a *Time* magazine cartoon from late 1954 depicted this inferiority theme simply but tellingly: it features a minister standing in a pulpit with a resigned expression on his face and pleading eyes cast heavenward and a caption that reads, "I'm no Billy Graham."[28] Other pastors were less concerned by comparisons of their own ministries to that of Graham than they were by the sincerity and longevity of the conversions that Graham "won" during his crusades. In particular, they worried that the newly converted may have responded to the evangelist's altar call because of mass psychology and religious emotionalism provoked by what they understood to be Graham's punitive, hellfire-and-brimstone presentation of sin and guilt in his sermons. Pastors also questioned the adequacy of the religious counseling that new converts received from BGEA volunteers immediately following their decisions, as well as the BGEA's haphazard referral of new converts to area churches.[29]

The ambivalence recorded by the *Christian Century*, however, points to a large, discerning group of Protestant ministers unwilling simply to endorse or to reject the colossal displays of religiosity that epitomized Graham's crusades. One Chicago pastor who wrote to the *Century* after the Detroit survey typified this lukewarm support for Graham and his work. He appreciated the *Century's* critical analysis of the Detroit crusade overall, but he thought the survey deficient in its understanding of Graham's evangelical function within the church and, accordingly, in its lack of "a more charitable attitude toward the so-called tangible results." He also reminded the *Century's* readers that Graham himself openly admitted that mass evangelism was less effective for instructing and retaining new converts than were sustained efforts at the parish level. But this

Chicagoan warned that there existed no fail-safe method or reliable scale of measurement for studying exactly how people "come to into the church." In light of these facts, to discourage the work of Graham, he continued, amounted to "cutt[ing] your hand off because it does not fulfill the function of the whole body."[30]

The sizable minority of pastors who unequivocally rejected Graham's crusading reveals still another important theological aspect of the Protestant clergy at midcentury. The author of the Detroit article, for example, highlighted the objections of a conservative pastor in the area who had attended three of Graham's services. He regretted that in "each [one] it seemed the important thing was to appease an irate God. Coupled with this was the emphasis on saving yourself as the prime motivation for being a Christian. This leaves me cold." He also deemed Graham's literalism and biblical interpretation "inadequate" for the care of a generation that had faced and continued to face "hellish events" in the post–World War II era. This conservative critic of Graham was rather unusual, as most right-leaning clergy—except for fundamentalists—stayed loyal to the evangelist. His specific criticism of Graham's born-again theology, though, mirrored that of many liberal and neo-orthodox pastors surveyed in Seattle and Detroit, as well as those of like mind serving in congregations across the nation. These disapprovals of Graham's simplified born-again theology, however, testified to a single fact: the existence of numerous congregations led by preachers who viewed human sin, divine grace, and individual conversion differently but no less seriously.[31]

Despite these detractors, Graham had the ear of a majority of American pastors, even if they listened critically. To be sure, the supporters who unreservedly embraced Graham's born-again theology and the moderates who found nothing really objectionable in it indicated a consensus among America's clergy about the importance of religious faith that was and is consistent with the general scholarly impression that the 1950s was an age of consensus. But this Grahamian consensus was built, at least in part, on the evangelist's unmistakable and ever-present message of sin and salvation.

The editors at *Time* and *Newsweek* gave dramatic visual representation of this midcentury religious consensus when they featured Graham on their respective covers in 1954. In those five breathtaking years after his Los Angeles campaign, he had risen from a successful but little known evangelist to, according to the *Time* article, "the world's No. 1 revival preacher." This rapid elevation to the pinnacle of American Protestantism had consequences for both the style and content of his ministry. Gone were the flashy suits of his early career—pistachio green and sky blue among the most garish—that had earned him the sobriquet "Gabriel in Gabardine." Gone, too, were the last vestiges of his fundamentalist past. For instance, he curtailed the exaggerated, literalist view of the Bible that once had led him to such excesses as providing in a sermon the exact dimensions of heaven at sixteen hundred miles square and sixteen hundred miles high. Instead, by the midfifties, Graham had emerged as an internationally known evangelist—he conducted only six domestic revivals compared to twenty overseas campaigns between 1954 and 1956— who enjoyed the respect of Christians around the world for his sincerity, his increasing ecumenicism, and his maturing theology. Graham's lower American profile during this period protected him from overexposure and allowed for an appropriate buildup to his most important crusade target to date: New York City. In recognition of the ambitious task before him, Graham cleared his schedule and devoted 1957 to the Big Apple alone.[32]

✠ Graham arrived in sin-stricken New York City in the late spring of 1957 as the underdog contender in a much-anticipated bout scheduled to open at Madison Square Garden. As one New York tabloid reported, "Evangelist Billy Graham squares off against Sin. . . . The bell sounds May 15th in a six weeks' knock-em-down and drag-em-out fight to the finish." In preparation for this moment, Graham had trained hard. Never had he been knocked down by a city, though he had faced some challenging "opponents." He had even evangelized in New York City earlier in the decade. Still, many expected Graham to fail, following in the footsteps of an actual pugilist by the name, coincidentally, of Billy Graham. This other Billy Graham, a former welterweight boxing champion, had fought successfully for a dozen years before suffering an embarrassing defeat at the Garden in 1955.[33]

Despite the boxer Billy Graham's loss at the Garden, the evangelist Billy Graham liked his odds. After all, God in the person of Jesus Christ did the actual fighting against the sins of New York City. The strength of Graham's faith did not, however, blind him to the extraordinarily high stakes of the crusade. He knew that failure in New York City or, more likely, an average performance in the so-called graveyard of evangelists would disappoint his followers and confirm the skepticism of his critics. Accordingly, he regarded New York as "the biggest and most important mission" of his life, and he steeled himself for the efforts of "all the forces of hell" to thwart his campaign. With an uncharacteristic note of messianism, he further declared, "If the climax of my ministry is to end in crucifixion, by God's grace I am ready."[34]

Round one went to Graham. On the morning of 16 May, the headlines of the city's papers announced that the first night had been a success. The *New York Times*, for example, reprinted Graham's opening sermon in full, an honor the newspaper rarely bestowed upon any preacher. The *Journal-American* recorded Graham's success with more gusto than the *Times* by completing the pugilistic metaphor. Their 16 May edition ran a cartoon depicting a triumphant, muscular Graham standing in a boxing ring opposite a bruised and frustrated devil.[35]

The devil never had another chance to best the evangelist. Although Graham "fully expect[ed] Satan to strike from an unexpected quarter" as the crusade continued, he delivered his message of sin and salvation for a stunning fourteen straight weeks. In that time, he worked tirelessly. He preached ninety-six times and put so much of his energy into the crusade that he lost thirty pounds from his already slender frame. His labors, however, did not satisfy his critics. They still carped over his theology and evangelical method—particularly the Graham team's million-dollar advertising budget that paid for such items as forty thousand bumper stickers—but few of them could dismiss the enormous scale of his audience. Night after night, Graham packed Madison Square Garden, breaking attendance records and becoming the longest-running event in the arena's history. He also drew record-shattering crowds to Wall Street (20,000), Yankee Stadium (100,000) and Times Square (125,000). The final tally indicated that more than 2 million people heard Graham live and that 56,000 made decisions for Christ; a staggering 96,000,000 watched one or more of the fourteen television broadcasts of his services, and 65,000 of those viewers pledged to accept Christ as a result of what they had seen in their living rooms.[36]

Through it all, Graham steadied himself with his tried and true message of sin and salvation. In New York, just as in Los Angeles in 1949, he set this tone early, preaching a sermon on the second night simply titled "Sin." For the rest of the summer, Graham consistently told New Yorkers that all had sinned and were in need of Christ. His sermon topics ranged from America's moral deterioration to problems in the home and juvenile delinquency, but he also maintained that original sin, what he called at one point the inescapable "disease of the soul," lay behind these problems.[37]

Yet Graham had difficulty balancing his emphasis on particular sins with this greater "disease of the soul." This feature of his ministry contributed to the impression that Protestantism consisted of a set of rules that divided "good" people from "bad" people. His sermon at Yankee Stadium, for instance, consisted of a moralistic screed against "divorce, crime, juvenile delinquency, the breakdown of honesty and integrity," and alcoholism, all of which he blamed for the crises that America faced in 1957. In other sermons, however, he acknowledged that individual and social problems were not so simply identified or solved. In fact, earlier in the crusade, he had criticized just that sort of moralistic, right-living theology: "You don't reform your way into God's family. You don't moralize your way into God's family." This dual emphasis on sins and original sin became so acute at times that Graham would offer his listeners the absolute assurance of Christ's power to change an individual's life for the better only to remind them in the same breath that "He [Jesus] doesn't remove your problems." Graham, however, rarely dwelled too long on this point, preferring to leave his audiences sure of the peace that he promised would accompany a decision for Christ.[38]

The peace Graham promised in New York, though, was no easy peace. It was instead the sort of peace suggested by the title of his best seller, *Peace with God*. This kind of peace, Graham believed, depended upon the sober reality of Jesus Christ's death on the cross and the even more sober recognition on the part of Christians that it was their sinful state of being that necessitated Christ's death. Graham articulated the cost of this peace most clearly in "The Offense of the Cross," a sermon that definitively summarized the preaching he had done at New York concerning Christ's crucifixion.

Graham began the sermon by repeating a comment that he had heard while attending a conference at Princeton Theological Seminary. During a discussion about the religious awakening of the 1950s, a fellow minister had argued: "I am convinced we are having a religious revival in America, but it is not the Christian religion." After quoting his colleague, Graham expressed his agreement with the sentiment by observing that Americans preferred the Jesus of "picturesque imagination" to the Jesus of the cross. Such a preference, Graham continued, was easily explained: the "cross of Christ condemns the world," and it "condemns us as sinners." Indeed, said Graham, "I know I am a sinner" because Jesus's life and death revealed that "all have sinned and come short of the glory of God." This truth of the cross, Graham preached, "humbles us," and yet the cross also "demands, the cross expects everything we have to be given to Christ." And for Graham, this was precisely why the cross offended and proved a "stumbling block to men who want to go to Heaven but are not willing to pay the price of the cross."[39]

From the perspective of some in the national media, Graham's message of repentance fell flat, no matter how many millions had heard it during the summer of 1957. The liberal *Nation* left no doubts about its opinion of the crusade, announcing in 1958 "Billy Graham's Fizzle." "The fact is," the editorial noted, "the New York churches spent $2.5 million to publicize another failure." The author based this assessment of the crusade on a 1958 *New York Times* survey of area ministers, which indicated that it was "dubious whether more than a handful of Graham's 56,000 'converts' (or 'decisions') in Madison Square Garden have been added to any church roll." The survey, according to the *Nation*, revealed that 64 percent of those who made decisions for Christ were already members of a church and that most of the remaining 36 percent never joined a church afterward. These "cold facts," the *Nation*'s editors hoped, would "break the charm" of Graham's crusades, and "another episode in American revivalism will be history." The editors, however, grossly misrepresented the results of the *Times* survey. Their percentages—which never appeared in the *Times*—were based on a sample of 3,997 "decisions," not the total of 56,000. Furthermore, the *Nation*'s claim that most of the previously unaffiliated converts did not join churches conflicted with the *Times*'s findings, which deemed the evidence "inconclusive."[40]

Life magazine also covered the results of the New York City crusade irresponsibly. Halfway through the campaign, a story reported that "New Yorkers have talked surprisingly little about Billy . . . Though he has had good crowds, a large portion of them have not come from New York City." One month later, in August 1957, a *New York Times* story detailed that locals accounted for 93 percent of the "decisions." Roughly ten thousand Manhattanites and another ten thousand from the remaining boroughs and Long Island went forward to receive forgiveness for their sins. Still another ten thousand or so came from New York's Westchester County and the nearby states of New Jersey and Connecticut.[41]

Although the *Nation* and *Life* had distorted the report card of the crusade, they did establish that the bulk of the "decisions" in New York came from within the Christian fold. Whether Graham's sympathetic audiences detracted from the value of his work in New York and in other cities was a moot question for the evangelist. Graham had never hidden the fact that he largely preached to the choir, and therefore he did not dispute the *Times*'s 1958 survey but called it "a very fair evaluation at this time." He nevertheless insisted that God had touched "many hundreds" and that, as he often said, "if one person's life was changed during the crusade, it would have been well worth the entire effort." While Graham's comment conflicted with his and the BGEA's usual and obvious interest in the numbers converted at the crusades, it was true that the quantity of conversions had never been a central motivation for his evangelism.[42]

From the vantage point of this study, however, the incredible numbers of "the choir" that Graham reached in New York do matter. The mass of churchgoing folk who attended the crusade, including those who made "decisions" for Christ, gave up a summer evening for what was likely their second church service of the week. Some number of these attended, to be sure, out of curiosity or out of conformity, and others did so, as cynics at the time pointed out, to escape the humid, fetid summer streets of New York for the air-conditioned Garden. But whatever the reason, these audiences knew that the Garden they entered on Seventh Avenue was no paradise and that Graham would explain that fact in the context of another, more famous garden of the Bible.[43]

The theme of sin that echoed to the rafters of Madison Square Garden followed those who made "decisions" for Christ as they made their way to the "inquirers tent." The "decision" process unfolded in this "tent," where the inquirers—Graham always resisted calling them "converts"—talked with religious counselors (usually laypeople) trained by the BGEA. The BGEA instructed counselors to avoid any inclination to "Proselyte or Condemn" the inquirers and instead provided guidelines for the counselors to discuss the full implications of a decision for Christ. This conversation included, of course, serious consideration of sin followed by an invitation for the inquirers to confess their sins using the "Sinner's Prayer." The prayer drilled home the essentials of Graham's evangelical theology: "I am a sinner. I need salvation. Jesus died to save me. By faith and belief in God's word, I accept Jesus in my heart as my Savior. I turn from sin. I renounce my sin. From henceforth I will live for Jesus and serve Him." Following the recitation of this prayer, the counselors reinforced its content with passages from the Bible that described "the fact of sin, the penalty of sin," and the evangelical claim that "Christ died to pay the penalty."[44]

Years later, in the 1960s, the BGEA conducted surveys of these inquirers as well as those of other campaigns to assess whether this message of sin and salvation had any lasting effect on their postcrusade lives. The project, spearheaded by Robert Ferm, a trusted BGEA official, consisted of a questionnaire that was hardly an objective research tool. The questions were clearly designed to elicit responses that fit the theological agenda of Graham and the BGEA. For instance, one question read, "Was there anything that made you think you needed Salvation?" Sample responses to the question, conveniently provided on the document, included "sickness, tragedy, failure." Another question was a variation on the same theme and asked the convert to "describe with detail your life before you made your decision, telling about moral and spiritual failures of human interest." The last three questions searched for signs of a postcrusade change in lifestyle, querying respondents about church attendance and "spiritual growth" measured by such things as "Bible study, Prayer, Witnessing." Finally, the survey asked whether others had "noticed a difference in your life?"[45]

Of the New York City inquirers who completed the survey, most answered the leading questions with Grahamian orthodoxy. In particular, their views of sin, like Graham's own, combined moralism with a general sense of being "lost in sin" prior to conversion.[46] Other collections of conversion stories echoed this attitude toward sin. Many of these testimonies came from teenagers—a large percentage, sometimes as many as half, of Graham's converts at a given crusade were under the age of twenty—a fact that troubled some of Graham's critics. Unlike these detractors, however, Graham and his supporters withheld any skepticism regarding conversions from youth, including that of a nine-year-old who, upon watching a sermon on television, wrote: "During the end of your sermon something happened in my heart. I have been having so many problems but all of them went away then."[47]

Still other New York respondents provided answers that indicated that their decisions for Christ were less about particular sins or a generalized sense of sin or youthful anxieties than they were about a deep awareness of the sin of pride. One male convert in his late thirties noted that he was the "worse [sic] type" of sinner, a "very righteous" feeling person. A woman, also in her thirties, wrote, "Even marriage and motherhood only pointed up the fact that I was able to love only one person—myself." Another woman mentioned that she had thought she was a Christian until Graham helped her realize that there was more to the Christian life than attending church and "doing good works and practicing the Golden Rule."[48]

Whatever the particularities of the answers given by New York converts, Graham's central theme of sin and salvation had clearly affected their lives, even several years after they had heard him in Madison Square Garden. Graham had observed this effect as early as 1957, noting in his diary that "there is a greater response to the invitation when I preach on judgment than any other subject . . . Perhaps the message of New York is judgment."[49] Graham's comment about the importance that he ascribed to warning against sin is quite telling. But the diary entry is also rather curious and naïve, as if he had just discovered the effectiveness of the message of judgment in 1957, when he had featured it consistently if not as prominently in earlier campaigns. Indeed, from surveys of converts from other campaigns, Ferm had reams of evidence that confirmed that sin and judgment were ever-present themes of his evangelism.[50] Taken as a whole, the responses of ordinary Protestants from New York and elsewhere to Graham's message lend credence to his frequent claim that countless lives would "never be the same" after a crusade had passed through a city.[51]

After New York, Graham's life was never the same either. The summerlong campaign established Graham as the undisputed face of Protestantism in America. At the end of the crusade, in fact, a Gallup poll, writes William Martin, revealed that 85 percent of Americans could correctly identify "Billy Graham; moreover, nearly three-quarters of that number regarded him favorably." These soaring approval ratings dwarfed those of President Eisenhower, and Graham even rivaled the president in spot news coverage that year.[52]

As the ranks of those who favored Graham swelled, so too did the number of his critics. Both before and after the New York crusade, the liberal *Christian Century* took frequent and hostile aim at his evangelism. Meanwhile, from the other side of the theological spectrum, fundamentalist leaders, such as Carl McIntire, John R. Rice, and Bob Jones, stridently voiced their own disapproval of his ministry. In their eyes, Graham had kowtowed to the center of Christian liberalism, especially in his cooperation with the liberal-leaning Protestant Council of New York.[53]

In addition to raising these general objections to Graham's ministry in New York, detractors also criticized him for doing too much or too little on the issues of race relations and poverty. Indeed, Graham's energies were not reserved for individual regeneration alone. Between his preaching appearances, he conducted dozens of "inspection trips" in an effort to better understand the social landscape of the city. For example, he visited Harlem to see "for himself the way things really were," and he addressed several thousand black residents there. He also explored the impoverished Bowery neighborhood and conducted a service at the Garden in Spanish for the benefit of a Latino audience of fifteen thousand. After his visit to the Bowery, he informed his Garden audience that "if Jesus were here today He would be down there much of the time with these people who need him so greatly."[54]

For a white, Southern evangelist of the 1950s, Graham's attention to the ethnic populations and to the poor was unheard of. Yet some leaders of the black community, in particular, were unimpressed. Because Graham's sermons lacked "social content," said one black pastor, they "would not touch our people." Evidently Graham agreed with this sentiment because partway through the crusade he hired Howard O. Jones, a black pastor from Cleveland, to organize his efforts among the city's black population.[55]

At about the same time and in a more dramatic and public fashion, Graham attempted to "touch" the African American community by sharing the Madison Square Garden stage with Martin Luther King Jr. Graham's decision to feature King for an evening attracted African Americans to the Garden that night and until the crusade's end. His invitation to King was not, however, simply a calculated move to bring more black faces in among the white ones that usually stared back at him in the arena. The occasion signaled yet again Graham's awareness of the great social sin of segregation—something that he had condemned in the pages of *Life* in 1956—and his approval of King and the cause of desegregation. Yet, true to form, Graham's endorsement of King was a cautious one: he had invited King not to preach, but to lead the audience gathered that night in prayer. Still, King made the most of the opportunity, praying for an increase in justice and love within America and asking forgiveness for the "lie" of racial inequality. He also gave thanks for the work of the crusade and the "dynamic preaching of this great evangelist." Graham stood calmly in the background, and as quickly as this historic moment had begun, it was over.[56]

Nothing earthshattering took place, no giant leap forward in the struggle for civil rights, but no one could harbor any illusions about where Graham's heart lay when it came to the problem of segregation. For his part, King understood the significance of Graham's gesture, remarking privately to the evangelist, "Your crusades do more with white people than I could do." In the end, however gradualist his approach to desegregation, Graham was a crucial ally of the civil rights struggle. The negative reactions of some Southern white Christians—and especially that of fundamentalist Bob Jones, Graham's old nemesis—confirmed the importance of the evangelist's support of desegregation. From their perspective, Graham seemed a full-fledged integrationist, and Jones predicted that Graham's association with King would effectively end his ministry in the white South.[57]

Graham's wholehearted effort to win Manhattan for Christ—from the Bowery to Wall Street to Harlem—exhausted him. For the rest of 1957, he convalesced at his home in Montreat, North Carolina. After this much-needed rest, Graham hit the sawdust trail with abandon once again. He began his 1958 crusading with a tour in the Caribbean, followed by a five-city swing through California and a stop in San Antonio, and he finished in Charlotte, North Carolina. He then went abroad for most of the next two years. He returned to the states in the early sixties for a few more high-profile campaigns, but none of those compared to the scale of the New York City crusade in 1957. By the midsixties, furthermore, Graham limited his campaigns to just one week.[58]

Graham may have slowed his evangelistic pace by the 1960s, but his preaching remained vital and consistent. While his core message of sin and salvation changed very little in the new decade, Graham did tinker with it a bit by incorporating some existentialist and psychological themes. His 1965 best seller *World Aflame*, for instance, sounded in some places eerily similar (though he would have been loath to admit it) to Paul Tillich's existentialist theology. Although Graham had always maintained that life without faith in God was empty, *World Aflame* emphasized the themes of emptiness and meaninglessness more prominently than any of his earlier work had. He, like Tillich before him, worried about the detrimental effects of a secular, technical society on the human personality. Americans, he wrote, were becoming anxious, helpless, and joyless automatons because of their spiritual investment in what he called the "pipe dream" of material welfare. This situation, thought Graham, proved Carl Jung's thesis that "the central neurosis of our time is emptiness." While Graham's existential and psychological analysis of modern America was superficial in comparison with Tillich's work in this area, in *World Aflame* he had articulated his opinion that contemporary culture pulled individuals apart at the seams, further disordering the already disordered personalities of Americans steeped in sin.[59]

❧ Although Graham preached to live "congregations" during his crusades and pitched his books at this same audience, his syndicated newspaper column My Answer constituted his most direct and personal ministry to lay believers. The idea for the column originated in the overwhelming amount of correspondence Graham received every year. In 1951, for instance, 178,000 letters poured into the Billy Graham Evangelistic Association; the next year, the number of letters sent to Graham nearly doubled. The column, sponsored by the *New York News–Chicago Tribune* syndicate, allowed Graham to "answer" his enormous body of correspondents.

After its debut in 1952, My Answer appeared five days a week in newspapers across America. In the fifties alone, the column generated fifteen thousand letters a week from a broad demographic of Christians and non-Christians alike. By the end of the decade, My Answer ran in more than 150 newspapers, reaching more than 16 million readers. The popularity of Graham's answers motivated Doubleday to publish a compilation of three hundred of them under the same title, *My Answer* (1960).[60]

The column followed a question-and-answer format. From the thousands of weekly letters, Graham and his staff selected a single question to feature in each column and then crafted an answer of 150 to 400 words in length. Astoundingly, though, Graham and his staff also replied to each of the letters that never saw print. Graham wrote many of the columns himself, but he also relied on some faithful assistants, particularly Robert Ferm, to produce the majority of the responses. Graham made no secret of this collective authorship; every year, he ran a column explaining the arrangement. Every column, however, passed through Graham's hands for final approval and editing. In fact, the *New York News–Chicago Tribune* syndicate would accept only columns with Graham's handwriting visible on the draft.[61]

The content of Graham's answers in the column shifted between a message of Christian triumphalism and moral perfectionism and a message of the deep and abiding presence and power of sin in Christian life. Thus, at times, he presented Christianity as a set of moral guidelines that, if completed, not only distinguished the believer as a good Christian but also promised a better life.[62] In the preface to the *My Answer* collection, for example, he boasted rather vaguely of the "overwhelming documented evidence" that demonstrated that his answers "based on the Bible" had helped "thousands."[63] At other times, he complicated his perfectionism—just as John Wesley, the father of modern notions of Christian perfectionism, had—by his firm belief in and articulation of the doctrine of original sin. In one of his columns, he bluntly and decisively argued, "Man's big problem centers in the ugly little word 'sin.' We all are sinners by nature, by inheritance, and by practice. If we say we do not sin, we simply make God a liar."[64] But Graham, like Wesley before him, had difficulty squaring the logical circle that was required by twinning perfectionism—the idea that Christians could progressively sin less—and original sin. Consequently, Graham vacillated between the idea that sin never ceased to afflict Christians and the belief that Christians could experience a life of increasing virtue and benefit.

Graham's faith in the power of Christianity to bring positive changes to the lives of the devout was not only consistent with his own evangelical theology but also typical of Christian theology in general. Niebuhr and Tillich also believed that Christians should and could experience a lasting, although fragmented, sense of freedom and fulfillment in their lives. Why else would they or any believer become a Christian? Still, while none of these three figures thought of Christianity as a means to an end, Graham's unqualified statements about the power of Christianity to solve complex individual and social problems came perilously close at times.

The nuclear dilemma was a classic example of Graham's utter faith in the Christian solution to any and all evils in the world. He often preached that mass conversions around the globe would eradicate the threat of nuclear war—a notion that Niebuhr consistently criticized as both fantastic and absurd. Provided that they accepted Jesus Christ as their savior, Graham promised equally definitive results, though on a smaller scale, to his My Answer readers.

Graham's My Answer correspondents generally shared the evangelist's blend of Christian perfectionism and belief in original sin. Their questions addressed a range of topics from the mundane and petty—the proper amount of lipstick in one case—to marital problems and from moralistic concerns about drink and sex to profound struggles with the recurrence of sinful behavior in Christian life.[65] But a strong minority of readers policed the column, writing letters of protest against aspects of Graham's ministry that they judged deficient. Among their complaints were concerns about his occasional lack of pastoral care, his simplicity and dogmatism, and astonishingly, his liberal theology.[66]

Graham's insensitive responses, although rare, are seen most often in discussions of infidelity. The most extreme example, a curious choice for reprinting in the pages of My Answer, concerned a woman plagued by her husband's incessant "unfaithfulness" during their nine years of marriage. Even for the patriarchy of the 1950s, Graham's reply was cold: "I must frankly say that your meek silence is in part to blame for your husband's philandering. He either thinks you don't love him, you don't care, or that you are not smart enough to know what is going on right under your nose." He advised her to show some "spunk" and confront her husband with an "either, or" ultimatum.[67] Graham's unkindness appeared again in response to a marital issue of a different sort. Worried about the fact that he had never attended church before his wife died, a recent convert wondered, "Do you think I am hypocritical?" "Certainly!" came the curt reply. "It seems a pity," continued Graham, "that it took such a tragedy to awaken you spiritually. Think of the fellowship you and your wife could have had, worshipping together!"[68]

This last case appalled two readers in particular, and they reprimanded Graham for his uncharitable response to the grief-stricken man. One lamented the "irreparable damage" likely done by these unsympathetic remarks to the bereaved man. The other pointed out the obvious inconsistency of Graham's theology. Christianity—indeed evangelistic Christianity—focused on repentance and conversion; but if "hypocrite" meant "changing one's way of living and meaning it," declared the reader, then "we are all hypocrites in one way or another."[69]

If Graham was unpastoral at times, he could also be quite simplistic and dogmatic in some of his answers. To a young man having difficulty making friends, Graham wrote, "Christians find their joy in giving themselves . . . and they are never without the joy and satisfaction of friends." Graham's simplistic confidence in the power of the Christian faith to effect positive change extended to other areas of life as well. For example, Graham argued, "Forgiveness is natural for the Christian and is contrary to the non-Christian." Fear of death no longer troubled the Christian, Graham guaranteed, "for the fear is removed" by the forgiveness of sins. Christians were destined for greater happiness and superior moral lives than were non-Christians. In fact, Graham claimed that Christians were "the only people in the world who have any right to be happy . . . as they know where they are now and where they are going." Responding to a thoughtful college student who found that "secular thinkers" held high ethical standards, sometimes higher than Christians, Graham countered, "On the average, you will find that the ethical and moral level of true Christians is now and always has been the highest."[70] To be fair, despite these optimistic and even fantastic declarations concerning Christian life, Graham also emphasized in his columns the principle that Christianity required incredible sacrifice. Yet Graham's theology of conversion, with its emphasis on the "new man" in Christ, could be easily mistaken for, if not self-help, then something akin to a simplistic "Christ-help."

Several readers objected to the simplicity and certainty of such answers. One woman griped that his answers did not have enough "meat" and that he needed to explain his Christian terminology more carefully. She was not alone. "Other readers objected to his "oversimplified" answers to complex issues, especially his lack of knowledge about the plight of the "average person."[71] Graham's certainty about heaven and hell also irked a number of readers, including those from both the right and the left. On the one hand, two left-leaning Christians from the South questioned his exclusivist view of salvation, asking about the fate of those who never had the chance to hear about Jesus Christ. On the other hand, a strong Calvinist berated Graham for his answer to a man who had attended a revival (unrelated to Graham) but failed to rise and accept Christ. The layman who did not rise confessed in his letter to Graham that he had felt uncomfortable and unsure when the pastor commanded those who knew they were destined for heaven to stand. Graham replied in his column that the "authority of the Word of God" assured born-again Christians of salvation: "Your uncertainty or anyone's uncertainty is caused by a failure to truly 'receive Christ.'" Angered by Graham's answer, his Calvinist critic noted that Graham might have the "top rating as being number one Preacher," but "in my rating you should not be allowed in the Pulpit." Graham, he continued, had failed to answer "this poor soul truthfully," for "God promised neither you nor anyone they would go to heaven."[72]

Many Protestants also questioned Graham's certainty about the immediate and lasting benefits of the Christian faith. They struggled to find, as one self-described "loyal church member" wrote, "the kind of peace [because of Christ's forgiveness of sin] that you are always preaching about." To his credit, Graham included dozens of probing letters from Christians who, like the "loyal church member," located their lack of peace in the persistence of sin in their lives. "I'm very mixed up in my spiritual life," one of these troubled Christians confessed. "I think I'm a Christian . . . Then I suddenly have a strong yearning to return to the old life of sin." Other believers distressed by sin wrote similar letters: "Must I always go on with this unrest in my mind?" Temptation plagued another: "I want to do right but I am too weak to overcome temptation. What hope is there for me?" Still others worried about, as one writer put it, "evil and wicked thoughts" that materialized regularly in their minds, even during prayer.[73]

Graham consoled these tortured souls by granting the complexities and challenges of the Christian life, but he invariably finished these thoughts with a triumphal call for them to accept Christ. For example, Graham replied honestly and compassionately to the Christian vexed by "yearning" for the "old life of sin": "Your problem is not too unusual although most people don't like to admit it." The battle of sin, Graham continued, "is present in us to a greater or lesser degree." After affirming these difficult realities, Graham announced that with God, "You can have complete victory!" and thus offered the solution that had sent this believer to him in the first place.

Another two readers wondered about Christianity's problem-solving power. They wrote that since they had become Christians, they had experienced more problems than ever before. Graham also affirmed the opinions of these correspondents, writing to one, "Any person who knows the Bible knows that the Christian life is likened to an athletic contest or to warfare, and neither one is easy." In his replies to both of them, Graham also admitted that Christianity would not necessarily solve individual problems but assured them that it did solve the most important problem of all: sin. Yet he also implied that perhaps something was missing in their faith. "The Christian life is most satisfying," he wrote to one of them, "but only when we actually go all out and all the way."[74] Here again, Graham's comment returned these questioners to the source of their initial concern.

Among the points made by Graham in these columns, three stand out. First, the Christian faith was not at all easy. Second, sin was a persistent force in the lives of all Christians. Third, Christians who believed hard enough could have "total victory" over sin and a "most satisfying life."

Graham's characteristic combination of ambiguity and certainty in these and other answers confused some readers and pleased others. Several of his correspondents, however, saw only the certainty with which Graham promised "total victory" and Christian satisfaction in such columns, and it angered them. These readers objected in particular to what they understood to be Graham's neglect of the total depravity of man, which, in their eyes, blocked any human participation in salvation. Redemption, said one critic, involved more than "walk[ing] down to the altar, say[ing] we accept Jesus as our saviour, and we are in and can't fall." Another of these critics, upset by Graham's view of sin and salvation, asked plainly: "When did our Blessed Lord assure sinners that the way of salvation would be easy and pleasant?" She complained further that Graham was just another of the "ministers who hedge around and are afraid to stand squarely and uncompromisingly for Divine Law." Graham, and others like him, she warned ominously, "will surely have to stand before the Judgment-seat some day and answer for your timidity, your cowardice, your failures to lead repentant sinners back to God."[75]

A third reader protested the glibness of Graham's articulation of the solution to the issue of sin after reading a column concerning the premature death of a non-Christian. While she granted that "because of Eve's sin we all are born in sin," she severely criticized Graham for telling a young woman that the reason that her unbelieving mother had died was because "the wages of sin is death." Graham's concrete distinction between Christians and unbelieving sinners left this devout but concerned reader in what she described as "desolation." It appeared to her that on the basis of Graham's answer, living a good life outside the Christian church "nets a big fat zero." The unsettling implications of that kind of theology dismayed her greatly and prompted her to ask desperately, "Where does one go from there?"[76]

In other columns, when Graham faced questions about sin and salvation, he responded in less absolute terms. One distraught Protestant wrote to Graham about the implications of First John 3:9: "Whatsoever is born of God doth not commit sin." The passage worried this correspondent because, as he put it, "I know that I have sinned. Does that mean that I am not a child of God?" This verse, Graham noted in his answer, confused many people. "What it actually means," he wrote, "is that whoever is begotten of God does not sin as a way of life or does not continually practice sin." He replied in kind to another correspondent, who disclosed his frustration with his "sharp temper and some of my old ways of doing things" and asked, "Must I go on living such a defeated kind of living?" Graham replied with an emphatic no, assuring the man that trust in God provided for "a victorious kind of Christian living." But, Graham continued, "victory in the Christian life is not faultlessness. The impact of sin makes deep impressions upon all of us, and they do not disappear in a moment." As if dissatisfied with his own reply, Graham reiterated the point, telling his correspondent that with God's help he would have victory over his temper, just not total victory. The Bible, Graham concluded, did not promise freedom from sin; it promised only that "sin shall not rule or dominate you."[77]

In this balancing of perfectionism and triumphalism with a firm conviction of the pervasiveness of sin, Graham finally reconciled his seemingly contradictory view of human nature. In fact, what he had articulated

—in the best tradition of Wesleyan theology—was a mature and straight-forward interpretation of Christian sanctification. Graham underscored this conviction of sin and sanctification in a reply to a reader who had objected to the idea of "everybody being a sinner" and argued that many wonderful people "certainly don't belong in the hoodlum and criminal class." The questioner's exceptionally poor grasp of the concept of original sin gave Graham the opportunity to spell out the doctrine once more. He presented two reasons for his insistence that "all have sinned." First, he cited scripture as sufficient evidence for his position. Second, he argued, "Human nature is best explained when you accept this view." Although Graham did not elaborate upon this point, it was reminiscent of Niebuhr and Tillich's theological anthropology. In the end, after the scriptural and theological arguments had been exhausted, Niebuhr, Tillich, and Graham appealed to empirical data—the undeniable tragedy of history and of humans' infinite capacity to bring destruction upon themselves and oth-ers—which unquestionably established for them the truth of human sin. Finally, near the end of the column, Graham offered his most definitive statement of his belief in the plain fact of human sin: "Any person that is not fully as good as Jesus Christ is a sinner."[78] Few could have misun-derstood his meaning: everyone, including himself and any Christian who ever lived, was a sinner.

While the tens of thousands who poured out their hearts to Graham each week ranged from those who considered makeup a matter of re-ligious significance to those who asked big questions about sin and salva-tion, the My Answer exchanges reveal the sincerity and the seriousness of Protestant devotion at midcentury. With regard to sin, however, it is true that the bulk of Graham's correspondents articulated their concerns in terms of "acts" rather than as "fact." For his part, Graham did not exactly disabuse these Christians of such a moralistic view of sin, but neither did he ignore the truth that sins were manifestations of the larger problem of original sin. In short, Graham's belief in sanctification meant that he mixed—often unevenly—the doctrine of original sin with the idea of Christian moral progress.[79] It stands to reason, though, that many or most of his pious readers shared his view of sanctification within the Christian faith. In other words, they would have understood both the power of original sin and the power of the Holy Spirit to ensure that, as Graham had written, "sin shall not rule or dominate" in the life of a Christian. Whatever the degree of correspondence between Graham's view of origi-nal sin and that of his audience, the column was a Protestant "confessional booth" that appeared in newspapers from coast to coast. Five times a week, confessions of sin—along with Graham's attempt at "absolution" —landed on millions of American doorsteps. For loyal readers, it no doubt served as an occasion to confess their own sin in solidarity with the confession in that day's column and to contemplate God's forgiveness.

✠ From the media's perspective, Graham was preaching to an audience far removed from the intellectual centers of America. Graham's relative youth, Hollywood good looks—in the early fifties he turned down a feature film offer as well as an NBC television program—well-tailored wardrobe, and expert delivery of polished, simplified sermons contributed to this impression of anti-intellectualism on the part of Graham and his audiences. Appearances aside, Graham's own words fed this image—none more so than his infamous comment: "I am selling the greatest product in the world; why shouldn't it be promoted as well as soap?" Less sensationally, but more typically, Graham's near literalism, articulated in his standard response "the Bible says" to any and all issues, reinforced his reputation for anti-intellectualism.[80]

Despite these tendencies, Graham was hardly the enemy of an intellectual approach to Christianity. In fact, he affirmed its importance to belief in 1965, writing plainly, "Faith is not anti-intellectual."[81] This view was built upon years of increasing openness to the life of the mind. While ministering in the 1950s, he had emphasized that turning to God involved the "mind, the affections, and the will." In that spirit, Graham evangelized at colleges and seminaries in addition to his regular city campaigns. He especially targeted America's elite institutions of learning, visiting Yale, Princeton, and Harvard in the late 1950s and early 1960s with, as usual, the intention of converting unrepentant sinners.[82]

Graham had spoken in an even more important venue a few years earlier, in 1954, when he addressed the faculty and students of the Union Theological Seminary in New York City. The liberal seminary, the academic home of both Paul Tillich and Reinhold Niebuhr, hosted Graham in the chapel, where Graham gave a forty-five minute talk. Tillich was there that day, and most likely Niebuhr was too, but it was their colleague John C. Bennett who wrote about the event for the *Union Seminary Quarterly Review*. According to Bennett, Graham "received one of the greatest ovations given in recent years" at the seminary, which caused Bennett to ask incredulously, "How could this be?" After all, Graham had walked head-on into the lion's den of neo-orthodox and liberal Protestantism.

Bennett explained this unexpected outcome rather cynically, hypothesizing that Graham "knows where to say what" and that the seminary community was "very much relieved to find that he was better than they had expected, or not as bad as they had feared." At one moment, though, Graham apparently forgot "where to say what" when he referred to the American Legion's back-to-God movement as a sign of religious revival, an opinion that his audience openly and sarcastically laughed at. Graham, oblivious to the derision, replied, "You must have had this in a class." As the article continued, however, Bennett softened his tone. He approvingly described how "Billy Graham's grasp of aspects of biblical truth" served as "a corrective for his involvement in American 'culture religion'" and how "his ecumenical outlook and strategy bring some correction to the worst aspects of his biblical authoritarianism." Although this was hardly a ringing endorsement, Bennett recognized Graham as something more than an American-way-of-life preacher. He highlighted, for instance, "a very fine openness" in Graham's social outlook, particularly his unwillingness to "allow religion to be a support for the racial status quo." By the end of the piece, it seemed as though Graham had won over Bennett, who humbly concluded that the visit "was a very good lesson for us. It may have helped us to realize more vividly, what we should have known from church history, that God can work powerfully through men who do not meet all our specifications."[83]

A year after Graham's visit at Union, historian Donald Meyer wrote of just how powerfully the evangelist's discussion of sin met the specifications of most Americans. As noted in chapter 3, Meyer, writing for the *New Republic*, argued that it was precisely this prophetic anti-liberal message that accounted for Graham's spectacular following. The out-of-touch intellectual culture that failed to see Graham in this way, Meyer asserted, missed the significance of the phenomenon of his evangelism. For example, to the critics obsessed with Graham's slick, all-American image, Meyer replied that it was exactly this image that allowed Graham to preach so successfully against what he considered to be the modern idols of individualism, materialism, and progress. As Meyer put it, "the sin for which you repent" at a Graham revival "is the sin of having fallen victim to the impossible vision of salvation portrayed in the beautiful, full-color magazine advertisements, where life is always slim and gleaming." Graham's sermons proclaimed, "You are not slim and gleaming," yet Graham, "because he is—can give you the nerve no longer to want to be. He can tell you to seek your salvation elsewhere." In fact, Graham's disenchantment with the unfulfilled promises of American culture matched that of any "post-liberal tragedist" and thus tapped into the "undissipated reservoirs" of pre-liberal, Bible-reading Americans. According to Meyer, then, intellectuals had to grapple with Graham's combination of evangelical realism, anti-liberalism, and Christian orthodoxy before they dismissed him and his audience as something less than substantive. After all, most Americans did not risk their souls lightly.[84]

As it turned out, Graham's anti-liberal Gospel also appealed to readers of the neo-orthodox *Christianity and Crisis* and, ironically enough, to those of the liberal *Christian Century*. In fact, none other than the president of Union Theological Seminary, Henry Pitney Van Dusen, voiced his support of Graham in the pages of *Christianity and Crisis* in the wake of Niebuhr's series of articles on Graham in the midfifties. Van Dusen considered Niebuhr's opinion of Graham overly critical, "presumptuous," and "unscriptural," not least because his colleague had ignored the "apostolic insight that there are 'diversities of gifts.' "[85] In other words, Graham was an evangelist, not a theologian like Niebuhr, and his vocation charged him with the task of spreading the Gospel as widely as possible.

Other Protestants rallied to Graham's defense as well. It seemed rather obvious to many of them, as it had to Van Dusen, that Niebuhr and Graham occupied two separate offices—both extremely necessary—in the Christian church. As one pastor put it, "We need men, both of Dr. Niebuhr's type as well as of the Billy Graham type."[86] Another correspondent, a seminarian from Georgia, highlighted the irony of Niebuhr's critique of Graham: "Your writings have made me aware of the sinful pretensions in my own life, including my own call to the ministry, and for this I am deeply in your debt. Yet, is it not somewhat in that vein that your article about Mr. Graham could be interpreted?"[87] Princeton theologian E. G. Homrighausen offered yet another prominent defense of Graham. Writing for the *Christian Century*, Homrighausen, despite his agreement with aspects of Niebuhr's overall critique, maintained that Graham's work was of greater significance and substance than Niebuhr had allowed.[88] Readers of the *Century* echoed Homrighausen's position, effectively staging a small mutiny within the liberal periodical.[89]

The mutiny turned into an all-out rebellion after the *Century's* publication of five scathing and patently unfair editorials about Graham and his New York City crusade. Only the first of these five articles contained any legitimate criticism. The author rightly questioned Graham's insulation from the public to which he preached and challenged Graham's message of antimaterialism in light of the BGEA's heavy reliance on the advertising industry to publicize his crusades. These points, however, were sandwiched between questions about Graham's integrity (by now a completely settled question) and his neglect of social issues, particularly the race question. The remaining editorials contained misinformation, irresponsible speculation, and character defamation, and they were often plagued by internal contradictions. Altogether, the editorials amounted to yellow journalism.[90]

The scurrilous articles sparked a lively and protracted debate in the Correspondence pages of subsequent issues of the Christian weekly. In total, the *Century* printed nearly eighty letters from its readers on the question of Billy Graham's ministry. As was the case after the publication of Homrighausen's article, the majority of writers supported Graham against the *Century*'s hostile opinion.[91] Although both the majorities were slight, they nevertheless signaled that the preeminent liberal Protestant magazine in America counted a strong pro-Graham community among its readers.

Taken together, the defense of Graham by Van Dusen, Homrighausen, and dozens of correspondents in the pages of the *Century* substantiated what Meyer had suspected about the evangelist's audience back in 1955. Graham's followers were not at all unsophisticated Protestants enthralled by the American way of life. On the contrary, Graham drew huge crowds to his evangelical campaigns because countless Americans appreciated his straightforward "pre-liberal" message of sin and salvation. While their reception of his preaching on sin may have been wrapped up in other anxieties and emotions, these everyday Protestants also identified with Graham's conceptualization and presentation of the doctrine of original sin. Indeed, Protestants who experienced wicked thoughts during prayer or selfish pride or a general sense of their own radical imperfections found in Graham's evangelical theology both the origin of and the solution to these and other problems. In sum, the evangelical view of sin mattered deeply to Graham's broad and varied constituency of lay theologians.

CHAPTER 6

Paul Tillich, *Seelsorger* in America

In 1964, Paul Tillich received an exceptionally moving letter from a World War II veteran who had recently read "You Are Accepted," Tillich's most famous sermon.[1] In his two-page typewritten letter, this former airman reported that just a few days before reading the sermon, he had crumpled under the "weight of guilt and shame and embarrassment" that arose from his memory of "the forgotten graves of the past." The graves, he revealed, were those of the victims of the saturation firebombings of Japan in 1945. For twenty years, this veteran had carried the burden of his participation in those air raids, and as the images of war flooded back into his consciousness, he framed the experience in terms of his deep personal conviction of sin: "I felt, I knew in my bones, that I was capable of murder, cowardice, hardness of heart—in short, that I am a sinner. I am a sinner; my sins, my capability for evil is not some extraneous blemish—it is bone of my bone and marrow of my marrow." Tillich's sermon, though, had helped him find release from this torment, and the veteran related his experience of "bow[ing] down" and confessing, "Forgive me, for I am a miserable sinner." The ultimate effect of this process of reading and prayer was a welcome sense of the "endless Grace of God."[2]

This veteran's encounter with the tragedy of human sin and evil exceeded that of Tillich's average religious correspondent, as did the sense of relief and forgiveness that Tillich's sermon brought him. Yet the source of this man's pain was by no means foreign to Tillich or to his readers. Familiarity with the horrors of war was not the only circumstance that could bring about an awareness of human sin and the experience of doubt and despair. In fact, such things were and are the very stuff of all human life. And, according to a writer for *Newsweek*, it was precisely this aspect of Tillich's work that explained his wide and diverse audience. "It is this contact with the man in despair," the author held, "that has made Tillich's message, for all its complications, as appealing to the everyday Christian

as to the modern intellectual without a theological home."[3] His sense of
Tillich's appeal to both "the everyday Christian" and the "modern intellectual" was essentially accurate. Like the veteran, armies of civilian readers and listeners found solace in Tillich's analysis of and response to the
human predicament.

Indeed, it is hardly surprising that Tillich proved so attractive to so
many. He was, in his native German, a *Seelsorger*—a caretaker of souls.
For him, the single greatest threat to human well-being was sin, or what
he more often called "estrangement." Thus, he reinterpreted this ancient
problem for a modern age that had neglected the view that Christianity
was, as he observed, "always the religion of sinners."[4] Tillich did not stop,
however, at a mere diagnosis of the problem of human sin/estrangement.
He also provided an answer for it through his reinterpretation, using a
modern vocabulary derived from the German Protestant theological tradition, of the classical Lutheran doctrine of "justification by faith."[5] In
fact, this theology inspired his two best-known aphorisms: "accept your

acceptance" and "the courage to be." Tillich's American readers and listeners studied his writings and flocked to his lectures precisely because they were hungry for the solace that came from his analysis of and response to the human situation as they had personally experienced it.

✣ While Tillich had achieved some renown in 1950s American culture—especially after publishing his best-selling book *The Courage to Be* in 1952—his fame reached its peak in the late 1950s and early 1960s. The clearest markers of this cultural prominence were his 1958 article "The Lost Dimension in Religion" for the *Saturday Evening Post* and his appearance on the cover of *Time* in 1959. After these two events, interest in his work surged and remained high until his death in 1965. Consequently, the record of Tillich's considerable influence within American lay and pastoral circles is strongest for the last seven years of his life. Tillich's importance in American religious life in the later years of his career can be traced through an analysis of the *Post* and *Time* articles, his popular books, and his many speaking engagements at universities and churches, and, of course, through his readers' and listeners' responses to him. In each publication and lecture, the themes of sin, guilt, and forgiveness suffused Tillich's message—although he regularly translated these terms into the language of estrangement and acceptance—and accounted for its popular appeal.

Tillich's "Lost Dimension" article appeared in the *Post*'s Adventures of the Mind series.[6] In this series, the *Post* departed from its usual lighter fare and introduced its millions of readers to the challenging work of eminent philosophers, scientists, and theologians. Tillich's article was no exception. He enjoyed full editorial control over his essay and obtained assurances from the editors at the *Post* that the articles in the Adventures of the Mind series would not be "simplifications" or "popularizations."[7] Tillich took the editors at their word and delivered a masterful summary of his broad theological vision to living rooms and newsstands across America. In a relatively short article, he managed to convey such key ideas as the meaning of faith and religion, his theology of culture, his symbolic view of certain foundational Christian beliefs, and, of course, the importance of the idea of human "estrangement" in his thought.

The article touched a nerve. Nearly two hundred letters from a wide range of Americans flooded into Tillich's office at Harvard University. A minority of the letters criticized or dismissed the piece, and he received a few crackpot notes. Overall, though, readers were positively disposed toward the article. Tillich's secretary at Harvard, Grace Leonard (Cali), summarized their contents for *Post* editor John Kobler, noting that a majority of the correspondents agreed with "Dr. Tillich's point of view" and showed "a deep reflectiveness and awareness of mankind's predicament today."[8] Several lay writers, for example, reported that their church study groups had used the article as a centerpiece for discussion. These positive responses were not limited to Tillich's stack of mail. Kobler and associate editor Richard Thruelsen recorded similar observations about the correspondence generated by the article. Thruelsen wrote to Tillich of one Protestant official who had requested eight thousand copies of "Lost Dimension" from the *Post*, presumably for distribution throughout the denomination's congregations.[9]

The article continued to have an impact long after its initial publication. It appeared in the companion volume put out by the series editors, *Adventures of the Mind* (1959). More tellingly, many readers saved it as a cherished expression of faith, describing its importance to themselves and to others in letters to Tillich well into the 1960s.[10] One letter writer from Montana, although not uncritical of the piece, captured the opinion of many of these faithful readers when he referred to Tillich simply as the "spokesman for humanity."[11]

What makes the laity's respect for Tillich's article all the more significant was that he severely criticized the state of midcentury Protestantism and challenged what he saw as a naïve American optimism about the human situation. These readers, in other words, welcomed Tillich's intellectually sharp and penetrating analysis of their faith and of the wider religious and secular culture. They agreed most of all with his contention that the post–World War II religious revival generally lacked depth— hence his title "The Lost Dimension in Religion." Thus, Tillich's critique of the state of American Protestantism, like that of Niebuhr's, was also a constitutive element of that very same Protestantism.

But what exactly did these readers agree with? For Tillich, American Protestantism had lost the dimension of depth in the 1950s because it had become narrowly defined "as the belief in the existence of gods or one God, and as a set of activities and institutions for the sake of relating oneself to these beings in thought, devotion, and obedience." This narrowing of the scope of religiosity to a gray-haired man in the sky or to certain prescriptive behaviors and institutions, in other words, limited belief to tangible objects and rituals. As a result, the depth of faith and its abiding question of ultimate meaning, or what Tillich called "ultimate concern," were lost amid the appearance of religious devotion. This circumscribed Protestantism, moreover, had its origins in the modern and peculiarly American faith in what he called the "horizontal dimension." As a "horizontally" rather than a "vertically" oriented society, America valued "movement ahead without an end, the intoxication with speeding forward, without limits." Americans, therefore, derived meaning not from ultimate questions about existence—including the fallen nature of the human condition—but from trust in scientific and technological progress or the marketplace or both.[12]

This marriage of Protestantism and the horizontal dimension, Tillich argued, had devastating consequences for human autonomy and the religious spirit. "Man," he contended, "becomes a thing among things . . . a bundle of conditioned reflexes without a free, deciding and responsible self." Worse still, man in this state becomes provisionally aware of the emptiness of life on this horizontal plane and finally "feels that he has lost the meaning of life, the dimension of depth."[13]

The dimension of depth, however, was not totally absent from midcentury America. According to Tillich, it could be found wherever the question of ultimate meaning was asked and wherever that question led to an answer that brought about the "radical realization of our predicament."[14] The predicament of which Tillich wrote was human estrangement and separation from "the ultimate source of meaning," or, to translate Tillich's distinctive language, estrangement or alienation from God as a consequence of original sin. He reinforced this message in a letter to a laywoman who had confessed that Tillich's *Post* article and his "questioning theology" had shaken the foundations of her faith as well as that of some fellow congregants. He wrote in response, "The only 'unshakable' is the infinite distance between God and man—a distance which shakes everything we say or do in relation to God."[15] Tillich's reply further illuminated the theology behind the *Post* article: only awareness of the "infinite distance between God and man," and of the estrangement that resulted from it, could restore to religious faith the dimension of depth that the culture and superficial religion tried to avoid and sometimes actively suppressed.

In the article, Tillich clarified this complex argument about the relationship between human estrangement and the dimension of depth with several examples from the realm of culture. Indeed, Tillich believed that the "narrow" church had so disconnected itself from an understanding of the estranged situation of humanity that it would have to relearn this aspect of Christianity from the "theology" of serious writers, poets, artists, musicians, and philosophers who might or might not be Christian. His description of "the poet's" recovery of the dimension of depth exemplifies the theological profundity that Tillich found beyond the church sanctuary: "It is the religious question which is asked when the poet opens up the horror and the fascination of the demonic regions of his soul, or if he leads us into the deserts and empty places of our being, or if he shows the physical and moral mud under the surface of life, or if he sings the song of transitoriness, giving words to the ever-present anxiety of our hearts."[16] Passages like this one, which drew on the perspective of cultural theologians,[17] ensured that even those unfamiliar with Tillich's distinctive, nontraditional theological vocabulary could grasp his argument about the loss of depth in religion.

Tillich's themes of religious loss and cultural superficiality partially explain the positive response of the public to the article. Americans of the modern and postmodern eras have frequently chastised themselves about the loss of something or other and have longed vaguely for a return to the good old days. Yet the majority of Tillich's correspondents had become aware that they were not simply pining for a bygone era. The heartfelt notes of appreciation and the dozens of lengthy and sometimes ponderous letters that he received in response to "Lost Dimension" indicate that his analysis of the estranged character of human existence resonated with many American Protestants.

One such letter came from an elderly Methodist from rural West Virginia who praised the "splendid article." In a shaky longhand, he informed Tillich of his own "survey of the same thing" within the Protestantism he knew. "The church," he wrote, "has failed to keep in mind the distinction between sin and the results of sin." This confusion meant that the church, "instead of a discisive victory over the intruder [sin], unwillingly, plays the role of a quack Dr. with a rich patient, except in this case the patient's health and growth threatens the world's well-being."[18] Though his last thought is not entirely clear, it appears that he objected to the "quack Dr." church's attempts to palliate the symptoms of sin without addressing the root cause of the illness. This logic closely parallels, in its own way, Tillich's insistence that as the first and most crucial step in regaining the dimension of depth, Christians must come to an awareness of their estranged predicament.

Clear across the country in Washington State, Tillich's "Lost Dimension" inspired a thoughtful letter from a remarkable mother of six. In addition to tending her brood and managing with her husband their twenty-three-acre orchard in central Washington, she had been active in a local church, and it was out of this context that she wrote to Tillich. His critique of a religiosity limited to the horizontal dimension had especially appealed to her. She admitted that at one time she had been "right in there pitching with the rest," until she realized that "escape was futile, and I must face the meaning of life, or die." That realization had led her to her current church, which, she claimed, borrowing a phrase from the article, did not "cover up the truths" about the human predicament "by secular or religious ideologies." She went on to comment on Tillich's symbolic interpretation of the Creation, the Fall of Adam and Eve, and the Resurrection. She noted that although her church "actually believed" these stories about the earth's origins, sin, and the Son of God, they had lost their "validity" as revelations of humanity's true condition. The problem, in her view, was that these doctrines had been "confused and misinterpreted" at an earlier time in the history of the Christian church.

Although this woman identified with Tillich's presentation of the Christian message, her own thoughts were not entirely clear. On the one hand, she apparently disagreed with Tillich's symbolic view of the core elements of the Christian faith, on grounds of what seemed to be a literal interpretation of the Bible. On the other hand, she repeatedly thanked Tillich for his "thoughtful arguments" and emphasized again that her church "appeals to minds which are not afraid to ask questions." But she had to cut her letter short because, she explained, "the baby is awakening, the apricot pickers are picking madly and will soon be wanting checks written, already I have been interrupted several times by those who want to buy apricots, and so life must go on, and this letter can not."[19] Before sealing her letter, she dropped in a "little tract" about the Christian faith that she had written in her spare time. This image is worth more than a thousand words: a busy rural woman of relatively humble social position squeezing in contemplation about important Christian questions raised by the learned émigré theologian into her busy day.

Tillich received this orchard matron's letter with enthusiasm. At the bottom of her letter, he jotted a note to his secretary instructing her to "acknowledge this very fine letter very positively and tell her why I can not answer immediately. But I am looking into her booklets [sic] with great interest."[20] His genuine interest in the letter and in the "little tract" that came with it is no surprise in light of Tillich's understanding of his own vocation. The woman was Tillich's kind of Christian—a thinking one. More to the point, she clearly identified with his warnings about the limited horizontal dimension and its masking of the tragic reality of the human predicament. In keeping with that analysis, she entertained his symbolic interpretation of, among other things, the biblical account of original sin, even if she did not fully endorse it.

The reactions of conservative Christians to "Lost Dimension" reveal another side of the sin-consciousness of American Protestants at midcentury. Many in this group were unimpressed by Tillich's interpretation of the faith and by his nontraditional language. They wanted the fundamentals of Christianity; they wanted more forthright and explicit discussion of the problem of sin and the answer of Jesus Christ. In short, they wanted Billy Graham's Christian message. For his part, Tillich hardly endeared himself to this community by referring to Graham's work in the article as "primitive theological fundamentalism."[21]

Yet the critical rejoinders from conservatives served to demonstrate their serious consideration of the doctrine of original sin. Shortly after the publication of "Lost Dimension," Billy Graham's father-in-law, L. Nelson Bell, devoted his *Christianity Today* column to an assessment of the article. He severely criticized Tillich for what he perceived to be a lack of plain sin-talk in the piece: "Not once in Tillich's article is there a mention of the ugly word 'sin.' . . . He makes no reference to the world's basic problem and no intimation that man is a sinner both by inheritance and practice. Yet sin is evidenced in every area of life. We see it manifested in our own hearts and on the pages of our daily newspapers, a terrible blight from which man cannot extricate himself either in act or consequence."[22] Other conservative evangelicals reinforced Bell's analysis, expressing their "disgust" at Tillich's apparent evasion of the term "sin." A laywoman from Texas even sent Tillich a copy of Bell's column, writing: "Please Mr. Tillich read this article. I read yours and feel so sorry for you."[23]

Within conservative and traditional Christian circles, however, positive responses to the article were not unheard of. After Bell's critical assessment of "Lost Dimension," *Christianity Today* published a few letters over the course of several weeks that defended Tillich, including one from a theologian at the Perkins School of Theology at Southern Methodist University in Dallas, Texas.[24] A few of Tillich's other lay correspondents demonstrated in their letters that they, too, were capable of balancing a critical appreciation of Tillich's theology with their own more conservative positions. Writing from Ohio, a laywoman by the name of Mrs. Anderson exhibited such a nuanced understanding of "Lost Dimension." She opened her three-page letter humbly: "I won't pretend to understand everything you said in your recent Post article." Still, she wished to share her thoughts concerning the issues of depth and meaning in the Christian life. To Anderson's mind, the answer to "our problems regardless of how big or little they may be" was for humans to cease "trying to second guess our Lord." Anderson's solution followed the usual rhetoric of conservative evangelicals: absolute faith in God steered believers through the challenges of life. Yet she complicated the idea of faith as an expedient resolution to life's problems by noting, as Tillich had in his article, the "shallowness of the recent Christian movement in our country." She pointed out further that most contemporary signs of piety reflected "the modern whim for more"— an obvious gesture to Tillich's definition of the horizontal dimension—as opposed to "faith in God." She blamed this mockery of God's sovereignty on the fact that "few ministers dare to speak out against sin."[25]

For Anderson, the one exception to the hollow Christianity of midcentury and a shining exemplar of the faith was Billy Graham. Graham was preaching "the submission of self," she wrote, "sensational tho' he may be." Present-day ministers, she contended, should follow the example of Graham and "worry less about increasing their church membership and worry more about the conditions of the souls of the members." Anderson hoped that Tillich would not think her a "Pharisee"; she assured him that she understood her own sin and "half-hearted" Christian ways. But, with the help of God, she professed, "I will continue to seek that goal of 'one with Christ' and cast off the sinfulness which continues to bind me." She closed by asking Tillich for a letter of reply: "Maybe I need to know if my ideas are right even tho my actions are not."[26]

Although she read Tillich through the lens of Billy Graham, Anderson shared the theologian's suspicion of the captive revival and its neglect of sin. Her views, in fact, reveal the influence of both Graham and Tillich. Her goal of "casting off sinfulness" echoed the straightforward theology of Graham, while her view of the persistence of sin in Christian life reflected an appreciation of Tillich's understanding of the religious dimension of depth. Compared with other lay writers, Anderson may have been exceptional in her ability to draw on both Graham and Tillich to nourish her own spiritual life, but she was quite typical in her serious contemplation of the separation between God and humanity as a consequence of sin. Although Graham and Tillich differed in many respects and their audiences came from dissimilar theological communities, these polarities could fall away in the context of their beliefs—and those of their constituencies—about human nature.

Not quite a year after the *Post* article, Tillich landed on the cover of *Time*, and once again his seemingly novel treatment of sin and salvation appeared on newsstands and in living rooms throughout America. The banner headline that greeted the countless readers of *Time* read, simply and tellingly, "A Theology for Protestants." The accompanying article fairly represented that theology, noting Tillich's views that the traditional concept of God was dead, doubt was inevitable, and idolatry widespread. Yet the center of Tillich's work, according to the author, was the problem of human estrangement: "What Tillich has been trying to do all his life is to make the Christian message meaningful for 20th century man in all his 'estrangement.'" For his part, Tillich agreed with the author's assessment of his theological project and wrote a letter to *Time* praising the article, which the editors gladly published in a subsequent issue of the magazine.[27]

Whether Tillich's theology was indeed "a theology for Protestants" was open for debate. For one large group of believers, it certainly was not their theology, and they let *Time* know it. For four consecutive weeks, the magazine published largely negative reactions to the article, including several letters from outraged Protestant ministers. These pastors argued uniformly that ordinary Protestants neither had any interest in Tillich's theology nor could they comprehend it. One of them mockingly cited Philippians 4:7: "In one sense he [Tillich] is like the peace of God, for he passes all understanding."[28]

The response of an equally outspoken group of religious readers suggests that these ministers misjudged the views of ordinary Protestants. A majority of the more than seventy laypeople who wrote directly to Tillich after his cover appearance voiced their support of Tillich's overall approach to theology, and many appreciated his understanding of the human situation in particular. Within this cohort, even some critics of Tillich found common ground with his theology of sin. One curmudgeonly layman, for example, began by speculating about Tillich's level of sobriety when he wrote the article. Still, this man wrote that he appreciated Tillich's explanation of the "Protestant Principle"—the sinful tendency of humans and groups to claim divine dignity for their morality, sanctity, or doctrine—while emphasizing that it was "nothing new." Rather, he wrote, "it has always been fundamental in a believers faith before God."[29] Another critic with fundamentalist inclinations initially disputed Tillich's conception of sin. But as he continued, his dogmatic tone shifted to one of inquiry, and he listed a series of theological questions, including, curiously, "What exactly is sin?" He asked the question to determine whether "what I believe in is false or true." This man's query about sin suggests that Tillich's thought had given this conservative pause and, at least for a moment, bridged their theological divide.[30]

Like these two readers, an elderly woman who identified herself as "Grandma Hoff" stopped short of total rejection of Tillich's theology. She opened her letter by expressing sorrow for Tillich and what she saw as his needlessly complicated perspective on Christianity. Although she advised him to pursue "that old time religion" and the "simple teachings of Jesus," she insightfully observed that the "old time religion" was in fact nothing other than "ultimate concern." Part of her own "ultimate concern," she further explained, was the fact that America made "graven images" in the "shape of guns/bombs/etc." Despite their many differences, Tillich's theological casting of Christian faith as addressing ultimate concern had stirred something within this old-time believer and helped her articulate her concerns about the dangerous graven images that she thought Americans worshiped in the cold war era.[31] Plainly, Tillich's account of humanity's separation from God was not as isolated from the values of ordinary believers as conventional views of his audience have assumed.

If some curmudgeons, fundamentalists, and Grandma Hoffs were ambivalent supporters of Tillich's theology, most of his correspondents were unequivocally enthusiastic about his work. Several of these writers strongly protested the negative letters published in *Time*. One Texan, for instance, was dismayed by the "deplorable" fact that pastors had authored so many of the critical letters that saw print. He argued that Tillich, not unlike "Jesus, Servetus, and Roger Williams," was a victim of organized religion's perennial resistance to innovation.[32]

In addition to expressing general support for Tillich's theological stance, some of these lay writers commented directly on his views of sin, often with a colloquial flair that lent a cryptic quality to their opinions. One resident of Independence, Kansas, first thanked Tillich for his "intellectual approach to Christianity," which assured her that she was "still in the fold" despite feeling like a "lost sheep." She also expressed her appreciation for what she saw as Tillich's "lack of dogma," remarking: "You can have that 'Old Time Religion.'" She then offered an idiomatic and at first glance puzzling approval of Tillich's theology: "I prefer to live modern, passing up thinking man's filter cigarettes and home laundries that can think, for Professor Tillich's brand of beliefs which can stand the tests of time and philosophic thought. That's my idea of progress."[33] Although seemingly incoherent, her dismissal of advances in the material world in favor of "Professor Tillich's brand of beliefs" suggests that Tillich had convinced her that progress was a matter not of technological advance but of coming to terms with the reality of the human condition.

The *Time* article, despite its sobering description of Tillich's theology, avoided portraying him as a misanthrope by also presenting his insistence on the original, underlying goodness of humanity. Tillich, the author reported, understood human beings as a combination of an "essential self" (good) and an "existential self" (prone to sin). This vision of the human experience caught the attention of one Mrs. Engelhard, a housewife from Virginia. She sent Tillich a long letter describing her own opinion of the "essential and the existential" and their importance for religious life. She first voiced her frustration with what she asserted was the Lutheran tradition's—and her own pastor's—disregard for this understanding of human nature. The message of both was too steeped in the idea that, in the words of a common church confession, "We are by nature sinful and unclean." She preferred instead a view of human nature that balanced a recognition of the sinful self with an acknowledgment of the "divine" or "true" self. Engelhard asserted that, for her, sin was a consequence of withdrawing from her "Christ self." Yet, she exuberantly observed, awareness of the Christ self, "of being a part of the infinite," gave "rest, peace, [and] joy!" The Christ self, she continued, put the sinful self in a "place of 'second importance,'" which, she suggested, "is where it belongs." She ended her letter by thanking Tillich "for caring enough about what the laity think to read this."[34]

Tillich did read Engelhard's letter and was impressed by it. He asked his secretary, Grace Leonard, to convey to her (he was teaching in Europe) that he had enjoyed reading the letter and felt "that you have worked out your thoughts carefully and well."[35] What Engelhard had worked out was a keen sense of the ambiguity of human nature. Her statement of Christian freedom—that "rest, peace, [and] joy" depended upon an awareness of human sin—matched Tillich's own views, as did her contention that sin was of "secondary importance" in light of the "Christ self." Tillich had emphasized this point in the article and repeated it countless times elsewhere. Perhaps as a fellow Lutheran—Tillich's own denominational heritage—Engelhard had grasped, even unknowingly, his reformulation of the traditional doctrine of "simultaneously justified and sinful."

The "Lost Dimension" article and the *Time* feature were breakthrough pieces in connecting ordinary Americans to Tillich's theology of sin. From the perspective of a twenty-first-century world of innumerable publications and information overload, it may difficult to imagine the lasting impact that these articles in the then-dominant mass media had on believers. Writing from the small, historic fishing town of Astoria, Oregon, Ardie Stangland, a middle-aged housewife, recorded just how powerfully Tillich's work had affected everyday Protestants in her corner of the country:

> I have been surprised, not in the controversy stirred up by the article which Time magazine carried about you, but by the very one-sided letters of criticism. Perhaps it is because lay persons like myself do not often write "fan" letters in this field.
>
> However, I feel I must tell you that regardless of the criticisms from theologians, what you have to say means a great deal to many laymen.
>
> For instance, after your article, entitled "The Lost Dimension in Religion", appeared in the Saturday Evening Post, I happened to mention it to a friend—a housewife like myself. With considerable feeling she replied, "I read it too, and that man makes sense. If this is what the church can offer, I'll stick with it a while longer!"
>
> Much of any theological writing is extremely difficult, of course, for the average layman, as he lacks the theological vocabulary and the theological concepts to understand it. However, in spite of this difficulty, the broader meanings of what you have to say seem to come through to us, and we are eager to learn and to understand more.
>
> We hope that you will continue to have time to write occasionally for people like us, who are just as concerned, though perhaps more bewildered than the theologians, in our struggle to discover the meaning of life and a faith to live by.[36]

✠ Tillich wrote several books specifically for those of the laity who were searching, as Stangland wrote, for "the meaning of life and a faith to live by." The more popular of these included two monographs, *The Courage to Be* (1952) and *Dynamics of Faith* (1957), and three edited collections of sermons: *The Shaking of the Foundations* (1948), *The New Being* (1955), and *The Eternal Now* (1963). Tillich wrote these monographs, or his "little books" as he often called them, as distillations of his theology for everyday Protestants, who he assumed would not consult his massive and highly complex *Systematic Theology*. In that same vein, Tillich published his collected sermons at the behest of colleagues, students, and laypeople who had found them to be moving examinations of the human experience as well as illuminating but more accessible representations of his larger theological system.

The Courage to Be was Tillich's most popular and critically acclaimed book—and as he told one correspondent, his own favorite among the many that he wrote.[37] Widely praised in both the religious and the secular press, *Courage* quickly became a best seller and has not yet lost its appeal (to date, the book has sold more than a half million copies).[38] When the book first appeared, theologian W. Norman Pittenger, writing in the *New Republic*, called Tillich "the most germinal thinker of our day . . . a prophetic voice speaking with compelling power to our generation."[39] The book, in fact, attracted not only disaffected college students, as is sometimes thought, but also a wide audience reaching across generations. It sold well within various denominations and became a standard text in many church education classes across the religious landscape.

Tillich expected a lot from his readers. Although *The Courage to Be* was a short book, Tillich's erudition and his sophisticated philosophical and theological approach to Christianity were on full display. Chapter 1, for example, focuses only on the word "courage," guiding the reader through a history of various philosophical and theological interpretations of that quality. The intricacy of the argument notwithstanding, the book consisted of three straightforward components: First, Tillich explained why life is hard. Next, he argued that the various answers of collectivism (group social life) and individualism (self-assertion) fail as satisfying responses to the hardship of life. Finally, he explained why a particular form of Protestant courage was the best hope for human beings in light of the profound difficulties of human existence.

At the center of this tripartite analysis of the human situation was Tillich's theology of estrangement, or sin. That life was hard was simply a fact of existence for Tillich. The reason for this was that nonbeing—a philosophical term that Tillich defined as the threat of nothingness—framed every life. This experience of the threat of nonbeing, or nothingness, that made human existence so difficult came in three basic forms: the anxieties of fate and death, of emptiness and meaninglessness, and of guilt and condemnation. These manifestations of nonbeing, according to Tillich, touched every human life. No one was immune from the fear of death, from the loss of confidence in someone or something that previously had "given meaning to all meanings," or from failures in life that produced guilt and "self-rejection." In all three instances, these anxious expressions of nonbeing came to life because of an underlying human estrangement. Tillich made this point most clearly in his analysis of the anxiety of emptiness and meaninglessness: "This threat is implied in man's finitude and actualized by man's estrangement." But all three types of anxiety," he continued, "are implied in the existence of man as man, his finitude, and his estrangement."[40]

The central place of estrangement necessarily informed his critique of both collectivist and individualist answers—whether Christian or not—to the human predicament. He understood that collective social life and individual self-expression have their places; as a consequence of estrangement, however, no group or individual could manifest the courage required to displace the threats of nonbeing from the center of human existence. In fact, the very belief that collectivism or individualism could resist nonbeing was itself symptomatic of estrangement: it placed confidence in the self or the group instead of in God.[41] Even an attempt to balance collectivism and individualism fell short of successfully combating the threats of nonbeing that afflicted humankind: "Under the conditions of human finitude and estrangement," such a balance was impossible because "that which is essentially united becomes existentially split." Inevitably, he continued, "the courage to be as a part separates itself from unity with the courage to be as oneself, and conversely." He concluded, therefore, that the anxieties of nonbeing that temporarily had receded once again would be "unloosed" and become "destructive."[42]

In contrast to the collectivist and individualist solutions to the human situation, Tillich advanced an explicitly Protestant form of courage in response to the three threats of nonbeing. The courage to be, he asserted, "is an expression of faith," a faith defined by "the self-affirmation of being in spite of the fact of nonbeing."[43] This type of courage, in other words, did not eliminate the threefold anxiety of nonbeing—that was the meaning behind his use of "in spite of." Instead, the courageous acknowledged their estranged condition and accepted the fact that the anxieties of fate and death, guilt and condemnation, and emptiness and meaninglessness would shadow them throughout their lives. Most important, Tillich stressed, this faith came from without. An individual could not generate a courageous faith from within the self; he must be "grasped" by God. This infusion of faith supplied the power for man to affirm himself in spite of nonbeing "because he knows that he is affirmed by the power of being-itself [God]."[44] This stance of faith avoided the historically unsuccessful and, religiously speaking, idolatrous search for redemption in human forms, whether corporate or individual.

As noted earlier, Tillich's phrase "the courage to be" was an innovative reworking of the classical Lutheran doctrine of justification by faith, but one that avoided the conventional and, for many, clichéd connotations of that concept. Tillich freely admitted this intellectual debt in his account of the anxiety of guilt and condemnation and fate and death. In the context of the anxiety of guilt and condemnation, he wrote, "One could say that the courage to be is the courage to accept oneself as accepted in spite of being unacceptable. . . . [T]his is the genuine meaning of the Pauline-Lutheran doctrine of 'justification by faith.'" He confirmed this point by concluding, "The courage to be in this respect is the courage to accept the forgiveness of sins . . . as the fundamental experience in the encounter with God."[45] It is true that Tillich's explanation of the courage to be in the face of doubt and meaninglessness had less to do with the forgiveness of sins and more to do with his theological understanding of God—not as an object among others, but as "the God above God"—and the crucifixion of Jesus Christ. Yet this emphasis on the nature of God and the crucifixion, especially the latter, assumed the importance of forgiveness and justification, since the anxieties of doubt and meaninglessness were themselves expressions of a fundamental human estrangement that only forgiveness and salvation could overcome. In sum, Tillich's essentially Lutheran-Protestant analysis of the courage to be underscored the radical sinfulness of humanity, whose only remedy lay in the radical grace of God—the "acceptance of what was unacceptable." The seemingly untraditional formulation, "the courage to be," was Tillich's way of communicating to a modern audience that courageous, affirmed living despite human sin was possible only because of God's justification of the sinner by faith through grace.[46]

Tillich's timely analysis and interpretation of the anxieties of human existence in Courage resonated deeply with thousands of ordinary Protestants living in the Age of Anxiety. One of these, Mary Baker, of Illinois, had recently returned to the church after an absence of nineteen years and discovered Tillich's thought through an adult education class, which had read Honest to God (1963) by Anglican bishop John A. T. Robinson. Robinson's book, a controversial best seller, quoted Tillich liberally, and Baker found Tillich's words to be "like a beakon [sic] through a fog." She was especially taken with Tillich's ability to "say with great ease and simplicity what others try to say with effort and verbosity." She approached her pastor about her interest in Tillich, and he lent her a copy of *The Courage to Be*. She studied the book for five months, typing up difficult passages, writing her own interpretations of them, and checking with her pastor to measure how well she had comprehended the material. "When I had finished," she reported, "I had 49 pages of typewritten comments." Baker included this information in her letter to Tillich because she wanted him to know "that your long efforts are bearing the kind of fruit which inspired you to share your wisdom with all of us."[47] Baker did not enclose her commentary, but it is clear that she must have absorbed something of Tillich's view of human sin and salvation from her close reading of his work.

Another laywoman, Carol Rice Seamons, did include her typewritten commentary on *Courage* along with her letter of appreciation. Unfortunately, Tillich never had the chance to read this interpretation of his work because she posted it on the day of his death, 22 October 1965. In her essay, Seamons focused on the last chapter of the book—Tillich's account of the courage to be in light of nonbeing—which she described as "a 'taking-off point.'" She opened her exposition of *Courage* by writing, "Courage-in-spite-of is but love of God-in-spite-of." While her subsequent interpretation of this idea was a bit confused, Seamons concluded her analysis cogently: "We then expect only human performance of ourselves and of others since our craving for Absolute Love, Absolute Perfection is met in our relationship to God." Although Seamons never used the term "sin" or Tillich's language of estrangement in her letter, she seemed to grasp Tillich's essential religious viewpoint. "Man's highest potential," she wrote, "can not be realized through any earthly means: not through man's own efforts, not through another human being, not through thought, reason or knowledge." She observed, moreover, that the human experience of "restlessness, discontent, emptiness, anxiety, and guilt," while real, could be overcome by faith in God. Revealing how carefully she had read the last chapter of *Courage*, Seamons argued that these experiences could not "slough off" the part of humanity "that is divine, is God-entwined," and is the "source of our greatest strength and deepest fulfillment." Indeed, for Tillich, the courage to be depended upon such awareness of the profound disquiet of the estranged human experience as well as the acceptance of God as the power that conquered estrangement.[48]

Another layman, better-read, followed the example of these two exegetes. He wrote a four-page letter on how *Courage* had clarified the lessons of his previous theological and philosophical investigations. He discovered in *Courage* the relevance of the "basic classical Christian doc-trines of the fall, sin and salvation." These insights concerning "man's basic existential estrangement" convinced him of "man's need of a Chris-tian experience" founded on "a willingness to take the existential anx-ieties of fate, death, guilt, condemnation, doubt and meaninglessness upon ourselves and live with them and in spite of them." This reader's quite stunning recapitulation of the book not only accurately rehearsed the essential theme of *Courage* but also recognized a more subtle point: the courage of which Tillich wrote was not a one-time achievement, but one that required frequent renewal in the face of and in spite of the ever-present anxieties brought on by sin.[49]

Christians undertook thoughtful studies of *The Courage to Be* in church basements and fellowship halls, just as they did in private homes. A pastor from a Congregational church in Minneapolis, Minnesota, for instance, reported that members of his adult education class had been "enriched by comprehending some of your book." As if to prove his point, the pastor included in his letter a poem that represented the discussants' views of the book. Two of the stanzas provide a window into the group's struggles with the text but also convey their clear understanding of the fundamen-tal message of *Courage*:

> Herr, [*sic*] Tillich, you bewildered us
> With talk of finitude and being.
> We struggled in an anxious fuss
> Over the ontological meaning.
>
> But, what a lovely time we had,
> This group, collectively a part.
> We found Non-Being not all so bad
> Since Being, thereby makes a start.

The last stanza, whatever its literary quality, indicates a plain comprehen-sion on the part of these midwesterners of the courage to be as a justifying faith or, in Tillich's words, as "the self-affirmation of being in spite of the fact of non-being."[50]

✦ *The Courage to Be* was but one of several texts by Tillich that were read with enthusiasm by pastors and lay theologians alike. In his collections of sermons, *The Shaking of the Foundations* (1948), *The New Being* (1955), and *The Eternal Now* (1963), and in his long essay, *Dynamics of Faith* (1957),

Tillich continued to teach everyday Protestants by translating the Christian message into the language and conceptual framework of the mid-twentieth-century world. But in these works, as in *Courage*, the centrality of the doctrine of original sin and Tillich's faith in the Christian message as the answer to sinful estrangement were hardly lost in translation.

The influence of the collections of sermons, taken together, rivaled that of *The Courage to Be*. By the early sixties, sales of the three volumes totaled more than fifty thousand copies.[51] Reviewers praised the books for their accessibility, although a number of them cautioned prospective readers that this accessibility by no means limited the depth of Tillich's interpretation of the biblical text. A reviewer from *Presbyterian Life*, for example, warned readers that *The Shaking of the Foundations* was "no milk-and-water preaching to leave the smugly pious undisturbed. This will tear up a smug, placid faith by the roots."[52] Unintimidated, the selection committee for the Religious Book Club chose *Shaking* as the book of the month for June 1948.[53]

The adage that pastors preach the same sermon every week, while overdrawn, applied to Tillich as much as to any parish cleric. In all three volumes, Tillich returned again and again to the issues of estrangement and reconciliation.[54] The most famous of his sermons, "You Are Accepted," appeared in *The Shaking of the Foundations* and centered upon what he called "the all-determining facts of our life: the abounding of sin and the greater abounding of grace."[55] In his sermon "The New Being," reprinted in the volume of the same title, he summarized the essence of the Christian Gospel, citing Galatians 6:15: "It is the message of a 'New Creation.'" For Tillich, as for St. Paul in the first century, humans in union with Jesus Christ participated in a new reality, a new way of living. The old, sinful self was, however, still present: "We belong to the Old Creation," Tillich wrote, but the "demand made upon us by Christianity is that we also participate in the New Creation."[56] Theodore Gill, editor of the *Christian Century* and reviewer of *The New Being* for that publication, recognized the similarity of the central message in the two collections, noting that each sounded the theme of liberation from "the quaking bog beneath particular existences and general existences."[57] *The Eternal Now*, the final volume in the sermon series, returned to Tillich's familiar territory of sin and salvation. Part one of the text consisted of six sermons on the theme of the human predicament, including "The Good That I Will, I Do Not."

Tillich's sermon collections did much to shape American Protestant church life and individual spirituality during the 1940s, 1950s, and 1960s —especially through their influence on the clergy. In the postwar decades, the bookshelves of Protestant pastors almost invariably contained one or all of these volumes. And these pastors, stationed in churches rural and urban and in every region of the country, often brought Tillich's theology as expressed in these sermons to the ordinary congregational level. Sometimes this occurred indirectly, as they borrowed and integrated elements of Tillich's sermons into their own preaching and teaching. One of these clergymen, a Presbyterian pastor writing from the hinterlands of South Dakota in 1948, spoke for many when he thanked the German theologian for the way in which *Shaking* had stimulated his "spiritual thought beyond measure," something he prayed that he might "sometimes mediate to my flock."[58]

Congregations also directly encountered Tillich's sermons in Bible studies and adult education classes, some led by pastors and some by laypeople. During a pastoral vacancy in his church, an ambitious layman in Yonkers, New York, for instance, organized a study group around all three volumes of Tillich's sermons. Another congregation, this one in Illinois, opened and closed each Bible study class, as a laywoman reported to Tillich, by "reading one of your sermons aloud."[59] Likewise, the religious education director of a church in Ohio enthusiastically related her incorporation of Tillich's sermons into the church's curriculum. She described her church as one trying to "come alive in these tense times, opening itself to a fresh 'word from the Lord.'" Even having achieved that goal, she continued, the church "would be a lonely outpost without you." She especially appreciated Tillich's views on the ambiguity of the human condition, writing, "This business about ambiguities is so right and from so many of your writings. I'm trying to gather together what your outline of self-integration, self-creativity, self-transcendence—might be in detail. It's fun and I'm growing." In her postscript, she assured Tillich that there was no need for him to reply because "you have been writing to me for years."[60]

The prevalence of the theme of human estrangement in Tillich's sermons sometimes provoked specific reactions like the ones above, but more often they elicited only general reactions from his readers. Yet these general responses, too, revealed readers' engagement with Tillich's analysis of the human condition. Correspondents informed Tillich of the assistance that his sermons provided in the "search for meaning" and during the "storm and stress" and "dark periods" of life.[61] Such comments, although vague in one sense, alluded to readers' appreciation of Tillich's emphasis upon the existential struggle of life, a struggle consistently framed in terms of sin and estrangement.

In *Dynamics of Faith*, Tillich attempted to tackle the preacher's task from another angle. Rather than sermonize about the good news of redemption, he wrote an essay that unpacked the meaning of faith. For Tillich, the meaning of the word "faith," like that of "sin," had suffered distortions over the years. He thus set out to rehabilitate the term because, as he suggested, "It belongs to those terms which need healing before they can be used for the healing of men."[62] He aimed the book at a popular audience and accordingly kept its length at just over a hundred pages. Although less well-known than *The Courage to Be*, *Dynamics* was his second-most-successful book in terms of sales. In 1961, Tillich's editor at Harper and Brothers reported that it was selling at the rate of a thousand copies per month, with total sales of more than forty-five thousand.[63]

Tillich's effort to rescue the idea of faith depended upon three primary strategies. First, he broadened the concept of faith, relying on his "intentionally ambiguous" language of "ultimate concern." With this concept, Tillich wanted to call attention to the nature of faith, a pledge or devotion to something that conditioned everything else in life. For example, he wrote, "if a national group makes the life and growth of the nation its ultimate concern, it demands that all other concerns, economic well-being, health and life, family, aesthetic and cognitive truth, justice and humanity, be sacrificed."[64] The nation, in other words, becomes a god. Although the term "ultimate concern" did broaden how the nonreligious as well as the religious might conceive of faith, the object of faith was still narrow for Tillich: "In true faith the ultimate concern is a concern about the truly ultimate; while in idolatrous faith preliminary, finite realities are elevated to the rank of ultimacy."[65]

Tillich's distinction between "true and false ultimacy" related to the second objective of the book: the attempt to combat idolatrous faith. In its basic religious form, idolatry violated the distance that separated humanity from God by dragging God down to the level of the finite. Tillich reminded his readers that such activity contradicted the essence of Protestantism, what he called "the Protestant Principle." For Tillich, the Protestant faith was a "faith" because it recognized that God came to the estranged human on God's terms, not the reverse. Humans had nothing to contribute—not their religious inclinations, good behavior, spiritual discipline, or success—to the work of salvation. For "the very heart of Christianity" was the belief "that in spite of all forces of separation between God and man this is overcome from the side of God."[66] To understand faith otherwise was a sign of estrangement in the form of unbelief, which implied the idolatry of the self.

Finally, *Dynamics* emphasized the importance of doubt in the life of faith. Tillich explained the matter directly: "Serious doubt is confirmation of faith." Indeed, doubt was the precondition necessary for upholding the Protestant Principle. Absence of doubt implied "possession" of faith, and true faith was something that could never be possessed; otherwise, it would no longer have the character of faith—that is, of trust, not ownership. Doubt related, moreover, to the condition of human estrangement. Humans would always doubt God, as a function of their separation from God in sin. Claims of final certainty about God suggested that an individual had surmounted sin and thus, ironically, discounted the need for a redeeming God by removing the "in-spite-of element" of faith.[67] In short, lack of doubt undermined the importance of the love of God that saves despite human estrangement.

Though reviews were mixed, *Dynamics* was generally well received across the Protestant Christian community. The *Pastoral Psychology* Book Club selected it as the book of the month for March 1957, and it inspired the theme for Religious Emphasis Week at the University of Nebraska in 1958. *Dynamics* received a cordial review from the conservative periodical *Christianity Today*, and the book found a place on the syllabus of the philosophical classics course offered at the bastion of conservative evangelicalism—and Billy Graham's alma mater—Wheaton College.[68] The harshest and most inaccurate critique came from Harold Weisberg in the *New Republic*. Weisberg's misrepresentation of the book was a consequence, it would appear, of his having neglected to read it. For example, Weisberg faulted Tillich for overlooking the "shopworn truism that faith in this sense has led men to evil as well as good." Perhaps Weisberg stopped reading before reaching page sixteen: "The danger of faith is idolatry and the ambiguity of the holy is its demonic possibility. Our ultimate concern can destroy us as it can heal us."[69]

Tillich's treatment of doubt and idolatry as expressions of estrangement evoked a range of responses from readers similar to that stirred up by his sermon collections. Again, lay theologians thanked him for providing guidance and solace as they worked through their despair, grief, or self-disgust, not to mention the mystery of faith itself.[70] Many readers felt enriched by and reveled in the depth of Tillich's analysis of faith—even though some plainly comprehended only part of Tillich's argument. They understood that faith was a complex matter, full of mystery, questions, and tension. Though the book legitimated for many the dynamics at play in faith, such ambiguities could not easily be admitted to in polite church company and thus were restricted to private correspondence.

That several readers from the South, in particular, expressed such sentiments should complicate our understanding of the Bible Belt in postwar America. Although comprising only a small sample and possibly an atypical one, correspondence from Tillich's following in the South suggests groups of "underground" believers unconvinced by the tidy rhetoric of their region's prevailing forms of evangelical Christianity—including that that of Billy Graham's ministry—regarding matters of doubt and sin. In fact, this underground may not have been as small as one might suppose. As Robert Ellwood notes in *The Fifties Spiritual Marketplace* (1997), Graham's neat resolution of sin and doubt in many of his sermons was "expected and discounted" by evangelicals, especially Baptists, as part of the preaching craft. In short, many evangelicals knew that reconciliation with God was not as easy as Graham or other popular preachers made it seem.[71]

Among Tillich's southern correspondents, two lay theologians in particular exemplify this subtle and important qualification to one-dimensional accounts of Bible Belt piety. W. R. MacIlrath, of Washington D.C., "like a lot of slightly educated would-be Christians," appreciated Tillich's intellectual approach to Christianity. He had not yet read *Dynamics* but had recently ordered the book, predicting, "I shall probably mark your *Dynamics of Faith* all up when I get it." His marks would have been mostly positive, if his letter was a fair indicator of his views. He articulated a strong resistance to the self-righteousness and dogmatic opinions of the "Holy Rollers" at his local Baptist church. The certainty with which these "Holy Rollers" pronounced on sin, their relationship with God, and the orthodoxy of their "brand" of religion infuriated MacIlrath: "The Holy Roller type of Pretestant is approachable also, in the first stages, and is expecting a quick convert to HIS BRAND of religion. When he don't get that right quick he is off you like a dirty shirt." From his perspective, such attitudes were "as authoratative about it [Christianity] as Joe Stalin ever was in his most inspired moments about communism."[72] If nothing else, when MacIlrath got his hands on *Dynamics*, he would have appreciated

Tillich's insistence that doubt was essential to Christian faith and that the absence of it was a sure sign of pharisaism and the estranged idolatry of certitude.

Geri Cranford, of North Carolina, had begun marking up her copy of *Dynamics* with the intention of harshly criticizing Tillich. After having read the book once, she had concluded that Tillich was "unsaved." Her initial judgment faded, however, as she "read [*Dynamics*] again and again." Like many who wrote to Tillich, she apologized for her "simple way of writing" and her inability to comprehend parts of the book. She believed that God was "using your book to show me what I presume to be the remarkable insight that He has given you. Man does not know himself." Faith, Cranford knew, came from God's action, not her own. But she also confessed that she trusted God's promises only "now and then," mostly when "the adding machine breaks, market drops or coffee boils over."[73] However folksy her theological reflection, this southern evangelical was bluntly honest about her faith and doubts. In that spirit, she further acknowledged that sin plagued the "saved" person as much as the unsaved: "Before salvation—we sin and get by with it, after salvation, you may do the same things, but it nauseates you." She also noted that God promised nothing to those striving for perfection who attempted to offer something of their goodness to God. In that case, "Christ's death then becomes useless." All these reflections mirrored Tillich's conclusion in *Dynamics* that in relation to God, "we are always receiving and never giving."[74]

Tillich replied to Cranford with a standard form response recommending his three volumes of sermons.[75] Nevertheless, the communication and apparent mutual understanding between Cranford and Tillich had bridged a gap, one supposed by most accounts of midcentury Protestantism to be insurmountable. Tillich, the internationally renowned theologian with a Ph.D. in philosophy, a licentiate in theology, and thirteen honorary doctorates, and Cranford, a married woman of limited education and social standing in North Carolina, shared a basic view of faith and sin.[76]

Perhaps the most impressive examples of lay interest in Tillich's books came from those who read and studied his three-volume *Systematic Theology* in adult church classes. Few had expected that lay believers would show any interest in these massive and intricate volumes. But not all critics found *Systematic Theology* to be prohibitively difficult. A reviewer for *Time*, for instance, judged *Existence and the Christ*, the second volume of the three and the one that outlined Tillich's more systematic interpretation of sin, "accessible to any serious reader." A writer for *Christianity*

Today made an even stronger claim, calling it, astonishingly, "the most readable book that Paul Tillich has yet published."[77]

These assessments were borne out by a few of the lay groups that selected the *Systematic* for their adult education forums. These classes—many but not all of them led by former students of Tillich's—attracted a range of congregants. A Methodist church group in rural California, for example, met weekly to read and discuss the *Systematic*. Perhaps aware of the widespread impression of the improbability of such a thing, the group's pastor wrote to Tillich and detailed the composition of the class, which included twelve members ranging in profession from a medical doctor to several high school teachers and a few housewives.[78] Another Methodist pastor, Robert Chiles, wrote to his former teacher about his Ohio congregation's passionate interest in *Existence and the Christ*. As proof of their diligent reading, Chiles included a glossary of Tillichian terms that the class had written to facilitate its understanding of the text. Of the thirteen who participated in the project, Chiles reported that only five had college training and that at least one had not finished high school. Tillich wrote approvingly of the glossary in his reply to Chiles and his class. With that endorsement and some editorial help from Chiles, the class went on to publish the glossary in the journal *Theology Today*.[79]

⁜ The impact of Tillich's thought on those who studied his books, including even the formidable *Systematic Theology*, suggests that Tillich ministered to a considerable national "congregation" far beyond Boston, Chicago, or New York. Like Reinhold Niebuhr, Tillich shaped many pastors' theologies, which they in turn shared with their parishioners. But Tillich was also in direct personal contact with many members of his extended congregation. Unlike Niebuhr, whose speaking engagements were limited after he suffered a debilitating stroke in 1952, Tillich enjoyed relative good health, and his seemingly boundless energy allowed him to travel nearly every weekend of the academic year to address clerical and lay audiences in every region of the country.

Because Tillich was manifestly a minister to ministers, his thought shaped many congregations directly, often through his own former students. A pastor from Michigan who once had sat spellbound in Tillich's classroom reported, "Now there are few of us who are not deeply indebted to you for insights and categories which we use almost automatically in our everyday theological thinking, whose adequacy we discover in actual experience."[80] Another former student testified to the utility of

Tillich's interpretation of estrangement during his career in the pulpit. Decades after his graduation from Union, this pastor assured Tillich "that the concept of estrangement has been used constantly since I first heard you use it. I have been questioned for many things, I suppose, but not for that. Always thanked for that."[81]

Tillich informed the theology of still more pastors in his role as a respected leader of the movement for continuing education for clergy. In 1958, for example, at the University of North Carolina at Chapel Hill, ministers from as far away as Florida, Georgia, and Virginia attended a seminar led by Tillich and designed around the theme of "lay theological education." According to the campus chaplain, Tillich's presentations there had created a concern among local church members to hear "straight-forwardly about the findings of biblical scholarship and theology."[82] At an event held at the Pacific School for Religion in 1963, Tillich addressed a crowd of more than twenty-five hundred, most of whom were clergy who had come to hear his three-part lecture series, "The Relevance and Irrelevance of the Christian Message." Predictably, part of the relevance of Christianity was a clear understanding and articulation of the conflict between essential being and estranged existence.[83]

Although countless Protestants experienced Tillich's theology at second hand, through their ministers, Tillich's zeal for public speaking meant that laypeople had ample opportunity to hear him in person. Most of these events took place on college campuses, often during an institution's Religious Emphasis Week, and Tillich became a revered figure among undergraduates at schools large and small, known and unknown. In many of these college settings, Tillich predictably emphasized the theme of estrangement. At the University of Oregon in 1956, for example, he opened the school's Religious Evaluation Week with the address "Man and God in Protestant Christianity." This relationship between man and God, Tillich asserted, depended first and foremost upon the knowledge that "there is no good in man which man can boast of in front of God" because "you cannot find a special part of man that is not under the law of estrangement." In fact, Tillich contended, "nothing is only good or only bad in man," an intermediate state that accounted for "the ambiguity of life."[84] Eight years later, speaking at Mundelein College, an unheralded school in Chicago, he had not lost his focus on the "fallen condition" of humanity, noting that "there are elements of good in bad and bad in good and this is 'estrangement.'" He summed up his remarks there by drawing on Luther's idea of the Christian sinner-saint: "In reality [and] in life, there is always the mixture; the saint is a sinner in spite of being a saint."[85] The collegiate settings for these events were not indicative, however, of a separation between town and gown in matters of lay theology. The overflow crowds that met Tillich at these engagements were a mixture of local townspeople and ministers as well as members of the campus community.[86] In conjunction with these occasions, moreover, Tillich often preached or taught at a local parish in the host city.

Tillich's 1962 visit to the University of Colorado at Boulder offers a representative sample of the impact that he had on college students and on the surrounding communities of the faithful across the country. Over that weekend, Tillich delivered the lecture "Types of Man's Self-Interpretation in the Western World." As usual, attendance was high, and the audience was, as University of Colorado philosophy professor John Carnes described in his letter to Tillich, "deeply moved, not only by your words, but perhaps more by you as a person." Carnes also relayed his particular gratification at witnessing the reactions of undergraduates, many of whom had read Tillich's work but discovered only through his presentation that "Paul Tillich is not just a great theologian but also a truly great human being." Carnes also noted that members of his own church, St. John's Episcopal— many of whom attended classes led by Carnes about the "general theological position of Paul Tillich"—numbered among those profoundly affected by Tillich's lectures at the university.[87]

Another congregation in Boulder, First Methodist Church, also had conducted a class on Tillich's theology. In advance of his lectures and as part of the church's ongoing Current Theological Thinking forum, the group read *The Courage to Be*. In addition to preparing for Tillich's talks, the participants had extra incentive to read carefully: Tillich had agreed to attend the final class on the book. According to one member of the class, the occasion was, not surprisingly, a "rewarding experience" for all.[88]

Walter Lehmann, a pastor in Louisville, Kentucky, also testified to the impact that Tillich's college lectures could have on those who heard the eminent theologian. Lehmann had traveled from Louisville to Lexington, Kentucky, to see Tillich at Transylvania College in 1965. He later wrote of the importance of this event and of Tillich's work generally to his faith journey: "You have answered so many of my personal conflicts and problems by pointing to the ambiguities of life and the answer that transcends them. Because of personal conflicts and policies as well as a shaking of the foundations of my fundamentalistic theology I passed through a midnight of the soul and out of the despair of Nothing I heard the Eternal speak a soul saving word. The journey was guided a great part of the way through your writings."[89] Lehmann's account reveals yet another instance in which Tillich's words concerning the human condition provided consolation and guidance during a crisis of the ambiguity of the self and the soul as a consequence of estrangement.

Tillich's visits to churches were not always the byproduct of his college lectures. Beginning in the early 1950s, he preached annually to the First Unitarian Church of Germantown, Pennsylvania, which not only had invited Tillich to visit several times but also had attracted other theological luminaries of the day—including Reinhold Niebuhr. This theologically inclined congregation eagerly listened to Tillich's sermons and pressed their pastor, Max Daskam, to obtain copies of them for the congregants' continued edification. The liberal aspect of Tillich's thought, no doubt, explains part of what endeared him to these Unitarians. Yet Tillich's decidedly non-Unitarian vision of human nature also appealed to this congregation. In one instance, following a sermon on just this subject, Daskam urged Tillich to send a copy of it quickly: "Your sermon yesterday prompted dozens of us sinful souls to sign up for copies. Everyone seems to want to read it."[90] Dozens of other congregations hosted Tillich, and hundreds more wished for his presence among them.[91] These Protestant communities, both those that enjoyed a personal encounter with him and those who hoped for one, together with the tens of thousands of devoted readers and lay theologians who knew him only on paper, composed Tillich's vital national congregation.

One sterling congregant, Dody Zachmann, exemplified the wisdom that emanated from the pews of American Protestant churches and captured the inspiration that lay theologians could enjoy after reading Tillich's ruminations on the human condition. Zachmann, aged thirty-eight, was a housewife and mother of three, with three years of college education. Though professing that she lacked a "great intellect," she turned to Tillich's theology in search of "something more than a new way to bake a cake." Zachmann opened her correspondence by rejecting the idea that Tillich appealed only to theologians, scholars, and graduate students. She felt, instead, that truths could be found in his writings by "all who read, think, search and are aware of a need for new approaches to the age old search for a reason for Being—for God—for the meaning of prayer and faith." Zachmann regretted that many ministers, including those who had protested Tillich's 1959 *Time* cover article, did not share her view of Tillich's accessibility. In her mind, it was the practice of such ministers to "tip toe along," overly dependent on older ways of communicating the Gospel, and unjustifiably proclaim, "Tillich is not for the average laymen." Ministers, she continued, must not claim authority as "the only ones to interpret—theology—for man in 1959."

Despite Zachmann's frustration with pastors who underestimated the "layman's use of theology," she gratefully acknowledged that her own minister nurtured theological exploration. She also took comfort in the fact that others cared as much as she about the basic questions: "Why am I here, What is God, and What does Christ mean to me." These questions, she opined, were asked in many "Great Books discussion groups" and in "study groups in the churches." But, she continued, in the absence of these opportunities, individuals could ask them on their own "for the cost of a paper back or a library card."[92] Like many of Tillich's correspondents, Zachmann admitted that she had not understood everything in Tillich's writings, but she thanked him all the same because "it was through your interpretation of The Fall, Ressurection [sic], Faith and all the many other parts of [the] story of man and his struggle that I gained insight into the Bible." Tillich's theology meant that she "had to go the long way around while others can take the orthodox short cut, but I have had and am having a much greater journey going the long way!"[93]

Zachmann was a particularly searching and reflective Christian, but not an atypical one among Tillich's readers. Like so many other lay theologians, she pursued the very questions, chief among them the question of human nature, that Tillich argued were universal or, as he put it, "implied in existence." He had undertaken as his central theological task a rearticulation of the traditional Christian message—not least of all the Fall—in a language common to the believer, the nonbeliever, the educated, and the uneducated. Though Tillich regarded his life's work ambivalently, his overflowing file marked "Fan Mail" testified to his success in communicating the doctrine of original sin and returning it to the forefront of the Christian imagination.[94]

✣ Tillich's congregation—composed of the Zachmanns, the Andersons, the Stanglands, the Cranfords, the MacIlraths, and many others like them—was a robust group of lay theologians attracted to the depth and force of Tillich's thought. The strength of this congregation also owed much to the aging theologian's own productivity and effort to reach a mass audience beyond academia. Three events, one that took place just a few months before his death in 1965 and two others from 1963, illustrate just how popular his ideas had become and how thoroughly embedded they were in American culture.

In 1965, at the age of seventy-nine, Tillich addressed perhaps his largest audience ever. He was a commentator on the television program *Revolution in Religion*, which aired on the CBS network to millions of viewers in the Chicago area. The Illinois Bell Telephone Company sponsored the program and sent 1.5 million feedback surveys to selected customers, soliciting their opinions on the show and their "attitudes on religion."[95] Sadly, this trove of data appears to have been lost, but clearly Tillich had become a household name in Chicagoland, as he had in many other places in the United States.

In 1963, Tillich's short essay "Courage and a Dynamic of Faith" was included in *Faith Is a Star*, a compilation of faith statements by guests of the Southern Baptist network radio show *Master Control*. This show featured interviews with scholars, religious leaders, statesmen, artists, athletes, movie stars, and businessmen. The editors of the volume also included the testimonies of, among others, Michigan governor George Romney, entertainment mogul Walt Disney, FBI director J. Edgar Hoover, and singing cowboy Roy Rogers. Tillich's article, which summarized much of *The Dynamics of Faith*, naturally stood out among this assortment of less-sophisticated Christian reflections. He warned against idolatry—and perhaps not coincidentally, especially the idolatry of success. He also emphasized that the human situation was one of "finitude and estrangement" and that God alone, through Christ on the cross, "makes the courage of faith possible."[96] The other, less-reflective testimonials may have drowned out Tillich's more thoughtful contribution, yet his inclusion with this company of celebrities signaled his own iconic status within the culture of the early sixties.

Tillich's "Ambiguity of Perfection," delivered in May 1963 at *Time* magazine's fortieth anniversary celebration, solidified his high standing in the pantheon of midcentury personalities. To honor the occasion, *Time*'s publisher, Henry R. Luce, threw a lavish party at New York's Waldorf Astoria. The guest list consisted of 284 of the magazine's famous cover subjects, including Lyndon B. Johnson, Douglas MacArthur, Barry Goldwater, Bob Hope, Bette Davis, Casey Stengel, and Jack Dempsey. Luce assured Tillich that his speech would be the highlight of the evening and promised him that New York governor Nelson Rockefeller and Secretary of State Dean Rusk would be limited to five minutes and ten minutes, respectively.[97]

That night, the doctrine of original sin trumped both political power and star power. After the party's host had projected images of each guest's *Time* cover onto a screen in the Waldorf's ballroom, Tillich rose to deliver his address. This unlikeliest of audiences sat, according to one account, in "rapt silence" while Tillich reminded his listeners that "all life is ambiguity: the inseparable mixture of good and evil, of true and false, of creative and destructive forces—both individual and social." When he concluded his speech, the hall erupted in applause.

A subsequent issue of *Time* contained a photo spread of the event, inviting the American public to ooh and aah at the glamorous party and to marvel at the spectacular assembly of dignitaries and superstars. Embedded within the feature, however, were Tillich's remarks about the nature of human existence. This was the second time that Luce had marked a *Time* anniversary by giving attention to the doctrine of original sin, the first having been Niebuhr's cover appearance fifteen years earlier. To be sure, this was *Time*'s—or perhaps Luce's—distinctive vision of America, but these moments—one in 1948 and the other in 1963—demonstrate that the doctrine of original sin served, in a sense, to bookend the postwar years.[98]

The cultural prominence of Tillich's vision of the human condition made it all the more fitting that two years later—just four months before he died—Tillich received what he described as a "kind and moving letter" from Donna Petrie, a woman who asked, "Why is evil innate and good not?" He responded to this question as he had throughout his career in his books, articles, sermons, and lectures, by explaining that "no theologian would make the statement you imply in your question." Rather, he wrote, "*the good is innate,*" and "the bad is a distortion of the good and nothing independent." After explaining that "because of the many misinterpretations of the doctrine of 'original sin,'" neither he nor Reinhold Niebuhr used the term any longer, he continued with the most concise summary of his view of human nature that he ever wrote:

> Man is, this is my doctrine, essentially good. But under the conditions of existence in time and space he distorts his essential goodness; and this is a universal tragic destiny to which everybody is subjected. It is the destiny of estrangement from his true being. He, who knows a little bit about human nature and history cannot deny this fact. But this does not mean that man is only estranged, he is also reunited with his essential goodness. He is both, good and bad in every act. He is ambiguous; and ambiguity is the character of every life process. There is nothing only good and only bad.[99]

Although it is a helpful distillation of his understanding of human nature, to appreciate the full meaning of this passage requires knowledge of Tillichian theology and its distinctive terminology. He did believe in the essential goodness of human beings as a function of humanity's original creation in the image of God, but as he made plain in *Systematic Theology* and in this letter, that state of pure, essential goodness was never realized in human life. Instead, "under the conditions of existence in time and space he distorts his essential goodness," a universally "tragic destiny to which everyone is subjected." In short, all have turned away from their essential goodness, just as in Tillich's view of the Genesis story, the mythical Adam and Eve "turned" from God in Eden. The "universal tragic destiny" that Tillich consistently asserted was the "destiny of estrangement."[100] This fundamental separation from God was not mere theological abstraction, but a fact clear to anyone with a rudimentary knowledge of "human nature and history." But humans, he writes, are not only estranged but also reunited with "essential goodness," indicating his belief in the perseverance of the goodness of God's creation of humanity. Tillich's discourse on the ambiguity of the human condition synthesizes his double emphasis on the good and the bad of human nature, a vision that simultaneously acknowledges the universality and severity of human sin but also conveys his resistance to monolithic notions of "innate evil."

What did Donna Petrie think of this response? While it seems likely that she would have been elated that someone of Tillich's stature had taken the time to reply to her question, her reaction to his answer is unknown. Perhaps she was sufficiently familiar with Tillich's work, as so many Americans were, to incorporate his sophisticated analysis of the human condition into her own life. What is known is that she actively reflected on the issue of human nature and sought counsel from a leading theologian on the matter. Tillich, for his part, steered her away from what he understood to be damaging, misanthropic interpretations of the doctrine of original sin and insisted upon the goodness of human nature, albeit goodness radically compromised by existential estrangement.

Exchanges like this one and the others described in this chapter recover the sincerity and sophistication of religious thought and devotion at midcentury. The anxiety and search for meaning experienced by countless Protestants in America after the Second World War necessarily raised questions about human sin and evil. By reading, questioning, and embracing Tillich's analysis of the human predicament, many lay theologians came to choose a path of devotion that sent them, as Zachmann described it, the "long way around" to faith. Tillich had promised nothing less. The "courage to be," "accepting your acceptance," and the "dynamics of faith" met the reality of sin head-on and in all of its complexity, inviting believers to admit and acknowledge the ambiguity of human nature, the "good and the bad" in every person and in every "life process." Although Tillich's exploration of the depths of human existence was informed by his extensive theological learning, he believed that this essential point could be grasped by anyone. After all, who is not amazed and disturbed by the dark recesses of the heart and mind? The surprise, then, is that we should be surprised at all that Tillich, a compelling *Seelsorger* in America, reached such a diverse and large Protestant congregation with his conceptualization of original sin.

CONCLUSION

In the mid-twentieth century, the historic doctrine of original sin acquired new relevance in American culture. The doctrine's resurgence was attributable to a number of factors, including the advent of the Age of Anxiety and the personal popularity of its chief expositors, Reinhold Niebuhr, Billy Graham, and Paul Tillich. In few other periods in American history had average citizens experienced losses and gains as extreme as those encountered by the midcentury generations. In the span of three decades, they had stood in breadlines, fought in two major hot wars, and threaded their way nervously through a cold one. Yet by the end of the 1950s, they also enjoyed ballooning savings accounts, broader access to homeownership, and expanded opportunities in the most powerful nation on the globe. For Niebuhr, Graham, and Tillich, this vertiginous world and, indeed, the vertiginous experience of being human were best understood in the context of original sin. Many everyday Protestant lay theologians agreed, and they, under the guidance of Niebuhr, Graham, and Tillich, created a theological revival that rivaled the influence of the captive revival of the postwar great awakening.

Without question, Reinhold Niebuhr, Billy Graham, and Paul Tillich drove this theological renascence. In addition to their talent, energy, and charisma, the likes of which have yet to be seen again in a public religious figure, all three brought the explanatory power and commonsense appeal of the doctrine of original sin to bear on the Age of Anxiety. They believed that the doctrine of original sin was the most accurate description of the human experience. The long record of destruction, avarice, violence, licentiousness, and animus in human history made arguments for the goodness of humanity seem empirically questionable, even unsustainable. This reality of human corruption was as undeniable as the sordidness of history—and was, in fact, the reason for it—and it was confirmed for them by the readily observable manifestation of unbelief, hubris, and

189

concupiscence in all people. What was writ large for Niebuhr, Graham, and Tillich was also, in their view, imprinted on the hearts and minds of every individual.

Yet their analysis and unrelenting exposition of the problem of human sin was almost always an entrée to the Protestant answer of justification by grace. It was, then, this balance of judgment and mercy that centered their respective ministries and won them the attention and often the admiration of legions of everyday lay theologians. For a large number of Americans at midcentury, Christian faith was not a pie-in-the-sky escape from reality but a challenging, arduous orientation that conditioned their lives. This demanding life of faith required of its followers an awareness of themselves as always and already failed Christians whose existence was framed by the ongoing drama of temptation, guilt, repentance, and forgiveness. It was the drama's culmination in forgiveness that prevented these Christians from falling into the mire of hopelessness and self-contempt. Indeed, the doctrine of original sin as articulated by Niebuhr, Graham, and Tillich was also a welcome and ultimately liberating diagnosis for these believers. It reassured them that although they were perpetual sinners, they were not uniquely rotten human beings but simply typical specimens of a fallen humanity to whom God had offered the unmerited gift of grace. Niebuhr, Graham, and Tillich intended this message of self-knowledge to lift the heavy weight of perfectionism from the shoulders of these Christians, and they hoped that it would free their audiences to live constructive lives in a world in which no one and nothing even approached perfection.

When viewed from the perspective of the theological revival and its constituents, the careers of Niebuhr, Graham, and Tillich look very different from the conventional portrayals of them. In the eyes of lay theologians, Niebuhr was less a realpolitik political philosopher than a prophet-pastor deploying a specifically Christian gospel of pessimistic optimism about the ambiguous condition and prospects of humanity and the world; Graham was less a theatrical revivalist playing on the emotions of a fearful public to thicken his stack of decision cards than a genuine evangelist communicating both the severity of sin and the power of Jesus Christ to conquer sin; Tillich was less a liberal, abstruse theological experimenter who catered to avant-garde cultural revisions of the Christian message than a translator of the classic doctrine of original sin for a modern age and a *Seelsorger* articulating the "God above God's" gracious acceptance of the unacceptable.

The existence of this large and disparate group of serious lay theologians also subverts many common scholarly assumptions about the faith of everyday believers. Most important, they dispute the notion that theological concerns are limited to those who occupy pulpits or lecterns or to those of elevated social position and advanced education. In fact, such hierarchal categorizations simply cannot account for the range of theological reflection that cuts across such divisions. Lay theologians instead confirm what historians and theorists in the field of print culture have known for some time: that the social ladder is not a reliable indicator of the reading habits of ordinary people. If lay theologians read without regard for the social ladder, they also thought about sin in defiance of it. Sin, after all, is a democratic concept. It hardly takes special credentials to ponder the darkness of the human heart and mind.

These "disobedient" Protestants who incorporated the theology of Niebuhr, Graham, and Tillich into their own spiritual imaginations, moreover, add a theological dimension to the categories of popular religion and lived religion. While these approaches to the study of religion have been indispensable for illuminating the religious worlds of those Americans who wear neither a collar nor a bow tie and who perhaps do not even attend church, both categories presume that the religion of ordinary people is mostly, if not completely, atheological. That a large number of midcentury lay theologians seriously reflected upon the nature of sin and its meaning for their lives and their faith disputes that assumption. The dynamic exchanges between lay theologians and Niebuhr, Graham, and Tillich represent, therefore, popular lived theology.[1]

Finally, in addition to refashioning perceptions of Niebuhr, Graham, and Tillich and unveiling the lived theological worlds of everyday believers, this book demonstrates that theological substance animated Protestants and their communities in this period. While the argument presented here does not deny the existence of captive expressions of Protestantism in these decades, it resists the dominant historical narrative's cynical reduction of postwar belief to such forces as the red scare, social conformity, the celebration of the American Way of Life, or all three. Attention to the theological revival and its core message of original sin, in other words, breaks the interpretive stranglehold that the captive revival has had on postwar Protestantism for more than half a century. This study insists instead that the faith of many Christians in this era was driven by the fact that, as a respected colleague often says, people actually believed this stuff—and they did so thoughtfully and critically.

This redrawing of the Protestant landscape via the theological revival contributes as well to the ongoing revision of the enduring, if inaccurate, *Leave-It-to-Beaver* image of post–World-War II America. Although a handful of scholars have documented the vibrancy of the intellectual and artistic environment of the era, both within the academy and outside it, the period is still seen as one of stultifying consensus and conformity. Even those scholars of the period who note the abundance of public intellectuals and important novelists often criticize them—interestingly enough—for their captivity to the sociopolitical conventions and consensus-ethic of the day. Indeed, even though the generation of these years has been mythologized by the phrase "the Greatest Generation," somehow this greatest of generations of the twentieth century is viewed by the general public as the most insipid in recent memory and has long served as the butt of jokes about shallow suburbanites. This is not to deny the reality—at times repressive—of the social forces of consensus and conformity within mid-century culture. But the intellectuals and novelists of those years and their large reading publics who helped forge that culture did so after having witnessed the struggles of the Depression years, the crushing devastation of the Second World War, and the potential for a worldwide conflagration during the cold war. In that context, consensus and conformity—in the positive sense of affinity and agreement—were fostered as possible avenues toward greater sociopolitical stability and civility.

At the center of this culture of moderation stood Niebuhr, Graham, and Tillich and their mass of constituents. Together they valued the power of original sin, as the historian Alan Simpson put it in 1957, to "teach the limits of the possible" in personal and social relations. By acknowledging these limits, they did not mean that humans should cease striving toward the greater good with the promise of establishing ever more just societies. Instead, they urged their attentive followers to be suspicious about what could be achieved in the name of humanity and hopeful about what might be achieved in the name of Christian humility.

Yet this theological revival captained by Niebuhr, Graham, and Tillich ended in 1965. Tillich died in that year, and the world lost of one of the more enterprising theological minds of the twentieth century. Niebuhr lived until 1971, but he published his last focused discussion of sin in 1965 with *Man's Nature and His Communities*. Graham, of course, went on crusading, but by the midsixties, he no longer pushed himself to the brink of total exhaustion. He organized fewer crusades and cut back from multiweek extravaganzas to more modest, weeklong events. And although he retained his status as the undisputed father and leader of modern evangelicalism, he was soon joined by a host of televangelists who began leading old-time religion with less humility and an even greater emphasis on particular sins.

The moment may have ended, but its legacy is with us. Neither Niebuhr, Graham, nor Tillich has fallen into historical obscurity. Reinhold Niebuhr's work continues to inspire and influence conversations about social justice and America's role in the world. Graduate students still produce dissertations on his theology, and books such as Langdon Gilkey's *On Niebuhr: A Theological Study* (2001), Elisabeth Sifton's *The Serenity Prayer: Faith and Politics in Times of Peace and War* (2003), and Martin Halliwell's *The Constant Dialogue: Reinhold Niebuhr and American Intellectual Culture* (2005) indicate that his thought continues to influence intellectual life in America.[2] His name is frequently invoked—especially in the wake of the Iraq war—in such influential publications as the *New York Times*, the *New Republic*, and the *Christian Century*. The four strongest advocates for Niebuhr since his death have been Martin Marty, the late Arthur Schlesinger Jr., *New York Times* columnist David Brooks, and Andrew Bacevich of Boston University, all of whom have lamented the lack of a prophetic voice of equal stature to replace him.[3] In addition, Niebuhr has surfaced in the novel *Saints and Villains* (1999) and, surprisingly, in *Horizon*, an off-Broadway production based on his life and work.[4]

Paul Tillich's thought, though less visible in American culture than Niebuhr's, has nevertheless remained influential. The religion sections of most bookstores still carry *The Courage to Be*, which was reissued in 2000 by Yale University Press. Undergraduates at Christian colleges and seminarians alike continue to read his books, especially *Courage* and *Dynamics of Faith*.[5] The North American Paul Tillich Society has operated since 1975, publishing a quarterly newsletter and holding an annual conference devoted strictly to scholarship concerning Tillich. Like Niebuhr, Tillich has been the subject of numerous dissertations and books—though they are mostly specialized studies in the fields of theology and psychology.[6] There are signs—not least of all that President Barack Obama claims the German émigré, along with Reinhold Niebuhr, as an influence—that his intellectual contribution is beginning to make inroads into the public sphere once again.[7]

Billy Graham continued to crusade, preach, and write for more than thirty years after the deaths of Niebuhr and Tillich. His message of human sin and divine forgiveness weathered the storms of the counterculture movement, Watergate (though he naïvely continued to support Nixon through much of the scandal), and the extremism of elements of the new Christian right. In the twenty-first century, after nearly sixty years in the public spotlight, Graham continues to be astonishingly and incredibly relevant. His opinions on matters religious and nonreligious have carried as much weight as those of presidents and prime ministers; his face has graced the covers of major periodicals (among them *Newsweek* and *Time* in 2006 and 2007, respectively); and the Billy Graham Evangelistic Association has remained the premier evangelical organization on the planet. Finally, the world awaits news of his approaching death—Graham turned ninety in the fall of 2008—in a fashion usually reserved for the pope.[8] This monumental public life recently has drawn the attention of scholars and journalists, who are just beginning to take the measure of his singular career, an endeavor that will not end anytime soon.[9]

This midcentury theological revival and the legacies of Niebuhr, Graham, and Tillich serve as potent reminders of the importance of theological doctrine as a shaper of private and public life in American history. Indeed, a personal sense of sin has been and continues to be an astonishing source of energy—even if, at times, it has also been a source of inertia—that has mobilized countless individuals not only to change their cast of mind and lifestyle but also to change their societies. The notion of sin has pushed Christians into public life both in the everyday worship and social ministry of church life and in large-scale reform movements, including the struggle for civil rights that coincided with the original sin moment chronicled here.[10] In other words, the doctrine of original sin, for good or for ill, has had and continues to have significant influence over the direction of individual and community life in America. After all, Christianity was then—and to some degree still is, even in an age of pluralism—a point of common experience for many Americans, and the basic ideas of the tradition, including original sin, inform their interpretation of and actions in the world more readily than do other cultural institutions and authorities.

This is borne out in contemporary American culture. Although another figure of the stature of Niebuhr, Graham, or Tillich has yet to appear, the doctrine of original sin has remained a vital force in American culture. A cohort of high-profile academics, journalists, and ministers have insisted on the doctrine's importance as a concept that has informed much of Western history. Likewise, everyday Americans both within and outside Christian circles continue to believe it—and to doubt it—as a universal feature of human character. And it is likely that the issue of original sin will continue to inspire, as it has for centuries, debates about its truth and its worth for understanding the human experience.[11]

For a time in America, in the middle of the Age of Anxiety and the theological revival of the mid-twentieth century, the balance of this historic debate tipped in favor of affirmations of the doctrine of original sin. As a final note, there is no better illustration of both the content and the cultural power of the theological revival than John Updike's classic novel *Rabbit, Run* (1960). The book captures the inner turmoil of everyday people in the postwar era through its depiction of the travails of Harry "Rabbit" Angstrom. Indeed, Rabbit represented "Kierkegaardian man," as his last name, *Angst*-rom, suggests. With a dead-end job and an equally dead-end marriage, Rabbit was unhappy and listless. His dissatisfaction, as Updike later noted, was a function of the fear, dread, and "perpetual restlessness" of the human condition.[12] Niebuhr and Tillich—two thinkers who influenced Updike—as well as Graham, who did not, assessed the human situation similarly. They explained this unhappiness and angst through the prism of what they understood as the universal affliction of humanity: original sin.

In addition to an archetypical character, Updike provides a memorable scene in which the captive and theological revivals clash. Midway through the novel, Reverend Eccles, the local Episcopal priest and Rabbit's current pastor, visits his Lutheran colleague and Rabbit's boyhood minister, Fritz Kruppenbach, to discuss Rabbit's adultery. As Eccles waits in his colleague's den, he ponders why he "likes Kruppenbach least" among the ministers in town. The hulking pastor finally greets Eccles gruffly and asks simply, "What?" Eccles launches into what he thinks are the reasons for Rabbit's infidelity, explaining that Angstrom's athletic success in high school, his unimaginative wife, his doting parents, and his meddlesome in-laws spelled a recipe for disaster. An air of conceit suffuses Eccles's diagnosis, and upon finishing it, he awaits Kruppenbach's approving reaction.

Kruppenbach entertains none of it. He scolds his fellow pastor for confusing the job of the minister with that of a psychologist, or worse—a moralistic cop. "It seems to you our role is to be cops, cops without handcuffs, without guns, without anything but our human good nature . . . Well, I say that's a Devil's idea. I say, let the cops be cops and look after their laws that have nothing to do with us." Kruppenbach continues his rebuke, instructing Eccles that the minister's role is nothing more than to be an "exemplar of faith." And the answer to be given to such confused and desperate parishioners as Rabbit is Christ crucified and risen: "'Yes, he is dead, but you will see him again in Heaven. Yes, you suffer, but you must love your pain, because it is *Christ's* pain.' . . . Make no mistake. There is nothing but Christ for us. All the rest, all this decency and busyness, is nothing. It is Devil's work."[13]

Kruppenbach's impromptu sermon captured the essence of the theological revival. In fact, the single sentence "There is nothing but Christ for us" was the bare-bones message of its ministers under the leadership of Niebuhr, Graham, and Tillich. Although they had their differences, these three giants of postwar Protestantism shared Kruppenbach's vision of the Gospel and preached it to untold numbers of readers and listeners. In the end, they convinced their respective audiences of the simultaneously sinful and righteous natures of all people and, like Kruppenbach, believed that there was only one answer for such sinner-saints: "There is nothing but Christ for us."

NOTES

To represent the geographic diversity of Niebuhr's, Graham's, and Tillich's correspondents, I have noted in brackets the states from which the letters originated, when this information is available.

ABBREVIATIONS

BG	Billy Graham
BGCA	Billy Graham Center Archives, Wheaton, Ill.
PT	Paul Tillich
PT papers	Paul Tillich Papers, Andover-Harvard Theological Library, Harvard Divinity School, Cambridge, Mass.
RN	Reinhold Niebuhr
RN papers	Reinhold Niebuhr Papers, Collections of the Manuscript Division, Library of Congress, Washington, D.C.

INTRODUCTION

1. "Faith for a Lenten Age," *Time*, 8 March 1948; "Evangelist Billy Graham," *Time*, 25 October 1954; "To Be or Not to Be," *Time*, 16 March 1959.

2. The term "neo-orthodox" originally referred to the theology of Karl Barth, but also has been employed to describe the theology of Reinhold Niebuhr, Paul Tillich, Dietrich Bonhoeffer, Emil Brunner, Rudolf Bultmann, and others. Despite Niebuhr's and Tillich's criticism of the term and the scholars who have characterized both of them as liberals or neoliberals, I have chosen to rely on the term "neo-orthodoxy" in relation to Niebuhr and Tillich because it was and is the most widely used descriptor of their work. On this point, I am following the work of Douglas John Hall. See Hall, *Remembered Voices*.

3. The exception is H. Shelton Smith's *Changing Conceptions of Original Sin.*

4. Herberg, *Protestant, Catholic, Jew*; Eckardt, *Surge of Piety in America*; Marty, *New Shape of American Religion.*

5. Butler, "Jack-in-the-Box Faith?" 1357–78.

6. See Ellwood, *Fifties Spiritual Marketplace*, 8, 12–13, 70, 80–81; Hudnut-Beumler, *Looking for God in the Suburbs*, 57, 59–60, 65–71; Wuthnow, *After Heaven*, 40–41. See also Silk, *Spiritual Politics*; Allitt, *Religion in America since 1945*; Ahlstrom, *Religious History of the American People*, 2: chap. 56.

7. Mark Noll's concept of "elite popularization" is most germane here. See his *Old Religion in a New World*, 198–99. David Hall, Lawrence Levine, Roger Chartier, and Guglielmo Cavallo, among others, have also challenged assumptions about "elite" and "popular" cultural forms and their respective audiences.

8. PT, *Systematic Theology*, 2:46.

9. Nourie and Nourie, *American Mass-Market Magazines*; Marty, Deedy, Silverman, and Lekachman, *Religious Press in America*; Hulsether, *Building a Protestant Left*.

10. On balance, women wrote to Niebuhr, Graham, and Tillich more often than men, supporting Ann Braude's contention that in America "women go to church." Yet their audiences were by no means exclusively female. Lay men and male pastors frequently wrote to them, as well, making it difficult to generalize about the gender dimensions of their appeal. See Braude, "Women's History Is American Religious History," in Tweed, *Retelling United States Religious History*, 87–88.

11. William A. Holmes to PT, 29 September 1961, bMS 649, PT papers; Bennett, "Two Revivals," *Christianity and Crisis*, 28 December 1959, 193.

12. RN, *Beyond Tragedy*, 147–48; PT, "Intellectual Autobiography of Paul Tillich," in Kegley and Bretall, *Theology of Paul Tillich*, 21.

13. PT, *On the Boundary*, 71–72.

14. Walls, *Hell*, 2; Jeffrey Burton Russell, *Paradise Mislaid*, 18, 135. See also Marty, "Hell Disappeared."

15. Walls, *Hell*, 3. Walls notes a 1990 Gallup poll that found that 60 percent of Americans "professed belief in hell."

16. RN, *Pious and Secular America*, 10.

17. Rowland, *Land in Search of God*, 4.

CHAPTER 1

1. Leuchtenburg, *Troubled Feast*, 104. For contemporary comment on the Age of Anxiety, see Schlesinger, *Vital Center*.

2. Peyser, *Bernstein*, 182.

3. Wuthnow, *Restructuring of American Religion*, 43. Wuthnow continues, "In the press, forecasts tended to emphasize the darkness more than the light. Only one editorial in seven, an analysis of newspaper opinion revealed, expressed genuine optimism about the immediate future." See also Leuchtenburg, *Troubled Feast*, 103–15.

4. "The New America," *Newsweek*, 12 December 1955, 56; Handy, "American Religious Depression."

5. John C. Bennett, "Two Revivals," *Christianity and Crisis*, 28 December 1959, 192–93. Part of the inspiration for expanding Bennett's notion of a theological revival came from Roozen, Carroll, and Roof, "Fifty Years of Religious Change in the United States," in *Postwar Generation and Establishment Religion*, 63–64. Roozen, Carroll, and Roof's essay identifies a "neo-orthodox" and conservative evangelical "consensus" based on suspicion of easy optimism, "renewed respect" for biblical authority, and vision of faith as a collective endeavor. Ellwood briefly alludes to the two revivals phenomenon in *1950: Crossroads of American Religious Life*, 114.

6. Johnny Mercer first popularized the song in 1945. Bing Crosby later reprised it in 1962.

7. For a general account of the bomb's impact on American culture, see Boyer, *By the Bomb's Early Light*. For the impact of the cold war and the atomic bomb on everyday families, see May, *Homeward Bound*.

8. Gambone, *Greatest Generation Comes Home*, 153–59.

9. "Who Won What War?" *Time*, 4 February 1946, 25. See also McPherson, *For Cause and Comrades*, 90. McPherson summarizes surveys of World War II soldiers that support the *Time* article's conclusion that average GIs fought for a variety of reasons, the majority of which had little to do with patriotism or democracy. See also O'Neill, *Democracy at War*.

10. Wilson, *Man in the Gray Flannel Suit*, 92–95. John Dower recounts grisly souvenir practices in *War without Mercy*, 65. David Halberstam's and David Castronovo's work alerted me to the war scenes in Wilson's novel: see Halberstam, *Fifties*, 521–27; Castronovo, *Beyond the Gray Flannel Suit*, 25–27.

11. Wilson, *Man in the Gray Flannel Suit*, 98; Gambone, *Greatest Generation Comes Home*, 41. The psychological fallout of the war detailed in Wilson's novel was indeed staggering. During the war years, 1.1 million soldiers underwent treatment for "psychological disorders," and in 1945 alone, the armed forces rejected almost 1.9 million prospective soldiers for psychological reasons. See Herman, *Romance of American Psychology*, 69, 89.

12. "The New America," *Newsweek*, 12 December 1955, 56–57; Goldman, *Crucial Decade*, 16–26; Chafe, *Unfinished Journey*, 94.

13. "New America," 56–57. See also Donaldson, *Abundance and Anxiety*, chap. 9.

14. Chafe, *Unfinished Journey*, 117; Jackson, *Crabgrass Frontier*, 272–74; Jezer, *Dark Ages*, chaps. 8, 10.

15. Coontz, *Way We Never Were*, 36–37; Friedan, *Feminine Mystique*, 44, 58–59; Komerovsky, *Women in the Modern World*, 104–27; Lisansky, "Woman Alcoholic," 315.

16. Riesman, Glazer, and Denney, *Lonely Crowd*; Whyte, *Organization Man*.

17. Novick, *That Noble Dream*, chaps. 10, 11; Pells, *Liberal Mind in a Conservative Age*, chaps. 3, 4.

18. Russell Lynes, "What Are Best-Sellers Made Of?" *New York Times Book Review*, 27 December 1959, 2; Morris Dickstein as quoted in Castronovo, *Beyond the Gray Flannel Suit*, 20; Korda, *Making the List*, 84. Korda writes, "One of the things that the bestseller list certainly demonstrates is that American readers have been, since the 1940s, increasingly willing to be challenged and even attacked," commenting further that Americans were eager "for the literature of protest and of complaint." This self-consciousness extended into the early 1960s. See Ben Ray Redman, "Who and What Are We?—Essays on U.S. Culture," *Chicago Tribune*, 3 January 1960, G4; Farber, *Age of Great Dreams*, 15.

19. Arendt expanded her *New Yorker* article into the book *Eichmann in Jerusalem*.

20. "Existentialism," *Time*, 28 January 1946, 28–29; "Great Dane," *Time*, 16 December 1946, 62–63; William Barrett, "What Is Existentialism?" *Saturday Evening Post*, 21 November 1959, 49, 126, 129–30; Owen Barfield, "Rediscovery of Meaning," *Saturday Evening Post*, 7 January 1961, 36–37, 61, 64–65; Sykes, *Alienation*. For a useful overview of existentialism's impact in America, see Cotkin, *Existential America*.

21. Ernest Havemann, "Age of Psychology in the United States," *Life*, 7 January

1957. For an excellent discussion of the influence of psychoanalysis in America, see Hale, *Rise and Crisis of Psychoanalysis in the United States*. For a more focused discussion of psychology in this period, see Herman, *Romance of American Psychology*.

22. Leuchtenburg, *Troubled Feast*, 74. Often Americans' introduction to psychology was through marital counseling, an industry created almost overnight after the war. Coughlin, "Changing Roles in Modern Marriage," 110–11; Mudd, *Practice of Marriage Counseling*, 76.

23. Hale, *Rise and Crisis of Psychoanalysis in the United States*, chap. 16; Meyer, *Positive Thinkers*, 262–65.

24. For this reason, historian Donald Meyer locates Peale in the tradition of the Mind Cure movement of the early twentieth century. Meyer, *Positive Thinkers*, 262–68.

25. George, *God's Salesman*, 132, 138.

26. For an extended discussion of *Guideposts* and *The Power of Positive Thinking*, see George, *God's Salesman*, chaps. 4, 5; Margery Darrell, "Minister to Millions," *Look*, 22 September 1953, 86, 88–89.

27. Hutchinson, "Have We A New Religion?" *Life*, 11 April 1955, 157.

28. Peale, *The Power of Positive Thinking*; "Dynamo in the Vineyard," *Time*, 1 November 1954, 69; Norman Vincent Peale, "Why I Preach as I Do," *Christian Herald*, January 1956, 69; Norman Vincent Peale, "Why I Preach as I Do, Part II," *Christian Herald*, February 1956, 66.

29. "The Positive Thinker," *Wall Street Journal*, 7 May 1969, 25.

30. Curtis Gate, "God and Success," *Atlantic Monthly*, April 1957, 74–76;, Herbert Gold, "The Age of Happy Problems," *Atlantic Monthly*, March 1957, 58–61; William Lee Miller, "Some Negative Thinking about Norman Vincent Peale," *Reporter*, 13 January 1955, 19–24; Oates, "Cult of Reassurance," 72–82; Warren Weaver, "Peace of Mind," *Saturday Review*, 11 December 1954, 11, 49–50; Donald Meyer, "The Confidence Man," *New Republic*, 11 July 1955, 8–10; William Peters, "The Case against 'Easy' Religion," *Redbook*, September 1955, 22, 92–93; "Dynamo in the Vineyard" 68–71; Hutchinson, "Have We a New Religion?" 140, 143, 144, 147, 149–50, 153, 157–58; James M. Carmody, "Happy Little Peale-Agians," *America*, 17 March 1958, 661–62.

31. Miller, "Some Negative Thinking about Norman Vincent Peale," 19; "Dynamo in the Vineyard," 69.

32. George, *God's Salesman*, 145–46.

33. Norman Vincent Peale to PT, 23 April 1960, PT papers; PT to Norman Vincent Peale, 27 April 1960, PT papers. Peale's objection to Tillich's criticisms may have stemmed from the fact that his son, John Peale, a student at Harvard, admired Tillich. In fact, on the day Peale's letter arrived, Tillich, according to a note on the letter itself, was scheduled to meet with John at three o'clock that afternoon.

34. George, *God's Salesman*, 147.

35. R. J. Rushdoony, "Do-It-Yourself Religion," *Christianity Today*, 11 November 1957, 34–35; Lars I. Granberg, "Peale Faces His Critics," *Christianity Today*, 16 March 1962, 605–6.

36. For reader reactions, see "Peale's Appeal," *Time*, 22 November 1954, 6; "A 'New' Religion?" *Life*, 2 May 1955, 21–22; "The Age of Happy Problems," *Atlantic Monthly*,

June 1957, 27; "Peale and Niebuhr," *Reporter*, 24 February 1955, 12; "God and Success," *Atlantic Monthly*, June 1957, 29.

37. Hutchinson, "Have We a New Religion?" 147–48. Likewise, the young seminarian Richard John Neuhaus, later the editor of *First Things*, appreciated the *Atlantic's* exposure of the "shallowness of the 'positive thinking cult'" but wondered in a letter to the editor "with what do they fill the hole marked 'Religion'?" "God and Success," *Atlantic Monthly*, June 1957, 29.

38. Kenneth Hamilton, "The Common Ground between Norman Vincent Peale and Paul Tillich," *Theology and Life* 2 (November 1959): 298–306. See also Miller, "Some Negative Thinking about Norman Vincent Peale," 19; Oates, "Cult of Reassurance," 74–75.

39. George, *God's Salesman*, 104, 138.

40. Eugene Carson Blake, "Is the Religious Boom a Spiritual Bust?" *Look*, 20 September 1955; Miller and Nowak, *Fifties*, 87.

41. Stanley Rowland Jr., "Suburbia Buys Religion," *Nation*, 28 July 1956. See also Whyte, *Organization Man*, 365–67; Ellwood, *Fifties Spiritual Marketplace*, 178.

42. Rowland, "Suburbia Buys Religion," 77–80.

43. Waldo Beach, "Euphoria in Suburbia," *Christianity and Crisis*, 2 April 1956, 33–34; "Suburban Religion," *Time*, 15 July 1957, 78; "Church in Suburbia," *Time*, 27 January 1958, 52; Martin E. Marty, "The Triumph of Religion-in-General," *Christian Century*, 10 September 1958, 1016–19.

44. William R. Farmer, "Cynicism and the Revival," *Christianity and Crisis*, 2 April 1956, 35–38.

45. Correspondence, *Christianity and Crisis*, 30 April 1956, 61; ibid., 14 May 1956, 62–64.

46. "Dial Trinity 5-7561," *Newsweek*, 3 September 1956, 56.

47. Sittser, *A Cautious Patriotism*, chapter 5; Gerald H. Hinkle, "The Layman's Call and Ministry," *Theology and Life*, May 1958, 122–26; "What the Layman Expects from His Minister"; Frederick K. Wentz, "Lay Renaissance: Europe and America," *Christian Century*, 13 May 1959, 578–79; Howe, "Problems of Communication between Clergy and Laity." Of course, for some such lay activism signaled the American preference for pragmatism over theology. See "National Council Laymen Meet," *Christianity and Crisis*, 12 May 1952, 63; "Look Applauds the Layman's National Committee," *Look*, 16 October 1956, 16; "Methodist Laymen Hold Assembly at Nasson College, Springvale, Maine," *Zion's Herald*, August 1959, 6–7. On the liturgical renaissance, see "Liturgical Renaissance," *Christianity Today*, 15 April 1957, 26; see also Bains, "Conduits of Faith."

48. Castronovo, *Beyond the Gray Flannel Suit*, 119; Hudnut-Beumler, *Looking for God in the Suburbs*, 70; Mouw, "Bible in Twentieth-Century Protestantism," chap. 7 in Noll and Hatch, *Bible in America: Essays in Cultural History*, esp. 140, 142.

49. "Theological Awakening?" *Time*, 18 November 1946, 74.

50. "Radio Religion," *Time*, 21 January 1946, 75–76; "Calvinist Comeback," *Time*, 24 February 1947, 78.

51. "Sin's Return," *Time*, 17 September 1956, 108.

52. "The Road to Religion," *Life*, 7 April 1947, 36.

53. Whittaker Chambers, "The Devil," *Life*, 2 February 1948, 77–86.

54. Ibid., 78, 85.

55. [Whittaker Chambers], "Faith for a Lenten Age;" Hudnut-Beumler, *Looking For God in the Suburbs*, 65.

56. Charles G. Girelius, "A Plea for Human Nature," *Zion's Herald*, 10 November 1948, 1064–65; "Readers Write," *Zion's Herald*, 24 November 1948; "Readers Write," 15 December 1948, 1106, 1178. At the same time, the *Atlantic Monthly* had a debate in its pages about human limitation that was more Nieburhian than Deweyian. See W. T. Stace, "Man against Darkness," *Atlantic Monthly*, September 1948, 53–58; "Purpose in the Universe," *Atlantic Monthly*, November 1948, 35–39; "Repartee," *Atlantic Monthly*, January 1949, 16.

57. Lewis W. Gillenson, "The New Look in the Presbyterian Church," *Look*, 12 September 1950, 85–86, 87, 90; "Letters and Pictures," *Look*, 24 October 1950, 4.

58. Albert Q. Maisel, "The Battle against Sin," *Look*, 26 February 1952, 52–58. For reprints of the religious series in *Look*, see Rosten, *Religions of America*; Spence, *Story of America's Religions*. Harper's published a similar series, "Modern Religious Belief in America," which ran from February through May of 1959.

59. Leiffer, *Layman Looks at the Minister*, chaps. 4 and 8, esp. page 45. See the corresponding review article, "Pointers for Pastors," *Time*, 13 January 1947, 72, 74. It is worth noting that a Methodist minister wrote to *Time* after publication of the article and criticized the image of the pastor presented by Leiffer's book, declaring, "if this is what Methodists want in their pastors, then I am going to join the Presbyterians." "A Pastor Protests," *Time*, 10 February 1947, 8.

60. Halford E. Luccock, "American Methodism during a 50–Year Revolution," *Zion's Herald*, 22 February 1950, 4. In the same issue appeared Alexander Stewart, "Can We Curb the Liquor Advertising Rampage?" (11), offering another example of the parallel existence of the theological and captive revivals.

61. J. Paul Williams, *What Americans Believe and How They Worship*, 114–15.

62. Ibid., 114.

63. A. N. Wilder, "The Modern Sinner," *Christianity and Crisis*, 15 November 1954, 145–46; Winthrop S. Hudson, "Rauschenbusch—Evangelical Prophet," *Christian Century*, 24 June 1953, 740.

64. William Lee Miller, "The Irony of Reinhold Niebuhr," *Reporter*, 13 January 1955, 11–15.

65. Eugene Carson Blake, "Is the Religious Boom a Spiritual Bust," *Look*, 20 September 1955, 29, 28–31. Blake erroneously lumped Billy Graham with Norman Vincent Peale as a participant in peace-of-mind religion.

66. "Resurgent Protestantism: At Easter, the Wave of New Christian Orthodoxy," *Newsweek*, 28 March 1955, 55–59.

67. Roy A. Burkhart, "Toward a Healthy Theology," *Christian Century*, 19 December 1956, 1478–80.

68. Lloyd J. Averill Jr., "What Is a Healthy Theology?" *Christian Century*, 16 January 1957, 77–79.

69. Correspondence, *Christian Century*, 30 January 1957, 141; ibid., 13 February 1957, 203.

70. "And the angel said unto them, Fear not . . ." *Newsweek*, 23 December 1957, 52–53.

71. "The Word in Print," *Time*, 22 October 1956, 73–74.

72. Ibid.; Marty, Deedy, Silverman, and Lekachman, *Religious Press in America*, 57–59, 176; Hulsether, *Building a Protestant Left*; Toulouse, "Christianity Today and American Public Life."

73. Schneider and Dornbusch, *Popular Religion*, 13, 17–19, 52, 159. The exceptions included work by Harry Emerson Fosdick, Victor Frankl, E. Stanley Jones, Bishop Fulton Sheen, and Elton Trueblood. See ibid., 162, 146, 76, 82, 84–85.

74. "Microphone Missionary," *Time*, 14 April 1952, 72. See, for example, Fulton J. Sheen, "Is America's Religion Religious," in *Life Is Worth Living*, Fulton J. Sheen Company, videocassette, 1956; Massa, *Catholics and American Culture*, chap. 4.

75. "Microphone Missionary," *Time*, 14 April 1952, 88.

76. Moore, *Selling God*, 239; "Religion Best-Seller Class," *Newsweek*, 1 October 1956, 60–61.

77. James Rietmulder to RN, 24 September 1956, collection 1, RN papers.

78. "Protestant Tradition," *Newsweek*, 19 September 1955, 114, 116–17.

79. Chad Walsh, "Apostle to the Skeptics," *Atlantic Monthly*, September 1946, 115–19; Clyde S. Kilby, "C. S. Lewis and His Critics," *Christianity Today*, 8 December 1958, 13–15; "Theological Thriller," *Time*, 10 June 1946, 52–54; Dorrien, *Remaking of Evangelical Theology*, 174. Dorrien discusses Robert Brow's contention that evangelicals of the last half century have drifted toward Arminianism as a consequence of Lewis's influential books, a dubious argument in light of the contemporary accounts listed above.

80. Herberg, *Protestant, Catholic, Jew* (1955); Eckardt, *Surge of Piety in America*; Marty, *New Shape of American Religion*; Berger, *Noise of Solemn Assemblies*; Winter, *Suburban Captivity of the Churches*.

81. Herberg, *Protestant, Catholic, Jew*, 260.

82. Berger, *Noise of Solemn Assemblies*, 100; Herberg, *Protestant, Catholic, Jew*, 121. For his part, Eckardt also confessed that the revival was not monolithic. He admitted the existence of a "renewal of intellectual interest in religion" but chose not to analyze that strain of Protestantism. Eckardt, *Surge of Piety in America*, 18.

83. Herberg, *Protestant, Catholic, Jew*, 75, 77–78, 88.

84. Hudnut-Beumler, *Looking for God in the Suburbs*, 207.

85. Eric Goldman, "Good-By to the Fifties—And Good Riddance," *Harper's*, January 1960, 27–28.

86. For some surveys of the 1960s, see Gitlin, *Sixties*; Farber, *Sixties: From Memory to History*; Farber, *Age of Great Dreams*; Matusow, *Unraveling of America*.

87. Peale, *Sin, Sex, and Self-Control*.

88. James Daane, "Sifting the Saints," *Christianity Today*, 19 January 1962, 41. See also Sweet, "1960s: The Crisis of Liberal Christianity and the Public Emergence of Evangelism." Sweet not only chronicles the interest in traditional doctrine among evangelicals in the 1960s but also maintains that there were two sixties. The second sixties, from 1967 through 1970, according to Sweet, was the era of real church decline.

89. J. Robert Moskin, "Morality USA," *Look*, 24 September 1963, 75, 76, 78. After publication of the article, Moskin informed Tillich that he received hundreds, as he put it, of "heartwarming" letters, convincing him of the import of the piece. J. Robert Moskin to PT, 16 October 1963, PT papers.

90. Harry Emerson Fosdick, "I Dare You to Be a Pessimist," *Reader's Digest*, April 1962, 50, 51, 52.

91. "Witness to an Ancient Truth," *Time*, 20 April 1962, 59–62, 65.

92. See Chappell, *Stone of Hope*; Branch, *Parting the Waters*, 81–86.

93. Robert W. Spike, "Our Churches Sin against the Negro," *Look*, 18 May 1965, 29–31.

94. "Color Is Skin Deep, Evil as Deep as the Heart," *Christianity Today*, 24 May 1963, 21.

95. T. George Harris, "The Battle of the Bible," *Look*, 18 May 1965, 18, 19, 20.

96. "Toward a Hidden God," *Time*, 8 April 1966, 82–89.

97. Oppenheimer, *Knocking on Heaven's Door*. See also Hudnut-Beumler, *Looking for God in the Suburbs*, 176–77; Ellwood, *Sixties Spiritual Awakening*, 34, chap. 2. Ellwood views the early 1960s as a continuation of the religious situation of the 1950s, though he continues that decade through 1963.

98. Oppenheimer, *Knocking on Heaven's Door*, 27. Changes did occur, according to Oppenheimer, but "what was countercultural in the mainline religions was often aesthetic, rather than political or theological. American religions underwent little theological or doctrinal change in the 1960s and 1970s. What changed was the form, not the content, of the religious traditions." For some specific statistics regarding the growth of mainline Protestantism in the early 1960s, see Flowers, *Religion in Strange Times*, 37–40.

99. John Cogley, "An Interview with Reinhold Niebuhr," *McCall's*, February 1966, 90–91, 166–71.

100. "Graham Heard by 116,000," *Chicago Daily Tribune*, 18 June 1962, 1.

CHAPTER 2

1. The doctrine of original sin as espoused in Western Christianity holds that human beings are born with a predilection to sin. They are born sinners, in other words. St. Augustine of Hippo codified the doctrine on the basis of his readings of Genesis and the epistles of St. Paul. For Augustine and subsequent "orthodox" interpreters, original sin is a preexisting condition that all humans share as members of a common lineage descended—literally—from Adam and Eve, humanity's original parents and original sinners, as it were. Billy Graham affirmed this view of the doctrine; Niebuhr and Tillich did not. They understood the Genesis event as a mythical story that was nevertheless symbolic of every human being's sinful nature. See chapter 3 for a fuller discussion of their views of the doctrine.

2. See H. Richard Niebuhr, "Idea of Original Sin in American Culture"; Smith, *Changing Conceptions of Original Sin*.

3. The full text of Winthrop's "Model of Christian Charity" can be found at "The Religious Freedom Page," *University of Virginia Library*, http://religiousfreedom.lib .virginia.edu/sacred/charity.html.

4. Jonathan Edwards, *Great Christian Doctrine of Original Sin Defended*; Smith, *Changing Conceptions of Original Sin*, chaps. 1–3.

5. See James Madison's *Federalist* no. 10, in *Federalist Papers*, 77–84. Reinhold Niebuhr indicated his debt to Madison in *Moral Man and Immoral Society*, quoting the statesman's belief that "the truth is that all men having power ought to be distrusted." RN, *Moral Man and Immoral Society*, 164. See also RN, "From Progress to Perplexity," 144.

6. Arminianism is named for the sixteenth-century Dutch theologian Jacob Arminius. It designates theologies that modify notions of original sin and accentuate instead the human role in salvation. In other words, "right living" is emphasized over justification by grace.

7. Saum, *Popular Mood of Pre–Civil War America*, 25. See also Dorrien, *Remaking of Evangelical Theology*, 5–9, 158–59. Noll and Holifield attend to both prophetic and pragmatic developments in early American theology and conclude that moralistic notions of sin dominated theological discourse in the period. Yet original sin was not absent from eighteenth- and nineteenth-century theology; in fact, the problem of sin—original or otherwise—was taken quite seriously in these periods. Noll, *America's God*, 266–67, 268, 275, 298–301; Holifield, *Theology in America*, 115–17, 130–33, 152–53, 263–64, 287.

8. Weiman, "Religion and Illusion," 187; Carter, *Spiritual Crisis of the Gilded Age*; Smith, *Changing Conceptions of Original Sin*, 164–65, 71.

9. Dorrien, *Making of American Liberal Theology*; William Hutchison, *Modernist Impulse in American Protestantism*. See also King, "Enthusiasm for Humanity," 49–77; Meyer, *Protestant Search for Political Realism*; Rauschenbusch, *Theology for the Social Gospel*; Smith, *Changing Conceptions of Original Sin*, 199–201; Cauthen, *Impact of Religious Liberalism*, 96–99.

10. Machen, *Christianity and Liberalism*; Dorrien, *Remaking of Evangelical Theology*, 159; Sandeen, *Roots of Fundamentalism*, 188–207; Weber, *Living in the Shadow of the Second Coming*. *The Fundamentals* (1910–15) protested against the modernist view of human sin as well. *The Fundamentals* reached roughly 3 million readers in America and abroad. See Whitelaw, "Biblical Conception of Sin"; C. B. Williams, "Paul's Testimony to the Doctrine of Sin."

11. Richard W. Fox, *Reinhold Niebuhr*, 14–22; RN, "Intellectual Autobiography of Reinhold Niebuhr," in Kegley and Bretall, *Reinhold Niebuhr*, 3–8.

12. RN, "Billy Sunday—His Preachments and His Methods," *Detroit Saturday Night*, 14 October 1916, 3, 10.

13. RN, *Leaves from the Notebook of a Tamed Cynic*, 36, 60–63, 94, 106, 115, 224–25.

14. RN, "Intellectual Autobiography," 8–9; Gilkey, *On Niebuhr*, chap. 7; Stone, *Professor Reinhold Niebuhr*, 67–68.

15. Norman Thomas, "Moral Man and Immoral Society," *World Tomorrow*, 14 December 1932, 565, 567; Theodore Hume, "Moral Man and Immoral Society," *Christian Century*, 4 January 1933, 18.

16. Richard W. Fox, *Reinhold Niebuhr*, 144–45.

17. RN, *Moral Man and Immoral Society*, 44–45, 54, 262, 271.

18. Martin, *Prophet with Honor*, 63–71.

19. *Ibid.*, 70–79.

20. *Ibid.*, 84–86.

21. PT, *On the Boundary*, 30, 13; Pauck and Pauck, *Paul Tillich*, 13; PT, *My Search for Absolutes*, 31–32.

22. PT, *My Search for Absolutes*, 33–34; Pauck and Pauck, *Paul Tillich*, 28–35.

23. Smith, *Changing Conceptions of Original Sin*, 189, chap. 8; "Dr. Herrmann and the Dominance of Ritschlianism," *Literary Digest*, 14 July 1900, 49–50; Welch, *Protestant Thought in the Nineteenth Century*, 4, 8, 11, 24–28; Dorrien, *Making of Liberal Theology*, 25–26, 42–52.

24. John J. Carey, *Paulus, Then and Now*, 5; PT, *On the Boundary*, 84; PT, *My Search for Absolutes*, 25; Pauck and Pauck, *Paul Tillich*, 33–34.

25. Pauck and Pauck, *Paul Tillich*, 49–50, 45.

26. PT, *My Search for Absolutes*, 25–27, 33, 37; PT, *On the Boundary*, 48–50.

27. PT, *On the Boundary*, 22; Pauck and Pauck, *Paul Tillich*, 67–75; PT, *My Search for Absolutes*, 41–42.

28. Heidegger and Tillich traded arguments through mutual students, who evidently reported to each scholar what the other had said in lecture. Pauck and Pauck, *Paul Tillich*, 98.

29. Pauck and Pauck, *Paul Tillich*, 100–102, 107, 110–15, 120.

30. PT, *My Search for Absolutes*, 46–47; Pauck and Pauck, *Paul Tillich*, 133–38.

31. Richard W. Fox, *Reinhold Niebuhr*, 234.

32. Carter, *Another Part of the Fifties*, 150.

33. Some theological studies include Scott, *Legacy of Reinhold Niebuhr*, xvii–xviii; Douglas John Hall, *Remembered Voices*," chap. 3; Gilkey, *On Niebuhr*. Some political science studies include Michael J. Smith, *Realist Thought from Weber to Kissinger*, 103; Epp, "Ironies of Christian Realism."

34. Stanley Hauerwas provides a reductive perspective in *With the Grain of the Universe*, 120–22, 133, 107n. For the most part, historians of midcentury America have not carefully analyzed Niebuhr's theology of sin.

35. Most scholars view Niebuhr as a conventional cold warrior. See, for example, Whitfield, *Culture of the Cold War*, 87, 99. For a more balanced view, see Richard W. Fox, *Reinhold Niebuhr*, 232, 234, 247.

36. See, for example, Ellwood, *Fifties Spiritual Marketplace*; Hudnut-Beumler, *Looking for God in the Suburbs*.

37. A copy of Niebuhr's article for *This Week* magazine is included in his correspondence with the editor, William I. Nichols. See Nichols to RN, 7 December 1954, collection 12, RN papers.

38. "Tent Revival Ends after Eight Weeks," *Los Angeles Times*, 21 October 1949, 20; Stanley High, "Answered Prayer?—a Case History," *Reader's Digest*, January 1956, 28; Martin, *Prophet with Honor*, 309. See collection 19, box 8, folder 1, BGCA, for letters addressed simply to "Billy Graham, Minneapolis, MN."

39. William G. McLoughlin, "Billy Graham: In Business with the Lord," *Nation*, 11 May 1957, 403–10. See also "Whose Billy Graham?" *Christian Century*, 21 November 1956, 1350–52; "In the Garden," *Christian Century*, 15 May 1957, 614–15; "Mass Con-

versions" *Christian Century*, 29 May 1957, 677–79; "Fundamentalist Revival," *Christian Century*, 19 June 1957, 749–51.

40. Eckardt, *Surge of Piety in America*, 50–51; Marty, *New Shape of American Religion*, chap. 1. Conversely, there is a vast evangelical literature too large to list here that rather uncritically assesses Graham's ministry. See, for example, Drummond, *Canvas Cathedral*.

41. McLoughlin, *Revivals, Awakenings, and Reform*, 186–90; Carter, *Another Part of the Fifties*, 143; Ellwood, *Fifties Spiritual Marketplace*, 13, 230. Here, Ellwood is inconsistent in his assessment of Graham, mixing fairness with questionable generalizations; Hudnut-Beumler, *Looking for God in the Suburbs*, 83–84. Peter Berger's *Noise of Solemn Assemblies*, a book closely analyzed by Hudnut-Beumler, quotes at length another study that maintains that Graham's view of sin was nominal, arguing falsely that Graham was not troubled even by drink, ambition, or money. See Berger, *Noise of Solemn Assemblies*, 99–100.

42. BG, *Peace with God*, 32–37, 45–46, 49; *Seven Deadly Sins*, 47, 66; BG, "Grace vs. Wrath," *Hour of Decision* (Minneapolis, Minn.: Billy Graham Evangelistic Association, 1951), 3, collection 191, BGCA; BG, *World Aflame*, 53, 56–59, 61.

43. Burkhead, "Development of the Concept of Sin," 101–2; Martin, *Prophet with Honor*, 574.

44. "Billy Graham: When Millions Pray . . . Then There's Hope for New York," *Newsweek*, 14 March 1955, 90–91; BG, "Greater Sin! Greater Salvation!" *Hour of Decision* (Minneapolis, Minn.: Billy Graham Evangelistic Association, 1961), 6–7, collection 191, BGCA. On sins as manifestations of original sin, see BG, *Seven Deadly Sins*, 47, 66; BG, *World Aflame*, 52. Timo Pokki provides a useful, straightforward analysis of Graham's view of original sin in *America's Preacher and His Message*, chap. 3, especially 73–83.

45. BG, *Peace with God*, 50.

46. "Is Our Religious Revival Real?" *McCall's*, June 1955, 25; " 'Faith Comes by Hearing' . . . ," *Newsweek*, 28 March 1955, 56–57; "Americans and Religion: State of the New Revival . . . As Billy Graham, Niebuhr, and LaFarge See It," *Newsweek*, 26 December 1955, 44–45. Niebuhr and Graham appeared together again in the *Los Angeles Times* when each was asked to select his favorite Bible passage. See "They Pick the Bible's Greatest Words," *Los Angeles Times*, 10 April 1955, J8.

47. Stanley High, "Our Prayers Could Change the World," *Reader's Digest*, February 1955, 56–58.

48. Newbill, "Theology of Billy Graham," 126–31.

49. RN, Editorial Notes, *Christianity and Crisis*, 5 March 1956, 18.

50. Silk, *Spiritual Politics*, 101, 105.

51. RN, "Differing Views on Billy Graham," *Life*, 1 July 1957, 92.

52. I develop this argument more fully in "The Prophet and the Evangelist: The Public 'Conversation' of Reinhold Niebuhr and Billy Graham," *Books and Culture*, July–August 2006, 8–9, 37–42. In "Niebuhr and Graham," Gary Dorrien covers much of the same territory discussed in my article—though he comes to more negative conclusions about their relationship.

53. RN, *Pious and Secular America*, 20–21.

54. Niebuhr offered an apology of sorts for his 1957 *Life* article in "After Comment, the Deluge," *Christian Century*, 4 September 1957, 1035.

55. "Theologians Don't Seem to Understand," *Saturday Evening Post*, 13 April 1957, quoted in Martin, *Prophet with Honor*, 228; Silk, *Spiritual Politics*, 105; Paul Hendrickson, "Billy Graham, Preacher's Progress," *Washington Post*, 28 April 1986, B1.

56. Martin, *Prophet with Honor*, 168–72.

57. RN, "A Proposal to Billy Graham," *Christian Century*, 8 August 1956, 921–22; BG, "Billy Graham Makes Plea for an End to Intolerance," *Life*, 1 October 1956, 138–62. Michael G. Long has recently argued that Graham was "largely opposed" to Martin Luther King's inclusive vision for America and especially the tactics King employed for realizing that vision. Long includes the above *Life* article to support his case and rightly highlights the gradualist tone of some parts of the article. Unfortunately, he ignores the passages that strongly indict racism and segregation and the Christian Church's complicity in both. See Long, *Billy Graham and the Beloved Community*, 115, 118, 125.

58. Pollock, *Billy Graham*, 157.

59. Niebuhr did finally and scathingly dismiss Graham in 1969, in protest against Graham's leading worship in the Nixon White House. See RN, "The King's Chapel and the King's Court," *Christianity and Crisis*, 4 August 1969, collection 35, RN papers.

60. RN, "After Comment, the Deluge," 1035. Niebuhr acknowledged the importance of individual rebirth elsewhere, especially in *Faith and History*, 125–26, 140, 144.

61. PT, "The Lost Dimension in Religion," *Saturday Evening Post*, 14 June 1958, 78–79; Gene Grove, "Theologian Tillich Warns of Trend toward Idolatry," *Columbus Citizen-Journal*, 8 April 1960, 1, box 902C, folder 28, PT papers.

62. Helen S. Farmer "Preacher Men," *New Yorker*, 19 September 2005, 9; Gene Grove, "Theologian Tillich Warns of Trend Toward Idolatry," 1.

63. Krister Stendahl, Mellon Professor of Divinity Emeritus, Harvard Divinity School, interview by author, 16 June 2003, tape recording in author's possession.

64. John Cooper, "The Witness of Paul Tillich," *Resource*, March 1966, 31, box 901, folder 69, PT papers.

65. McBride, "Paul Tillich and the Supreme Court," 245–72; the court case in question was *Welsh v. United States* (1970). "My Travel Diary: 1936," review of *My Travel Diary: 1936*, by Reinhold Niebuhr, *New York Times*, 10 May 1970, 6, 34; "Tillich Gave Simplicity to Urgent Issues," *Denver Post*, 24 October 1965, box 902D, folder 36, PT papers. See also "People Are Talking about . . . ," *Vogue*, 1 February 1962, 128, box 902C, folder 30, PT papers; A. C. Spectorsky to PT, February 2, 1965, PT papers.

66. "Ferré Says Tillich Is Most 'Dangerous Theological Leader,'" *Presbyterian Outlook*, 7 November 1955, 1, box 902A, folder 23, PT papers; A. Campbell Garnett, "Is Modern Theology Atheistic?" *Christian Century*, 31 May 1961, 680–82; Hill, "Paul's 'Second Adam' and Tillich's Christology," 13. Questions about Tillich's Christian identity reached a crescendo in 1963 with the publication of the English bishop John A. T. Robinson's controversial *Honest to God*. The book, inspired in part by Tillich's description of God as "the ground of being," further publicized the small but increasingly influential "Death of God" theological movement of the 1960s. For an adequate

summary of the phenomenon, see Ved Mehta, "The New Theologian," *New Yorker*, 13 November 1965, 63–153. Mehta later published his work in book form, *The New Theologian* (1966).

67. R. Allan Killen, "Tillich's Soteriology," *Christianity Today*, 22 July 1957, 34.

68. Hannah Tillich, *From Time to Time*, 223; Pauck and Pauck, *Paul Tillich*, 80–93; Lears, *Something for Nothing*, 307–8; Porterfield, *Transformation of American Religion*, 218–19; McCarraher, *Christian Critics*, chap. five. McCarraher curiously frames Tillich's indiscretions as a fuller blossoming of Eros, and one not wholly destructive.

69. Hannah Tillich, *From Time to Time*, 223.

70. Upon the publication of Hannah Tillich's memoir, many of Tillich's friends and colleagues claimed that Hannah's perspective was exaggerated. See Rollo May, *Paulus*. Tillich's biographers and friends, Wilhelm and Marion Pauck, give some insight into this side of Tillich's life and his marriage to Hannah. They regard Tillich's first wife's betrayal with one of his good friends as crucial to his later behavior. See Pauck and Pauck, *Paul Tillich*, 80–93. Grace Cali, Tillich's secretary at Harvard, debunks the more sensational accounts of Tillich's personal life and clarifies some of Tillich's views of marriage and sex in *Paul Tillich First-Hand*, 12–15, 20–21.

71. Rollo May, *Paulus*, 61, chap. 5.

72. PT, *Systematic Theology*, 2:33–38. See also PT, *Theology of Culture*, 210. Tillich writes: "Today the meaning of original sin, its universality, its tragic role in history, can be emphasized in a way that it could not be twenty years ago. For we are able today to use a concept which everybody understands, the concept of estrangement: estrangement from oneself, from the other man, from the ground out of which we come and to which we go."

73. PT, *Systematic Theology*, 2:56.

74. PT, "The Good That I Will, I Do Not," in *Eternal Now*, 50–51.

75. The one exception is a remark he made in 1963: "I would avoid the words 'original sin' completely . . . . But the tragic estrangement of mankind (that is what the words actually mean) is a reality we cannot deny." D. Mackenzie Brown, *Ultimate Concern*, 121. For his affirmation of the word and the concept of sin, see PT, *Shaking of the Foundations*, 153–54; PT, *Systematic Theology*, 2:46.

76. RN, "Biblical Thought and Ontological Speculation"; RN, "Protestantism and the Arts," *Christianity and Crisis*, 6 February 1956, 2–3.

CHAPTER 3

1. Throughout this chapter, I fluctuate between the use of "man" and the more inclusive "humanity." I agree with Richard Fox, who notes that the "male generic is sometimes unavoidable" and makes for smoother writing; moreover, it was the pronoun employed by each thinker discussed herein. Richard W. Fox, *Reinhold Niebuhr*, xii.

2. RN, *Man's Nature and His Communities*, 16. Niebuhr prefaced his quotation of the *Times Literary Supplement* by confessing that his use of the term "original sin" was a "pedagogical error." The problem, one he also noted in the preface to volume 1 of the 1964 reprint of *The Nature and Destiny of Man*, was challenging "modern optimism" with the outmoded language of original sin, a term loaded down by misinterpretations and misunderstandings of the historicity of Adam and Eve. Niebuhr's point was one of

semantics and method, not one of denial or disbelief in the conceptual truth of the doctrine of original sin.

3. RN, "Intellectual Autobiography," 3–23; PT, *Systematic Theology*, 1:3–11, 18–22, 168–71; Gilkey, *Gilkey on Tillich*, 24, 28–33; BG, *Peace with God*, chap. 1.

4. BG, *Peace with God*, 36–37; BG, *Seven Deadly Sins*, 47, 66.

5. RN, *Nature and Destiny of Man*, 1:267, 270, 272–74, 280, 255–60, 275; BG, *Peace with God*, 10–11, 32–35; BG, *World Aflame*, 52, 63; Pokki, *America's Preacher and His Message*, 73–83; PT, *Systematic Theology*, 1:258–59; PT, *Systematic Theology*, 2:33.

6. "Only in This Country," *Time*, 17 May 1963, 59–70; PT, *Systematic Theology*, 2:31–36; RN, *Nature and Destiny of Man*, 1:178–86.

7. PT, "Philosophical Background of My Theology," *Kirisutokyo Gaku* (*Christian Studies*), November 1960, 2–10, BX4827.T53 A1 no. 21, PT papers; PT, *On the Boundary*, 56–57. See also PT, "Person in Technical Society," 137–53.

8. PT, *Systematic Theology*, 2:34–35.

9. Ibid., 2:34–35, 46.

10. Richard W. Fox, *Reinhold Niebuhr*, 161–62, 257.

11. Ibid., 144–45. Meyer also makes this observation in *Protestant Search for Political Realism*, 242–43.

12. RN, *Reflections on the End of an Era*, 213–14, 281–82; RN, *An Interpretation of Christian Ethics*, 84–85.

13. For the purposes of this chapter, I have chosen to rely almost exclusively on volume 1 of *The Nature and Destiny of Man* to explain Niebuhr's theology of sin. Although *Faith and History* and *The Self and the Dramas of History* also outline Niebuhr's thought on the human situation, his ideas about sin remain largely consistent with those articulated in *The Nature and Destiny of Man*.

14. RN, *Nature and Destiny of Man*, 1:1.

15. RN, *Discerning the Signs of the Times*, 160, 170, 181; RN, *Nature and Destiny of Man*, 1:181–82.

16. RN, *Nature and Destiny of Man*, 1:181; RN, "Sorrow and Joy According to the Christian Faith," *Pulpit Digest*, January 1955, 16. This sermon was a variation on "Peace of God," found in *Discerning the Signs of the Times*, 174–94.

17. Martin, *Prophet with Honor*, 76, 118, 120, 569.

18. BG, *World Aflame*, 53, 56, 61. For references to these figures, see 26–56.

19. RN, *Nature and Destiny of Man*, 1:182.

20. PT, *Systematic Theology*, 2:48, 50. Tillich gives his ontological reason for the term "hubris" in "Sin and Grace in the Theology of Reinhold Niebuhr," in Landon, *Reinhold Niebuhr*, 38.

21. Niebuhr occasionally asserted that unbelief was the basis of sin, but most often he discussed pride as the first sin (RN, *Nature and Destiny of Man*, 1:174). Graham was even less consistent. For example, unbelief appears after his discussion of pride in *Peace with God*, 42–43. But his emphasis on the "facts" of faith as a counter to doubt and unbelief colors much of his work, including his famous sermon, "Facts, Faith, and Feeling," *Hour of Decision* (Minneapolis, Minn.: Billy Graham Evangelistic Association, 1957), collection 191, BGCA.

22. RN, *Nature and Destiny of Man*, 1:186–87.

23. Ibid., 1:192, 194.

24. Ibid., 1:188–94.

25. Ibid., 1:16, 194–95.

26. Ibid., 1:199–200, 121. See also Carnell, *Theology of Reinhold Niebuhr*, 74.

27. RN, *Nature and Destiny of Man*, 1:200, 202f.

28. BG, *World Aflame*, 70; BG, *Seven Deadly Sins*, chap. 1.

29. BG, *Peace with God*, 26.

30. BG, *World Aflame*, 35–40, 198.

31. BG, "Things God Hates," *Hour of Decision* (Minneapolis, Minn.: Billy Graham Evangelistic Association, 1955), 1, collection 191, BGCA.

32. BG, *Seven Deadly Sins*, 16, 18; BG, *Just as I Am*, 727.

33. References to these thinkers are scattered throughout *World Aflame*. See also BG, *Seven Deadly Sins*, 4, 6, where he alludes to psychology and the unconscious as confirmation of the "evil in our hearts." Martin, *Prophet with Honor*, 575, 157.

34. Silk, *Spiritual Politics*, 101, 105.

35. PT, *Systematic Theology*, 2:50–51.

36. PT, "The Spirit of Protestantism," box 406A, folder 19, 4, PT Papers; PT, "The Spirit of Protestantism," box 406A, folder 23, 4, PT Papers; PT, *Protestant Era*, introduction and chap. 11.

37. PT, "Protestant Approach to the Recent World Situation," 1–3, n.d., box 406B, folder 33, PT papers.

38. PT, "The Origins of Protestantism," 5–9, n.d., 406A/20. For one example among many, see his *New Being*.

39. PT, "Person in Technical Society," 153; PT, *Systematic Theology*, 2:59–84. Tillich's sermons are a rich source for his discussion of negative pride. See, for example, PT, "You Are Accepted," in *Shaking of the Foundations*, 153–63, as well as 21, 70, 72; PT, "To Whom Much Is Forgiven," in *New Being*, 3–14; Gilkey, *Gilkey on Tillich*, 130–31.

40. RN, *Nature and Destiny of Man*, 1:228–29.

41. Ibid., 232–33, 238.

42. Ibid., 235.

43. BG, "How Wise Is Man?" *Hour of Decision* (Minneapolis, Minn.: Billy Graham Evangelistic Association, 1960), 7, collection 191, BGCA.

44. BG, *Peace with God*, 1–8; BG, "Man Made Religion," *Hour of Decision* (Minneapolis, Minn.: Billy Graham Evangelistic Association, 1961), 1–2, collection 191, BGCA.

45. BG, *Peace with God*, 5, 7.

46. BG, *World Aflame*, 24.

47. Ibid., 187.

48. On sex and sloth, see BG, *Seven Deadly Sins*, chaps. 4 and 6.

49. BG, *Peace with God*, 91.

50. BG, *Seven Deadly Sins*, 75; BG, "How to Overcome Temptation," *Hour of Decision* (Minneapolis, Minn.: Billy Graham Evangelistic Association, 1960), 3, collection 191, BGCA.

51. BG, "America's Immorality," *Hour of Decision* (Minneapolis, Minn.: Billy Graham Evangelistic Association, 1964), 3, collection 191, BGCA; BG, "Man Made Religion," 2–3.

52. PT, *Systematic Theology*, 2:52, 53, 51–55.

53. Tillich pointed to the religious character of these cultural forms. He argued that "implicit" religious concern in "the visual arts, novel, poetry, music, [and] dance" revealed profound religious truths. PT, "The Religious Situation in the Post-War Era," 11 April 1962, 9, 1–5, box 406A, folder 7, PT papers. See also PT, *Theology of Culture*.

54. PT, *Systematic Theology*, 2:51, 53; Gilkey, *Gilkey on Tillich*, 128–29.

55. PT, "The Lost Dimension in Religion," *Saturday Evening Post*, 14 June 1958, 76; Gilkey, *Gilkey on Tillich*, 129–30; PT, *Systematic Theology*, 2:52–53.

56. PT, "The Lost Dimension in Religion," 76.

57. Gilkey, *Gilkey on Tillich*, 129; Gilkey quotes Tillich's phrase "swallowed up."

58. BG, "The Sin of Tolerance," *Hour of Decision* (Minneapolis, Minn.: Billy Graham Evangelistic Association, 1957), 10, collection 191, BGCA. see also BG, *Seven Deadly Sins*, 52; BG, *Peace with God*, 121–27; BG, *World Aflame*, 119–26, 143. Graham, however, hardly sentimentalized the cross and lambasted Christians who did. See BG, "The Cross and Its Meaning Today," *Hour of Decision* (Minneapolis, Minn.: Billy Graham Evangelistic Association, 1958), 3, collection 191, BGCA; BG, "The Suffering Savior on a Crimson Cross," *Hour of Decision* (Minneapolis, Minn.: Billy Graham Evangelistic Association, 1957), 3–4, collection 191, BGCA.

59. RN, "Differing Views on Billy Graham," *Life*, 1 July 1957, 92.

60. BG, *Seven Deadly Sins*, 51. See also BG, *World Aflame*, 126; Burkhead, "Development of the Concept of Sin," 126, 128. Still, as Burkhead explains, Graham's "fatherly admonitions" to Christian sinners are balanced by "the seriousness with which he speaks about Christians who deliberately and actively involve themselves in a sinful lifestyle."

61. BG, *Peace with God*, 127. Graham used this phrase again in *World Aflame*, 140.

62. BG, "Facts, Faith and Feeling," *Hour of Decision* (Minneapolis, Minn.: Billy Graham Evangelistic Association, 1957), 1–9, collection 191, BGCA. Graham used this theological construction often: see *Peace with God*, 131–35, and *World Aflame*, 103.

63. RN, *Nature and Destiny of Man*, 2:45.

64. The double aspect of the cross as a symbol of judgment and redemption appears frequently in both Niebuhr's and Tillich's writings. See, for example, RN, *Beyond Tragedy*, chap. 13; RN, *Nature and Destiny of Man*, 2:56, 204, 211–12; PT, *Systematic Theology*, 2:167–73; PT, *New Being*, chaps. 1, 2.

65. RN, *Beyond Tragedy*, 62. Tillich made similar observations about Christian sinners. See PT, *Systematic Theology*, 3:140, 280–82; PT, "To Whom Much Is Forgiven," in *New Being*, 3–14.

66. BG, *Peace with God*, 209.

67. RN, *Nature and Destiny of Man*, 2:49; PT, *New Being*, 18; PT, *Systematic Theology*, 2:167, 179; PT, *Systematic Theology*, 3:280–82.

68. RN, *Nature and Destiny of Man*, 2:100; PT, *Shaking of the Foundations*, 160–62; PT, *Courage to Be*, 172; PT, *Systematic Theology*, 3:226–29.

69. Donald Meyer, "Billy Graham—and Success," *New Republic*, 22 August 1955, 8–10.

70. PT, "Sin and Grace in the Theology of Reinhold Niebuhr," 37.

71. PT, *Theology of Culture*, 201–3; D. Mackenzie Brown, *Ultimate Concern*, 190–95. On Niebuhr's faith in the laity, see RN, *Leaves from the Notebook of a Tamed Cynic*, 216–17; RN, "Intellectual Autobiography," in Kegley and Bretall, *Theology of Reinhold Niebuhr*, 6–7.

72. PT, *Shaking of the Foundations*, 60.

CHAPTER 4

1. Judy Soles to RN, 22 March 1961, collection 11, RN papers; RN to Judy Soles, 28 March 1961, collection 11, RN papers.

2. Apart from the preface, Fox's most telling comments about Niebuhr's humility in relationship to students and laity are made not in the body of the text but in the afterword. Richard W. Fox, *Reinhold Niebuhr*, x, 330, 342, 353; Brown, *Niebuhr and His Age*, 262–63. See also Merkley, *Reinhold Niebuhr*, 203–5; Clark, *Serenity, Courage, and Wisdom*, 59. Merkley, like Fox, portrays Niebuhr as a public celebrity but also restricts his influence to "intellectuals." Clark comments on Niebuhr's "large reading public" but never explains or supports this contention.

3. Hordern, *Layman's Guide to Protestant Theology*, 156.

4. RN, *Leaves from the Notebook of a Tamed Cynic*, 216–17. Niebuhr recorded this incident again in his prefatory remarks written for Kegley and Bretall, *Theology of Reinhold Niebuhr*, 6–7.

5. RN to June Bingham, 17 September 1954, collection 26, RN papers; RN, *Self and Dramas of History*, quoted in Bingham, *Courage to Change*, 307–8.

6. "Niebuhr v. Sin," *Time*, 29 April 1946, 51–52; George R. Stephenson, "Ten 'Sermonic Essays,'" *New York Times*, 9 June 1946, 114; George Stephenson, "Dr. Niebuhr's Thought and Work," *New York Times Book Review*, 4 July 1948, 8. Stephenson wrote, "Today, however, thanks to the popular press, men are coming to speak knowingly of the works of this ethics professor. Whether they read his books is another question." Pastors and laymen, however, had opportunity to read Niebuhr's sermons in periodicals such as *Advance* and *Pulpit Digest* as well as in the edited collection *Best Sermons*. RN, "Sorrow and Joy According to the Christian Faith," *Advance*, 13 July 1953, 5–6, 27. Two years later, Niebuhr appeared on the cover of *Pulpit Digest*, and a variation of his "Sorrow and Joy" sermon was reprinted. RN, "Sorrow and Joy According to the Christian Faith," *Pulpit Digest*, January 1955, 15–20; RN, "Mystery and Meaning," in G. Paul Butler, *Best Sermons: 1946 Edition*, 52–62.

7. Stanley S. Jones to Ursula Niebuhr, 11 June 1971, collection 10, RN papers [Georgia].

8. Charles C. Brown's account is a partial exception, documenting Niebuhr's early pastoral days and his relationships with pastors, students, and the general public. See Charles C. Brown, *Niebuhr and His Age*, chap. 2, 65–67, 131–35; Marty, *Modern American Religion*, 3:285. Marty has elsewhere noted Niebuhr's awareness of the "intuitive and inherited wisdom and faithfulness of laypeople" but understands this as a rare occurrence and one used by Niebuhr as a rhetorical device to expose the "clerical idealist folly." See Marty, "Reinhold Niebuhr: Public Theology and the American Experience," 20–21. In fact, almost any general study, including religious studies, of

the postwar world characterizes Niebuhr as part of an elite group whose thought had little impact on most Americans.

9. Theodore P. Ferris to Ursula Niebuhr, 31 October 1971, collection 10, RN papers. Ferris, the rector at Trinity Church in Boston, recorded this exchange in the sermon "Not Only Selfish," preached in honor of Niebuhr.

10. The Chicago Sunday Evening Club was a long-standing preacher's venue begun in 1906 and held weekly in Orchestra Hall. By the midfifties, these events were televised locally. "Sunday Talks in 52D Season," *Chicago Tribune*, 5 October 1958, 44.

11. RN, "Intellectual Autobiography," in Kegley and Bretall, *Theology of Reinhold Niebuhr*, 3; RN to June Bingham, n.d., collection 26, RN papers.

12. Scherer, "Reinhold Niebuhr—Preacher," 323.

13. Niebuhr said as much in correspondence with June Bingham. See RN to Bingham, 15 November 1954, and RN to Bingham, n.d. 1957, collection 26, RN papers. Will Herberg made a similar observation in a review of *The Self and Dramas of History*: "[Niebuhr's] writings . . . in one way or another, are all concerned with rendering the biblical understanding of man and history relevant to contemporary life and thought." See Will Herberg, "Three Dialogues of Man," *New Republic*, 16 May 1955, 28. Niebuhr's prayers are indicative of the nature and expanse of his preaching. See Ursula M. Niebuhr, *Justice and Mercy*, chap. 3, 12, especially pg. 100.

14. See especially RN, *Nature and Destiny of Man*, vols. 1 and 2; RN, *Faith and History*. These convictions appear in most things Niebuhr wrote, however. See, for example, RN, "Spiritual Crisis in Our Culture," *New York Times Book Review*, 3 February 1946, 3; RN, "Piety and Secularism in America," *Atlantic Monthly*, November 1957, 180–84. This article was later expanded into *Pious and Secular America* (1958). See also RN, "The Christian Witness in a Secular Age," *Christian Century*, 22 July 1953, 840–43.

15. Preston King Sheldon, "Religious Careers Attract Students," *New York Times*, 2 April 1949, 16. Niebuhr is quoted on his view of the ministry: "Ministers must be concerned with the social needs of men and the evils of the world. They must strive to do away with all kinds of political and economic injustices. But the primary need is to help men and nations understand the fundamental problems of human existence. They must understand the relevance of the Christian Gospel to the ultimate questions of human experience."

16. This interpretation of Niebuhr's preaching is based primarily on two volumes of sermons published before his death. See RN, *Beyond Tragedy* and *Discerning the Signs of the Times*. See also Scherer, "Reinhold Niebuhr—Preacher," 311–32.

17. Gertrude L. Winslow to RN, 1 December 1933, collection 2, RN papers; Carey J. Chamberlin to RN, 7 December 1943, collection 3, RN papers.

18. RN, "Hazards and Difficulties," 131.

19. Lydia Fleer to RN, 10 February 1930, collection 6, RN papers. The remainder of Fleer's letter is somewhat incoherent, but what appears to have been the most affecting thing for her was Niebuhr's challenge to and affirmation of Christian "idealism."

20. Mrs. Charles Reed, 9 May 1941, collection 13, RN papers [Ohio]; Houston Peterson to RN, 16 December 1941, collection 10, RN papers [New York]; Bert Russell to RN, 15 April 1929, collection 10, RN papers [Michigan]; Charles Rubenoff to RN, 3 November 1928, collection 10, RN papers [Michigan].

21. Bingham, *Courage to Change*, 279. Bingham's contention that listeners often expressed a better self-understanding is confirmed by Hans Rosenhauht. See Rosenhauht to RN, 26 April 1954, collection 10, RN papers. Rosenhauht, who worked in Columbia University's office of admissions, wrote to Niebuhr: "Your sermon on Deceivers Yet True . . . [gave] me a better understanding of myself." Bingham also quoted a reaction by a Scottish woman who attended the Gifford Lectures: "I dinna understand a word ye said, but somehow I ken ye were making God great." Another worshipper muttered: "I didn't understand him but he made me mad." See Harkness, "Symposium on Reinhold Niebuhr's *The Nature and Destiny of Man*," 567.

22. Grace E. Williams to RN, n.d., collection 13, RN papers. Williams's letter was typed on Columbia University letterhead but with no indication of her connection to the school. Her letter and several others cited thus far appear to be from essentially middle-class educated individuals. Other letters, cited below, indicate a broader spectrum of Niebuhr disciples.

23. For obvious reasons, I have protected the identities of these two women. Miss K to RN, 21 October 1952, collection 3, RN papers [California]; RN to Miss K, 24 October 1952, collection 3, RN papers; Miss C to RN, 20 November 1955, collection 3, RN papers [New York]; RN to Miss C, 22 November 1955, collection 3, RN papers.

24. Miss K to RN, 21 October 1952, collection 3, RN papers [California].

25. RN to Miss K, 24 October 1952, collection 3, RN papers. See also RN, "Sin," in *Handbook of Christian Theology*, 348. Interestingly, he opened this short essay by noting that sex had been too closely identified with sin.

26. James M. Howard to RN, 20 February 1936, collection 7, RN papers [Florida].

27. Stone, *Professor Reinhold Niebuhr*, 76, xii. Of 320 surveys, more than 100 replies were returned. So influential was Niebuhr that his students, according to Martin Marty, sometimes hardened his thought into dogma. See M. Marty, "Thinker and Doer," *New York Times Book Review*, 17 December 1961, 4, 16; Brown, *Niebuhr and His Age*, 135.

28. Clarence Kilde to RN, 14 December 1955, collection 7, RN papers; Brown, *Niebuhr and His Age*, 172.

29. A. M. Lutton to RN, 18 September 1955, collection 8, RN papers. On Niebuhr's doubts about the "moral man," see Richard W. Fox, "Niebuhr Brothers and the Liberal Protestant Heritage," 101, 104. Niebuhr explicitly stated his change of mind in a letter to Professor Edmund Cahn of NYU Law School: "When I wrote Moral Man and Immoral Society I made this rather too absolute distinction between the moral capability of individuals and the group." RN to Edmund Cahn, 13 March 1961, collection 4, RN papers.

30. Dan Barfield to RN, 20 October 1956, collection 2, RN papers [Texas]; RN to Dan Barfield, 22 October 1956, collection 2, RN papers.

31. Wesley Sheffield to RN, 4 December 1954, collection 11, RN papers [New York].

32. Ralph Farrell to RN, 20 September 1929, collection 6, RN papers [Missouri]; Edgar T. Reed to RN, 20 May 1930, collection 10, RN papers [Maryland]; John C. Petrie to RN, n.d., collection 10, RN papers [Tennessee]; Stanley Reynolds to RN, 3 May 1957, collection 10, RN papers [Massachusetts]; James Bortell to RN, 15 January 1970, collection 56, RN papers [Illinois].

33. The pastors' conference was an annual event begun in 1920, with usually a dozen or more denominations represented by some 150 ministers from thirty or more states. "150 Ministers Meet Here," *New York Times*, 8 July 1941, 14. In addition to the 1953 conference address, Niebuhr published "The Security and Hazard of the Christian Ministry." Despite the similarity of the title of his address to that of the article, the two were not identical.

34. "The first difficulty . . ." see RN, untitled, collection 41, RN papers. This is the original text of the essay later published in *Justice and Mercy*. RN, "Hazards and Difficulties," 128–29.

35. RN, "Hazards and Difficulties," 130–31.

36. Bingham's comments about Niebuhr's realization of his own "self-centeredness" were notes she made to herself on a letter she received from Erich Fromm. See Fromm to Bingham, 26 December 1958, collection 26, RN papers; RN to Bingham, 29 October 1961, collection 26, RN papers.

37. Two typical book reviews include RN, "Under the Bo-Tree," *New York Times Book Review*, 7 May 1944, 6; RN, "There Is No Escape from the Eternal," *New York Times Book Review*, 8 October 1950, 7.

38. Louis Minsky to RN, 29 November 1945; Minsky to RN, 30 September 1948, collection 10, RN papers. Minsky was the managing editor of Religious News Service. By 1948, Niebuhr had expressed his wish to drop the column, and Minsky agreed, citing in part some difficulty in adding new subscribers. The State Department requested permission to distribute materials (esp. chap. 5) from *The Children of the Light and the Children of Darkness* (1944) in China, Japan, and Southeast Asia; meanwhile, the War Department wanted copies of *Beyond Tragedy* (1937), *Christianity and Power Politics* (1940), and *Discerning the Signs of the Times* (1946). William Savage to RN, 7 October 1946, collection 11, RN papers; RN to William Savage, 25 September 1947, collection 11, RN papers.

39. Richard W. Fox, *Reinhold Niebuhr*, 218; "ABC Plans a Series of Video Discussions to 'Explore Practicality of Religion,'" *New York Times*, 8 October 1949, 28. Another ABC radio show hosted by Quincy Howe publicized Niebuhr's book *The Self and Dramas of History*. See "Quincy Howe, American Broadcasting Company," collection 56, RN papers.

40. Richard W. Fox, *Reinhold Niebuhr*, 234.

41. [Whittaker Chambers], "Faith for a Lenten Age," *Time*, 8 March 1948, 70–76, 79.

42. Letters to the editor, *Time*, 29 March 1948, 6–8; Richard W. Fox, *Reinhold Niebuhr*, 233–34.

43. [Whittaker Chambers], "Faith for a Lenten Age," 71.

44. [Whittaker Chambers], "Sin Rediscovered," *Time*, 24 March 1941, 38.

45. Richard W. Fox, *Reinhold Niebuhr*, 215, 234. Fox confuses the issue further by contrasting the "sophisticated" readers of *The Nature and Destiny of Man* with the "less sophisticated," commenting that the latter group "reveled in the new stress [in volume two] on Jesus himself, the incarnate word." It is unclear to whom Fox refers as "less sophisticated"; but whoever they were, they apparently took comfort in the hope and promise of Niebuhr's articulation of salvation in Jesus.

46. National Conference of Christians and Jews, *Religious Book Week May 7–14*, 15–16.

47. Robert D. Knudson, "Not Orthodox," *Christianity Today*, 24 December 1956, 36.

See also Virgil A. Kraft, "Dear Mr. Niebuhr," *Zion's Herald*, 18 October 1950, 988–89; R. L. Duffus, "The Hope That Lives," *New York Times Book Review*, 28 March 1943, 6. Stone makes a similar point in *Professor Reinhold Niebuhr*, 141–42.

48. "Paperbacks," *Christianity Today*, 13 March 1964, 34.

49. Merlin M. Paine to RN, 17 October 1955, and RN to Merlin M. Paine, 21 October 1955, collection 10, RN papers. For a range of responses to Niebuhr's book, see J. G. Hall to RN, 1 July 1955, collection 7, RN papers [Michigan]; Lieutenant Colonel T. V. Smith to RN, 21 June 1943, collection 11, RN papers [Virginia] Smith included in his letter of appreciation a paper that one of his students had written on *The Nature and Destiny of Man*. See also Mathew Evans to RN, 10 November 1944, collection 5, RN papers. Evans, a professor of history at Stanford, reported that Niebuhr's visit to campus had "stimulated a depth of thought in the widest variety of people." He also suggested that Niebuhr publish a more accessible summary of *The Nature and Destiny of Man*. His students at Stanford, though provoked by the book, had difficulty with the text. This subtle criticism further supports my argument. The book was challenging to readers from elite colleges like Stanford on down to ordinary believers, but its difficulty did not deter many lay theologians.

50. Pierce Butler to RN, 24 April 1941, collection 1, RN papers [Illinois].

51. Helen N. Hartmann to RN, 8 February 1956, collection 7, RN papers [New Jersey].

52. RN, "Is There a Revival of Religion?" *New York Times Magazine*, 19 November 1950, 13, 50, 62; RN, "Religiosity and the Christian Faith," *Christianity and Crisis*, 24 January 1955, 185–86. For Niebuhr as the critic of the revival, see also "Americans and Religion: State of the Revival as Billy Graham, Niebuhr and Lafarge See It," *Newsweek*, 26 December 1955, 44–45; "Is Our Religious Revival Real?" *McCall's*, June 1955, 25.

53. Eugene McCarraher makes a similar point in his *Christian Critics*, 218. In a rare departure from the usual acceptance of Niebuhr's take on the revival, Martin Marty has argued that he constructed a "normative American religion precisely so he could discuss normative American religion." See Marty, "Reinhold Niebuhr: Public Theology and the American Experience," 28.

54. RN, Editorial Notes, *Christianity and Crisis*, 2 April 1956, 34. Niebuhr defended the sincerity of Ike's personal piety again in a 1955 *New Republic* article, though he also warned of its vague quality and unfortunate association with the "American way of life." See RN "Varieties of Religious Revival," *New Republic*, 6 June 1955, 14. The Eisenhower quote comes from Silk, *Spiritual Politics*, 40.

55. "Resurgent Protestantism: At Easter, the Wave of New Christian Orthodoxy," *Newsweek*, 28 March 1955, 55. For another charitable estimation of the church, see RN, "The Problem of the Modern Church: Triviality," *Christianity and Crisis*, 10 December 1962, 223–24. Within Niebuhr's critique of the triviality of the church, there is a kernel of regard for the church and its work. He notes that secular critics "could not fully appreciate the capacity of the church to establish integral communities in which individual selves, lost in the vast technical togetherness of urban civilization, could know themselves, could be 'completely known and forgiven,' could be guided through the anxieties of youth, maturity and age, and through the perils of death."

56. RN, "Is There a Revival of Religion?" 62.

57. RN, "Varieties of Religious Revival," 13–16.

58. Ibid.

59. Ibid., 13–16; letters to the editor, *New Republic*, 27 June 1955, 7.

60. Paul Brinkman to RN, 17 June 1955, collection 2, RN papers [Oregon]; Brinkman to RN, 3 April 1954, collection 2, RN papers; Brinkman to RN, 24 March 1954, collection 2, RN papers; Niebuhr replied to all of Brinkman's letters, see RN to Paul Brinkman, 24 June 1955, collection 2, RN papers; RN to Brinkman, 8 April 1954, collection 2, RN papers; RN to Brinkman, 29 March 1954, collection 2, RN papers. Niebuhr and Brinkman corresponded at least on one other occasion based on comments in Brinkman's letter of 24 March 1954, but no copies were present in the archives.

61. RN, "The Secularism and Piety of America," collection 17, RN papers. A note on the document indicates that the article appeared in the Dutch publication *Elsevier's Weekblad* in December 1956.

62. Ibid.

63. William Lee Miller, "The Irony of Reinhold Niebuhr," *Reporter*, 13 January 1955, 11.

64. Ibid., 11–15.

65. Biographers agree that Luce was a thoroughgoing conservative with a "city on a hill" vision for America. But his sense of sin, if anything, balanced this messianic view of the nation. See Herzstein, *Henry R. Luce*, 421; Baughman, *Henry R. Luce and the Rise of the American News Media*, 24; Cort, *Sin of Henry R. Luce*, 473; Swanberg, *Luce and His Empire*, 406.

66. RN, "A Faith for History's Greatest Crisis," *Fortune*, July 1942, 128. See also Henry Luce to RN, 8 January 1949, collection 8, RN papers. In this letter, Luce himself showed surprising doubt about American confidence in its role in the world. He remarked that America, "far from having a strong George-Washingtonian belief in the rightness of its cause at home and abroad, is actually very uncertain of itself . . . . I am not at all sure that America has the kind of deep quiet moral confidence." To be sure, this may have pushed Luce to bolster America's confidence with celebratory articles in his magazines, but his words complicate Miller's presentation of him.

67. RN to PT, 6 July 1963, PT papers.

68. Miller, "Irony of Reinhold Niebuhr," 14.

69. Miller, "Irony of Reinhold Niebuhr," 14. David R. Bains has recently defended Niebuhr's strong ecclesiology against the long-standing impression that Niebuhr had no doctrine of the church. See Bains, "Conduits of Faith," 168–94.

70. See the 26 December 1955 issue of *Life*, in particular, John Knox Jessup, "The World, the Flesh and the Devil," 140–43. Niebuhr had always balked at such oversimplification of the human personality, using precisely the term "bovine" to indicate that individual "wholeness" required a power beyond human contrivance, and he certainly objected to notions of a redemptive history as well as American self-righteousness. See RN, *Discerning the Signs of the Times*, 178. Response to the Christmas issue was overwhelmingly positive, though; in this instance, a majority of the letters seemed satisfied with a "civil" faith in "American morality."

71. Niebuhr also contributed short essays on "Freedom," and "Self." See *Handbook of Christian Theology*, 139–41, 342–45, 349–51. See also Arthur A. Cohen to RN, 1 October 1956, collection 17, RN papers.

72. Hordern, *Layman's Guide to Protestant Theology*, chap. 7.

73. Huston Smith, *Search for America*, vii–viii, 144, 153. The reprinted passage appears on page 63 of *Irony of American History*.

74. Fred R. Shapiro, a librarian at Yale, has stirred up the controversy again in an article for the *Yale Alumni Magazine*, "Who Wrote the Serenity Prayer?" in which he disputes Niebuhr's authorship of the prayer. See Laurie Goodstein, "The Serenity Prayer Stirs Up Doubt: Who Wrote It?" *New York Times*, 11 July 2008.

75. Richard W. Fox, *Reinhold Niebuhr*, 290; RN, "To Be Abased and to Abound," *Messenger*, 13 February 1951, 7. Fox's biography alerted me to this early printed rendition of the serenity prayer. Elizabeth Sifton, Niebuhr's daughter, recently wrote a book about her father and the prayer entitled *The Serenity Prayer*. Yet her views of her father and the prayer differ from my own. For example, she understands her father as a religious critic isolated from the mainstream of American Protestants.

76. RN, "To Be Abased and to Abound," 7.

77. See other Niebuhr prayers in Ursula M. Niebuhr, *Justice and Mercy*, 96–104, 112–18.

78. Richard K. Washburn to RN, 6 November 1953, collection 13, RN papers [Massachusetts]. For some other elite reactions from the left, see RN, "Christ vs. Socrates," *Saturday Review*, 18 December 1954, 7–8, 37–39; letters to the editor, *Saturday Review*, 8 January 1955, 15 January 1955, 8; Joseph Harder to RN, May 1956, collection 7, RN papers [New York]. For some conservative evangelical reactions, see A. Martin to RN, October 1931, collection 8, RN papers [Ohio]; Mrs. Lon Wellein to RN, 31 January 1936, 6 February 1936, collection 13, RN papers [Michigan]. On "Moral Gray," see letters to the editor, *Messenger*, 13 February 1951, 34; Fred All to PT, 13 March 1959, PT papers.

79. William J. Foster to RN, 27 February 1956, collection 6, RN papers [California]; RN to Foster, 29 February 1956, collection 6, RN papers. On Niebuhr's doctrine of responsibility despite inevitability, see *Nature and Destiny of Man*, 1:255–60.

80. RN, "Cultural Crisis of Our Age," 33–38. Three businessmen wrote in regard to the article, Robert E. Wilson to RN, 10 February 1954, collection 13, RN papers [Indiana]; Bruce P. Burns to RN, 17 March 1954, collection 2, RN papers [New York]; R. R. Raney to RN, 13 January 1955, collection 10, RN papers [Illinois]. On pride, see Jay Smith to RN, 25 May 1953, collection 11, RN papers [West Virginia].

81. Stanley D. Tappan to RN, n.d., collection 13, RN papers [Connecticut].

82. Anonymous to RN, 4 April 1948, collection 13, RN papers.

83. RN, "After Comment, the Deluge," 1034–35.

84. Ibid.

85. Ibid.

86. Richard W. Fox, *Reinhold Niebuhr*, 332.

87. Floyd Brown to RN, n.d., collection 2, RN papers; Brown to RN, n.d., collection 2, RN papers; Brown to RN, October 1956, collection 2, RN papers; Floyd Brown to RN, April 1957, collection 2, RN papers.

88. Eva H. Grant to RN, 27 March 1956, collection 10, RN papers.

1. Anonymous to BG, 14 August 1950, collection 74, box 3, folder 1, BGCA. My discovery of the wedding ring in the archives was quite unexpected and moving; of course, I turned the item in to the BGCA.

2. "Billy Graham: Barrymore of the Bible," *Look*, 5 May 1953, 95–96; BG, "How to Be Filled with the Spirit," in *Revival in Our Time*, 113, 117.

3. Thomas M. Elliot, "Graham Crusade Tribute to Layman," *Atlanta Constitution*, 30 October 1950, collection 360, reel 3, BGCA; Hoch, "Grim Billy Graham, Man of Many Contradictions," *Detroit News*, 47, 25 September 1953, collection 360, reel 5, BGCA. See also "Christianity Can Stop Reds Billy Graham Declares Here," *Pittsburgh Sun-Telegraph*, 7 September 1952, 3, collection 360, reel 5, BGCA; Martin, *Prophet with Honor*, 133.

4. Mitchell, *God in the Garden*, 193.

5. "Evangelist Opens Revival Crusade," *Los Angeles Times*, 26 September 1949, 24; BG, "We Need Revival," in *Revival in Our Time*, 70. Graham held seven earlier crusades in Grand Rapids, Mich. (1947), Charlotte, N.C. (1947), Augusta, Ga. (1948), Modesto, Calif. (1948), Miami, Fla. (1949), Baltimore, Md. (1949), and Altoona, Pa. (1949). He began his first large-scale Youth for Christ work in 1944 in Chicago, followed by several other events in the United States and two tours of Great Britain.

6. "Huge Audience Hears Evangelist Tell of the Sins of the World," *Augusta Herald*, 11 October 1948, collection 360, reel 1, BGCA. For example, see Mr. and Mrs. L. N. Hopkins to BG, n.d., collection 74, box 3, folder 1, BGCA. For additional letters of appreciation from this period, see collection 74, box 3, folder 1, which covers the years 1948 through 1950.

7. "Bowron Backs Young Evangelist's Revivals," *Los Angeles Times*, 25 September 1959, 2.

8. Martin, *Prophet with Honor*, 116.

9. Dorothy C. Haskin, "Spiritual Awakening in California," *Moody Monthly*, January 1950, 328–29; "Greater L.A.'s Greatest Revival Continues!" *Daily News*, 26 October 1949, 1 November 1949, collection 360, reel 1, BGCA. See also Martin, *Prophet with Honor*, 113–18.

10. "A New Evangelist Arises," *Life*, 21 November 1949, 97–98, 100; "Sickle for the Harvest," *Time*, 14 November 1949, 46.

11. Mel Larson, "Tasting Revival—at Los Angeles," in Billy Graham and others, *Revival in Our Time*, 13, 17; "Tent Revival Ends after Eight Weeks," *Los Angeles Times*, 21 November 1949, 20.

12. See, for example, BG, "The Home God Honors," "How to Be Filled with the Spirit," "Prepare to Meet Thy God," "The Resurrection of Jesus Christ," and "Judgment," in *Revival in Our Time*, 89–166; BG, "Sin," sermon delivered 20 October 1949, tape T211, collection 26, BGCA.

13. BG, "We Need Revival," in *Revival in Our Time*, 72–74; BG, "The Greatest Sin a Man Can Commit," sermon delivered 29 September 1949, tape T188, collection 26, BGCA; "That Old-Time Religion Goes Modern," *Daily News*, 30 September 1949, 3, collection 360, reel 1, BGCA.

14. BG, "Resurrection of Jesus Christ," 149–50; BG, "Judgment," 161; Haskin, "Spiritual Awakening in California," 328.

15. Martin, *Prophet with Honor*, 118. In 1949, Edwards and his famous sermon had received attention because of Perry Miller's biography, *Jonathan Edwards*. See also "The Sense of the Heart," *Time*, 26 December 1949, 54–55.

16. BG, "Sinners in the Hands of an Angry God," tape T234, collection 26, BGCA.

17. This analysis is expanded upon in my online essay featured on the Jonathan Edwards Center at Yale University Web site. See Andrew S. Finstuen "'Sinners in the Hands of an Angry God' Reprised: Billy Graham and the Los Angeles Crusade of 1949," http://edwards.yale.edu/files/finstuen-graham.pdf.

18. Cornwell, *Ruth, a Portrait*, 107. Cornwell calls Graham's rendition a "disaster." But it is unclear just how disastrous it was; the only direct recollection of the event that Cornwell reproduces is Ruth Graham's statement that her husband learned never to "replace the Bible with another text."

19. Martin, *Prophet with Honor*, 92, 136.

20. Hoch, "Grim Billy Graham, Man of Many Contradictions," 47; Lewis W. Gillenson, "God's Ball of Fire," *Look*, 18 July 1950, 27, 28; "Dynamic Billy Graham Heads War on Sin," *Sunday Oregonian Magazine*, 1950, collection 360, reel 3, BGCA; "Billy Graham Lists City's 5 Worst Sins," *Pittsburgh Sun-Telegraph*, 14 September 1952, 28, collection 360, reel 5, BGCA.

21. "Evil and Sinful Hub Flayed by Evangelist," *Record*, 10 January 1950, collection 360, reel 1, BGCA; E. A. Batchelor Jr., "Graham in City to Fight Devil," *Detroit Times*, 27 September 1953, 1, collection 360, reel 5, BGCA.

22. "Billy in New York," *Newsweek*, 27 December 1954, 37; "Billy Graham Wins 300 Converts," unidentified newspaper, 7 April 1950, collection 360, reel 1, BGCA; "The New Evangelist," *Time*, 25 October 1954, 60; "Watered-Down Christianity Assailed by Billy Graham," *Detroit News*, 22 October 1953, 53, collection 360, reel 5, BGCA.

23. "The New Evangelist," *Time*, 25 October 1954, 54; James Bassett, "Billy Graham Finds Crowds and Strange Company in L.A.," *Mirror*, 18 September 1951, 5, 20, collection 360, reel 3, BGCA; Jay Edgerton, "A New 'Billy' Spurs Religious Revivalism Boom," *Des Moines Sunday Register*, 22 April 1950, 12-G, collection 360, reel 1, BGCA; Hoke, "Harvesting at the Revival—in Columbia," 48–49, collection 360, reel 1, BGCA.

24. "Post Lauded for Revival Stories," *Boston Post*, 7 January 1950, 12, collection 360, reel 1, BGCA; "Letters Pour in from Admirers of the Rev. Billy Graham Praising Paper for Fine Coverage," *Boston Post*, 15 January 1950, collection 360, reel 1, BGCA; letters to the editor, *Detroit Times*, 10 October 1953, 6, collection 360, reel 5, BGCA.

25. "Two Bigs for Boston," *Zion's Herald*, 25 January 1950, 7; "Readers Write," *Zion's Herald*, 15 February 1950, 3; 8 March 1950, 2; 12 April 1950, 2; 19 April 1950, 2; 26 April 1950, 2; 3 May 1950, 2.

26. William E. McElwain, "Pittsburgh Fails to Repent, Says Billy Graham," *Pittsburgh Sun-Telegraph*, 4 October 1952, collection 360, reel 5, BGCA; "Not Proud, Billy Answers Bishop," *Pittsburgh Sun-Telegraph*, 6 October 1952, collection 360, reel 5, BGCA; "Bishop Pardue Assailed for 'Scolding' Graham," *Pittsburgh Sun-Telegraph*, 7 October 1952, collection 360, reel 5, BGCA. The bishop and Graham publicly reconciled and parted friends.

27. Robert Ellwood makes a similar point about Graham and Baptist rhetoric in his *Fifties Spiritual Marketplace*, 48.

28. "Prayer! Prayer! Prayer!" *Newsweek*, 6 September 1954, 46.

29. The ambivalent to negative results of the surveys in the *Century* was a function of its liberal bias, just as the overwhelming support of Graham crusades in such sympathetic periodicals as the *Southern Presbyterian Journal* depended on their conservative bias. See Arthur Lester Frederick, "Billy Graham's Seattle Campaign," *Christian Century*, 23 April 1952, 494–96; Frank Fitt, "In the Wake of Billy Graham," *Christian Century*, 1 December 1954, 1458–59; "The Campaigns," *Southern Presbyterian Journal*, 13 August 1952, 9–13; H. B. Dendy, "A Man with God's Message," *Southern Presbyterian Journal*, 13 August 1952, 3. Another *Century* article from 1952 further confused the evidence of pastoral support by reporting that after strong initial resistance among ministers in Pittsburgh, support for Graham had dramatically increased by the end of the campaign. See "The Clergy and Billy Graham," *Christian Century*, 15 October 1952, 1202.

30. Correspondence, *Christian Century*, 22 December 1954, 1556.

31. Fitt, "In the Wake of Billy Graham," 1459.

32. "The New Evangelist," *Time*, 25 October 1954, 54–56, 58–60; "Billy Graham: Young Thunderer of Revival," *Newsweek*, 1 February 1954, 42–46; "Personality," *Time*, 17 November 1952, 47.

33. Mitchell, *God in the Garden*, 33; On Billy Graham the fighter, see "Next-to-Last Stand, Maybe," *New Yorker*, 16 April 1955, 90. Graham the fighter attended one of Graham the evangelist's early crusade services: "16,500 Hear Graham Extol Moral Law," *New York Times*, 28 May 1957, 26.

34. Mitchell, *God in the Garden*, 23–25.

35. Ibid., 9, 52–53; Archer Speers, "Billy Graham's 'Invasion,'" *Newsweek*, 20 May 1957, 66; "Text of Billy Graham's Sermon Opening His Crusade in Madison Square Garden," *New York Times*, 16 May 1957, 22.

36. "Billy Graham's Target," *Newsweek*, 26 August 1957, 72; Mitchell, *God in the Garden*, 52, 9–10, 32; Martin, *Prophet with Honor*, 235–36; Jerrold Schecter and James Wallace, "Billy Graham Preaches to Wall Streeters but Not of Finance," *Wall Street Journal*, 11 July 1957, 1; "Graham Exhorts Wall St. Throng," *New York Times*, 11 July 1957, 27. The *Journal* estimated the crowd at between seventy-five hundred and twenty thousand. The *Times* reported that a Graham spokesperson thought between ten thousand and twelve thousand attended, but the *Times* also noted a policeman's estimate of thirty thousand. I chose the high end of the *Journal's* estimate, roughly splitting the difference between Graham's spokesperson and the New York police officer.

37. "What Did Graham Say?" *Moody Monthly*, September 1957, 8; Martin, *Prophet with Honor*, 233; Mitchell, *God in the Garden*, 132–33, 37, 175; "Graham Diagnoses Man," *New York Times*, 30 June 1957, 56; "16,500 Hear Graham on Power of Satan," *New York Times*, 19 June 1957, 71; "Graham Points to Sin," *New York Times*, 28 June 1957, 35; "Graham Calls Home Society's Basic Unit," *New York Times*, 27 May 1957, 33.

38. Mitchell, *God in the Garden*, 175, 157, 133; Schecter and Wallace, "Billy Graham Preaches to Wall Streeters but Not of Finance," 1; Stanley Rowland, "City Idolatrous Graham Asserts," *New York Times*, 19 May 1957, 53.

39. BG, "The Offense of the Cross," in Ferm, *Persuaded to Live*, 12–22.

40. "Billy Graham's Fizzle," *Nation*, 8 February 1958, 110–11; George Dugan, "Graham's Impact Termed Fleeting," *New York Times*, 26 January 1958, 1, 61; "Dedicated Deciders in Billy Graham Crusade," *Life*, 1 July 1957, 87; "Crusade Windup," *Time*, 9 September 1957, 60; Martin, *Prophet with Honor*, 237–38.

41. "Dedicated Deciders in Billy Graham Crusade," *Life*, 1 July 1957, 87; "Graham Figures Given," *New York Times*, 1 August 1957, 17.

42. Ferm, *They Met God at the New York Crusade*, 4.

43. "Graham Satisfied over City Crusade," *New York Times*, 28 January 1958, 23.

44. "Class for Counselors," David M. Howard notebook, collection 74, box 1, folder 26, BGCA. Howard's copy of the guidelines for counselors was for the crusade in Mexico in early February 1958. An almost identical pamphlet was in "Chicago Procedure Book," collection 16, BGCA.

45. Mitchell, *God in the Garden*, 142–43; "My Conversion Story," Robert O. Ferm Papers, collection 19, box 20, folder 3, BGCA.

46. "My Conversion Story," Ferm papers, collection 19, boxes 20–23, BGCA, contains the majority of conversion responses.

47. Mitchell, *God in the Garden*, 18, 67–70, 124, 125, 146–52; Aubrey Leon Morris, "A Study of Psychological Factors in the Evangelistic Preaching of Billy Graham," 336–37; Ferm, *Persuaded to Live*, chaps. 2–11; Ferm, *They Met God in New York*, chaps. 2–6.

48. "My Conversion Story," Ferm papers, collection 19, box 20, folders 8 and 10, BGCA. Folder 8 contains California testimonies, while folder 10 is for Connecticut. The individuals, however, state that they were converted at New York City. The Billy Graham Evangelistic Association does not allow the use of names when quoting these conversion stories.

49. Mitchell, *God in the Garden*, 134.

50. Ferm, "My Conversion Story," Ferm papers, collection 19, box 20, folder 21, BGCA. The folders are organized alphabetically by state. I selected the following sample for thorough review: Alabama, Alaska, Arizona, California, Colorado, Connecticut, Delaware, Florida, New York.

51. Quoted in Martin, *Prophet with Honor*, 238.

52. Martin, *Prophet with Honor*, 232. "Crusade's Impact," *Time*, 8 July 1957, 58.

53. Ibid., 239–41.

54. "Billy Graham's Finale," *Newsweek*, 22 July 1957, 57; Martin, *Prophet with Honor*, 234; Mitchell, *God in the Garden*, 111–12, 115; "Sermon by Graham Relayed in Spanish," *New York Times*, 14 July 1957, 87.

55. Martin, *Prophet with Honor*, 234–35.

56. "Martin Luther King, Jr., Prays Invocation," 18 July 1957, tape T495, collection 26, BGCA.

57. "Crusades Impact," *Time*, 8 July 1957, 57; Martin, *Prophet with Honor*, 234–35.

58. "The Night God Filled Yankee Stadium," *Moody Monthly*, September 1957, 8; Martin, *Prophet with Honor*, 224, 284.

59. BG, *World Aflame*, 45, chap. 3.

60. Martin, *Prophet with Honor*, 138; J. D. Grey, "Spiritual Guidance," *Christianity Today*, 27 March 1961, 34. See also Lippy, "Billy Graham's 'My Answer,'" 27–34.

61. BG, *My Answer*, 9–10; Pollock, *Billy Graham*, 149–50.

62. BG, My Answer, 7 December 1960, collection 19, box 8, folder 5, BGCA. He offered something like a test for a questioner who wanted to know "whether we are Christian or not?" According to Graham, if one read the Bible regularly, recognized one's wrongdoing and asked forgiveness, tithed, felt comfortable with other Christians, evangelized naturally, loved one's enemies, and remained faithful to the church, then one was probably a Christian. He added that he had applied these standards in his own life and that he hoped his correspondent could score 100 percent.

63. BG, *My Answer*, 9–10.

64. Ibid., 209. See also ibid., 9, 115.

65. For example, in the early 1960s, the column featured questions about makeup and Christmas trees. The column also focused in the late 1950s and early 1960s on such particular sins such as hate, alcohol, and sex and on questions of sin as punishment. See collection 19, box 8, folders 1, 2, and 4, BGCA.

66. See collection 19, box 8, folders 1–5, BGCA. These folders contain collections of correspondence sent by laypeople in response to My Answer.

67. BG, *My Answer*, 39. Graham's replies tended to favor men over women, irrespective of the sex of the adulterer.

68. BG, My Answer, *Tampa Tribune*, 13 November 1961, collection 19, box 8, folder 1, BGCA.

69. Jennie Gourley to Billy Graham Evangelistic Association, 13 November 1961, collection 19, box 8, folder 1, BGCA [Florida]; D. S. to BG, n.d., collection 19, box 8, folder 1, BGCA.

70. BG, *My Answer*, 126, 29, 167, 192, 199, 221, 223.

71. Mrs. D. W. Rhees to BG, 10 May 1961, collection 19, box 8, folder 5, BGCA [Connecticut]; Olga Nygren to BG, 11 November 1961, collection 19, box 8, folder 1, BGCA [Washington State]; Mary M. to BG, 17 December 1961, collection 19, box 8, folder 1, BGCA [Pennsylvania]. Another moving letter came from a woman who wished that Graham would recommend Alcoholics Anonymous rather than rely solely on Christian answers to the alcohol issue. See Mrs. Carl Williams to BG, May 1962, collection 19, box 8, folder 2, BGCA [Arkansas].

72. Horace J. Fenton to BG, 12 April 1962, collection 19, box 8, folder 5, BGCA [Florida]. For similar objections, see Everett E. Smith, n.d., collection 19, box 8, folder 5, BGCA [Tennessee]; Perry C. Long to BG, 19 November 1961, collection 19, box 8, folder 1, BGCA. Folder 1 contains several other protests against Graham's definitive statements about heaven.

73. BG, *My Answer*, 111, 112, 115, 119, 120, 122, 176. For additional examples of pointed questions about the trials of Christian life, see ibid., 113, 117, 125, 136, 141, 143, 151, 210, 213.

74. BG, *My Answer*, 113, 115, 116.

75. Allen Meger to BG, 7 September 1961, collection 19, box 8, folder 1, BGCA [Missouri]; Mrs. W. F. Billings to BG, 13 March 1962, collection 19, box 8, folder 2, BGCA [Texas]; Marjorie Kromholtz to BG, 21 May 1960, collection 19, box 8, folder 5, BGCA [Washington State]. Kromholtz's opinions were echoed by another layperson

who found Graham's view of sin too forgiving: A. V. MacPherson to BG, 17 May 1960, collection 19, box 8, folder 5, BGCA [California].

76. Mrs. T. W. W. to BG, 28 October 1964, collection 19, box 8, folder 3, BGCA [California].

77. BG, *My Answer*, 125, 137.

78. Ibid., 204.

79. Ibid., 228. For example, late in the book, Graham quoted I John 1:8: "If we say that we have no sin, we deceive ourselves, and the truth is not in us." But he continued the column, proclaiming that confession of that sin restores human fellowship with God. Many Christians lack this fellowship; but, he added, "there is no joy or ecstasy quite like that of daily fellowship with God. Try it!"

80. Martin, *Prophet with Honor*, 152; "The New Evangelist," *Time*, 25 October 1954, 55. This naïveté played right into the hands of his cynical critics. In 1957, William G. McLoughlin, who later made a career of studying revivalism, wrote a cover story for the *Nation* titled "Billy Graham: In Business with the Lord," *Nation*, 11 May 1957, 403–10. See also BG, "What Is Conversion?" in Ferm, *They Met God at the New York Crusade*, 9; "Billy Graham Answers His Critics," *Look*, 7 February 1956, 49, 50.

81. BG, *World Aflame*, 132.

82. *Ivy* magazine and the *Yale Daily News*, quoted in L. David Cowie, "Cynic, Sophisticate, or Seeker?" *Christianity Today*, 8 July 1957, 25; "The Gospel at Harvard," *Christianity Today*, 27 April 1962, 32; "Something to Wave a Flag About," *Christianity Today*, 13 March 1964, 565–66; "Billy Graham at Yale," *Newsweek*, 25 February 1957, 68.

83. Bennett, "Billy Graham at Union," 9–14; John C. Bennett, "Graham and Segregation," *Christianity and Crisis*, 29 October 1956, 142–43.

84. Donald Meyer, "Billy Graham—and Success," *New Republic*, 22 August 1955, 8–10.

85. Henry P. Van Dusen, "Billy Graham," *Christianity and Crisis*, 2 April 1956, 40.

86. Johannes Ringstad to RN, 24 April 1956, collection 10, RN papers. See also Correspondence, *Christian Century*, 11 July 1956, 830–33, and 29 August 1956, 999.

87. Paul E. Smith to RN, 12 April 1956, collection 11, RN papers.

88. E. G. Homrighausen, "Billy Graham and the Protestant Predicament," *Christian Century*, 18 July 1956, 848–49.

89. Correspondence, *Christian Century*, 11 July 1956, 830–31, 29 August 1956, 999, and 5 September 1956, 1027.

90. "Whose Billy Graham?" *Christian Century*, 21 November 1956, 1350–52; "In the Garden," *Christian Century*, 15 May 1957, 614–15; "Mass Conversions" *Christian Century*, 29 May 1957, 677–79; "Fundamentalist Revival," *Christian Century*, 19 June 1957, 749–51; "The Long Anticlimax," *Christian Century*, 7 August 1957; Correspondence, *Christian Century*, 10 July 1957, 846; Correspondence, *Christian Century*, 17 July 1957, 871.

91. Correspondence, *Christian Century*, 4 September 1957, 1044. See also Correspondence, *Christian Century*, 19 December 1956, 1483–84; 16 January 1957, 81; 27 February 1957, 270; 5 June 1957, 711–12; 7 August 1957, 944; 14 August 1957, 970.

CHAPTER 6

1. The sermon appears in chap. 19 of *Shaking of the Foundations*.

2. H. G. to PT, 15 January 1964, PT papers. As in this example, I will identify writers of sensitive letters only by their initials.

3. "A Protestant Message," *Newsweek*, 2 May 1955, 90.

4. Quoted in Williams, *Harvard Divinity School*, 110.

5. PT, *On the Boundary*, 48.

6. PT, "The Lost Dimension in Religion," *Saturday Evening Post*, 14 June 1958, 29, 76, 78–79.

7. John Kobler to PT, 2 November 1957, PT papers. See the attached "An Introduction to a Series of Articles to Be Published by the Saturday Evening Post."

8. Grace Leonard (Cali) to John Kobler, 26 June 1958, PT papers. See also Barclay D. Johnson, "How Americans Respond to Tillich." This undergraduate thesis is a serviceable compilation of the letters generated by the article, but in contrast to the present study, Johnson interprets them one-dimensionally, as emotional reactions to Tillich's piece.

9. Margaret Lyons to PT, 26 February 1959, PT papers [Massachusetts]; Eleanor Stevens to PT, 14 March 1959, PT papers [New Jersey]; Richard T. to PT, 8 July 1958, PT papers; Margaret Marshall to PT, n.d., PT papers [Pennsylvania]; Richard Thruelsen to PT, 8 July 1958, PT papers.

10. Mrs. Lennie Wyatt to PT, 22 June 1958, PT papers [Missouri]; Gary Weyer to PT, 28 September 1965, PT papers; Theodor Slen to PT, 5 March 1964, PT papers [Minnesota]; Mrs. N. Gordon Le Bert to PT, 30 September 1958, PT papers [Missouri].

11. Stewart Hurlburt to PT, 14 June 1958, PT papers [Montana].

12. PT, "Lost Dimension in Religion," 29, 76, 78–79. See also PT, "Vertical and Horizontal Thinking," 23.

13. PT, "Lost Dimension in Religion," 78.

14. Ibid., 79.

15. Mrs. N. Gordon Le Bert to PT, 30 September 1958, PT papers [Missouri]; PT to Mrs. N. Gordon Le Bert, 15 October 1958, PT papers.

16. PT, "Lost Dimension in Religion," 78.

17. Tillich elaborates on this notion in his *Theology of Culture* (1959).

18. Arthur Slonaker to PT, 18 June 1958, PT papers [West Virginia]. See also Vernelle Robertson to PT, March 1959, PT papers [Washington State]; Burrel Prince to PT, 15 July 1958, PT papers [Ohio]; Elsie Egan to PT, 10 June 1958, PT papers; Jane Bandy to PT, n.d., PT papers [Kansas]; Joseph Anderson to PT, 24 June 1958, PT papers [Michigan]. Like the Methodist Slonaker, these letters explicitly discuss sin, if syncretistically and colorfully, and convey a firm belief in the concept.

19. Helen Monson to PT, 24 July 1958, PT papers [Washington State].

20. Ibid. Tillich wrote his response on the bottom of Mrs. Monson's letter, and his secretary, Grace Leonard, transcribed it.

21. A. U. Davidson to Ben Hibbs, 16 June 1958, PT papers. Hibbs was the editor of the *Saturday Evening Post*. See William Carson Lantz (Fuller Theological Seminary) and S. E. Anderson (Northern Baptist Theological Seminary) in the *Post*'s letters to the

editor page, *Saturday Evening Post*, 19 July 1958, 4. See also "The Lost Dimension of Depth," *Christianity Today*, 21 July 1958, 20–21; David H. Freeman, "Tillich's Doctrine of Revelation," *Christianity Today*, 21 July 1958, 12–15; "Adventure in Religion," *Saturday Evening Post*, 19 July 1958, 4; PT, "Lost Dimension in Religion," 79.

22. L. Nelson Bell, "A Layman and His Faith," *Christianity Today*, 21 July 1958, 35.

23. Mrs. Furgason to PT, July 1958, PT papers [Texas]; A. U. Davidson to Ben Hibbs, 16 June 1958, PT papers. See also "In Search of a Dimension," *Christianity Today*, 7 July 1958, 18–19; "The Lost Dimension of Depth," *Christianity Today*, 21 July 1958, 20–21.

24. "Eutychus and His Kin," *Christianity Today*, 1 September 1958, 25.

25. Mrs. Anderson to PT, July 1958, PT papers [Ohio].

26. Ibid.

27. "To Be or Not to Be," *Time*, 16 March 1959, 46–48, 51–52.

28. "Of Tillich & God," *Time*, 6 April 1959, 8. See also "Fireman or Arsonist?" *Time*, 30 March 1959, 2; "Of Tillich & God (Contd.)," *Time*, 13 April 1959, 6–7; "The Tillich Controversy," *Time*, 20 April 1959, 8.

29. R. B. Gordon to the editor, Time & Life Magazine, 16 March 1959, PT papers.

30. "To Be or Not to Be," *Time*, 16 March 1959, 46–52; Charles Wells, letter to the editor, *Time*, 20 April 1959, 8; Rev. Will Dowty, letter to the editor, *Time*, 6 April 1959, 8; William J. Povey Jr. to PT, 18 March 1959, PT papers.

31. Grandma Hoff to PT, 15 March 1959, PT papers [Pennsylvania]; "To Be or Not to Be," *Time*, 16 March 1959, 48.

32. Ruth Bassett to PT, 26 March 1959, PT papers [California]; Jane Cromwell to PT, 9 April 1959, PT papers [New York]; Willard Day to PT, 20 June 1959, PT papers [Virginia]; Dorothy Sjogren to PT, 25 March 1959, PT papers [Minnesota]; Mary Cousley to PT, 14 March 1959, PT papers [Illinois]; Grace Leonard to Charles Kegley, 16 March 1959, PT papers.

33. "To Be or Not to Be," *Time*, 16 March 1959, 46; Collette S. Shukers to PT, 22 March 1959, PT papers [Kansas].

34. Anne Engelhard to PT, 16 March 1959, PT papers [Virginia].

35. Grace Leonard to Anne Engelhard, 22 March 1959, PT papers.

36. Mrs. Ardie Stangland to PT, 9 May 1959, PT papers [Oregon]. Special thanks go to Christopher Stangland for granting permission to reprint his mother's letter in full.

37. PT to Phil Moeller, 1 February 1958, PT papers.

38. Carey, *Paulus Then and Now*, 53. A new edition of *The Courage to Be* was issued in 2000 by Yale University Press. Frances Witherspoon, "Our Answer Is Affirmation," *New York Herald-Tribune Book Review*, 28 December 1952, box 903A, folder 5, PT papers; "The Courage to Be," *Theology Today*, January 1955, box 903A, folder 5, PT papers. *Pastoral Psychology* selected the book as its "book of the month": "The December Selection," *Pastoral Psychology*, box 903A, folder 5, PT papers. Not all reviews were positive. The *Christian Century*, for example, ran a measured review: R. E. Gilmore, "From Anxiety to Faith," *Christian Century*, 4 March 1953, box 903A, folder 5, PT papers.

39. W. Norman Pittenger, "Courage to Be," *New Republic*, 29 December 1952, 20. See also Pittenger, "The Why of Man," *New York Times*, 4 January 1953, 10.

40. PT, *Courage to Be*, chap. 2, esp. 48, 54.

41. Ibid., 163, 90, 125, 155–56.

42. Ibid., 90.

43. Ibid., 172, 155.

44. Ibid., 172–73.

45. Ibid., 164–65, 170.

46. Ibid., 188, 161–67, 172–73.

47. Mary Baker to PT, 26 November 1963, PT papers [Illinois]. See also Daisy Akin to PT, 31 October 1963, PT papers [Texas]; PT to Daisy Akin, November 11, 1963, PT papers.

48. Carol Rice Seamons to PT, 22 October 1965, PT papers [California].

49. William Brady to PT, 11 October 1965, PT papers [Massachusetts]. For another letter frankly discussing existential estrangement, see Martin E. Fuller, 16 April 1960, PT papers [California]. Fuller held a doctorate in chemistry. Other letters of interest include Dorothy Riggle to PT, 13 November 1962, PT papers [Pennsylvania]; Lorna Wearing to PT, December 1964, PT papers; Kathy Brown to PT, October 1965, PT papers [Illinois]; Dick Colton to PT, n.d., PT papers; Anna Navarro to PT, 20 September 1965, PT papers [Florida].

50. Thomas Walmsley to PT, 21 June 1963, PT papers. Walmsley was the pastor of a Congregational Church in Minnesota. Laura Stewart authored the poem (the original version consists of four stanzas). Another lay class in Boulder, Colorado, made a study of *The Courage to Be*. PT, *Courage to Be*, 155.

51. William Savage to PT, 4 April 1960, 12 May 1960, and 25 March 1964, PT papers.

52. Untitled, 13 November 1954, box 904A, folder 11, PT papers. For additional reviews of *The Shaking of the Foundations*, *The New Being*, and *The Eternal Now*, see box 904A, folder 11; box 903B, folder 11; and box 903C, folder 21, respectively, in PT papers.

53. "The June Double-Selection," *RBC Bulletin*, June 1948, 1, box 904A, folder 11, PT papers.

54. William T. Sanders makes a similar point: "All of Tillich's sermons presuppose that the human condition is one of estrangement and suffering." Sanders, "Paul Tillich: Apologetic Preacher of the Christian Faith," 243.

55. PT, *Shaking of the Foundations*, 153.

56. PT, *New Being*, 15. I am indebted to Sanders for highlighting this passage. See "Paul Tillich: Apologetic Preacher of the Christian Faith," 240.

57. Theodore Gill, "The New Being," *Christian Century*, 12 October 1955, box 903C, folder 21, PT papers.

58. Joseph Gray to PT, 6 July 1948, PT papers [South Dakota]; Duane Murphy to PT, 10 April 1962, PT papers [California]; Robert Dwight to PT, n.d., PT papers [Oregon]; H. Norman Sibley to PT, 29 August 1948, PT papers [New York]; J. L. Sandford to PT, 10 October 1962, PT papers [Kansas]; Robert Washer to PT, 7 January 1965, PT papers [New York]; Clyde Sindy to PT, 14 January 1964, PT papers [West Virginia].

59. Stanley H. Fein to PT, 17 January 1965, PT papers [New York]; Lois Wickstrom to PT, 31 May 1963, PT papers [Illinois].

60. Helen Wallace to PT, 13 October 1961, PT papers [Ohio].

61. For a specific response on the question of sin, see Harriet Gladding to PT, 14 July 1958, PT papers [Virginia], and Evelyn Tucker to Grace Leonard, 2 February 1959, PT papers. For some letters that generally reference the impact of Tillich's theology in the writers' lives, see Lila Kuxhausen to PT, 4 December 1962, PT papers; A. Childrey, 12 May 1965, PT papers; Gray Clark, 13 September 1965, PT papers; Katherine Stevens to PT, 20 April 1965, PT papers [New Hampshire]; June Burn, n.d., PT papers [Alabama]; Gilbert Cantlin, 1 May 1964, PT papers [Ohio]; Monroe Hall to PT, 3 September 1955, PT papers [New York].

62. PT, *Dynamics of Faith*, vii.

63. PT to Melvin Arnold, 26 December 1957; M. Arnold to PT, 28 November 1961, PT papers.

64. PT, *Dynamics of Faith*, 1. See also D. Mackenzie Brown, *Ultimate Concern*, 11, 7–16.

65. PT, *Dynamics of Faith*, 12, 38. In a later text, *Ultimate Concern* (1965), he clarified this dialectic between the broad and narrow aspects of ultimate concern. He granted that artistic expression or science or some other pursuit might constitute an individual's ultimate concern, yet if nothing else but art or science was involved, the individual "approaches the borderline of idolatry." D. Mackenzie Brown, *Ultimate Concern*, 15.

66. PT, *Dynamics of Faith*, 10–12, 29, 104. See also PT, *Protestant Era*, ix–xxv; PT, "The Spirit of Protestantism," 4, box 406A, folder 19, PT papers.

67. PT, *Dynamics of Faith*, 22, 16, 29, 78–79, 100–101.

68. E. G. Homrighausen, "Dynamics of Faith," *Pastoral Psychology*, March 1957, 55–56, box 903A, folder 8, PT papers; Dave Rhoades to PT, 29 January 1958, PT papers. Rhoades was the chairman of religious emphasis week at the University of Nebraska, and he informed Tillich, "There has never been more discussion on this campus about a religious emphasis week." L. B. Smedes, "Tillich on Faith," *Christianity Today*, 16 February 1959, 4. Smedes's cordiality included the following: "The book contains a discerning analysis of the subjective aspect of faith, and much profitable criticism of man's temptation to place his faith in things less than ultimate." But, he added, "it misses being a genuine analysis of Christian faith." Kenneth S. Kantzer to Melvin Arnold, 14 May 1959, PT papers. Kantzer was the division chairman of biblical education and apologetics at Wheaton. Arnold, Tillich's editor at Harper's, forwarded Kantzer's letter to Tillich.

69. Harold Weisberg, "Bartering Truth for Salvation," *New Republic*, 1 April 1957, 21–22, box 903A, folder 8, PT papers; PT, *Dynamics of Faith*, 16. *Newsweek* provided the closest approximation of Tillich's ideas: see "Three Cheers for Doubt," *Newsweek*, 14 January 1957, 74.

70. Marjorie Eve to PT, 22 January 1965, PT papers [Indiana]; Anonymous to PT, 25 May 1965, PT papers [California]; Billy Mullins to PT, 16 February 1963, PT papers [Virginia]; Veda Day to PT, 2 September 1958, PT papers [California]; Martha Sanders to PT, n.d., PT papers [North Carolina]; William Allen to PT, 28 February 1962, PT papers [Kentucky]; Andrew Bumpas to PT, 5 January 1962, PT papers [Kansas]. Lay theologians also asked questions about *Dynamics*: see Katherine Wheless to PT, 16 March 1957 [Louisiana]; Mrs. S. K. Eutsler to PT, 27 September 1962 [North Carolina]; Kelley Baily to PT, 15 August 1963, PT papers [Illinois].

71. Ellwood, *Fifties Spiritual Marketplace*, 48–49.

72. W. R. MacIlrath to PT, 21 June 1958, PT papers [Washington, D.C.].

73. Mrs. Geri Cranford to PT, 1964, PT papers [North Carolina].

74. PT, *Dynamics of Faith*, 105.

75. PT, *Dynamics of Faith*, 104; Mrs. Geri Cranford to PT, 1964, PT papers; PT to Geri Cranford, 8 December 1964, PT papers.

76. Pauck and Pauck, *Paul Tillich*, 34–35; Lyons, *Intellectual Legacy of Paul Tillich*, 16.

77. "The New Being," *Time*, 10 June 1957, 51–52 See also "Tillich's Soteriology," *Christianity Today*, 22 July 1957, 34.

78. Darrel McCorkell to PT, 19 January 1960, PT papers [California].

79. Robert E. Chiles to PT, 21 May 1958, PT papers [Ohio]; Robert E. Chiles, ed., "A Glossary of Tillich Terms," *Theology Today*, April 1960, 77–89. An anonymous reader alerted me to the fact that Chiles went on to publish *Theological Transition in American Methodism, 1790–1935* (New York: Abingdon, 1965), in which he criticized Methodists for their inattention to the doctrine of original sin. For another instance of a congregation's study of Tillich's *Systematic Theology*, see W. James Westhafer to PT, 6 April 1960, PT papers [Ohio].

80. Cornelius R. Loew, 19 August 1946, PT papers [Michigan]; Ralph S. Robinson to PT, 13 March 1952, PT papers [Pennsylvania]; "Rev. Mr. Cole Will Review Theology Book by Tillich," *Vindicator*, 9 February 1952, box 902A, folder 20, PT papers. The article reported that this monthly meeting of clergy would focus on *Systematic Theology*, vol. 1; Robert E. Chiles to PT, 21 May 1958, PT papers [Ohio].

81. Paul W. Yinger to PT, 6 August 1965, PT papers [California].

82. Robert L. Johnson to PT, 9 October 1958, PT papers [North Carolina].

83. "Earl Series—Evening Lecturer," *Oakland Tribune*, 20 February 1963, 14, box 902C, folder 31, PT papers; Tillich and Foster, *Relevance and Irrelevance of the Christian Message*.

84. "Dr. Tillich Starts Week's Program," *Daily Emerald*, 23 January 1956, 1, 8, box 902B, folder 24, PT papers.

85. Mary Etta Talarico, "Tillich Addresses Overflow Audience Emphasizing Being, Non-being Relation," *Skyscraper*, 25 November 1964, 1, box 902C, folder 32, PT papers. Interested institutions ranged from Princeton Theological Seminary to the University of Oklahoma Medical School, the former seeking Tillich's wisdom on "Man's Agony in Our Time," and the latter inviting "A Dialogue with Paul Tillich on the Nature and Destiny of Man." Tillich also contributed, for example, to the University of Michigan's 1964 forum on "Modern Man's Images and His Search for Identity." See Elmer Homrighausen to PT, 19 July 1959, PT papers; Robert H. Havert to PT, 11 August 1964, PT papers. See also Paul Tillich, "Freedom and Destiny," an address given at Case Institute of Technology, Cleveland, Ohio, 15 October 1959, box 405A, PT papers. For additional examples of campus interest in Tillich's views of the human condition, see boxes 902B and 902C, PT papers.

86. See, for example, the following reports from his visits to Cornell University in 1958 and 1962: C. Michael Curtis, "Tillich Lectures Stir Record Interest on Hill," *Ithaca Journal*, 16 May 1958, 1–2, box 902B, folder 26, PT papers; Ernest Werner, "Challenge of Evil Everywhere: Tillich," *Ithaca Journal*, 14 April 1962, box 902C, folder 30, PT papers.

87. John Carnes to PT, 19 November 1962, PT papers; Eugene H. Wilson to PT, 30 November 1962, PT papers. For another example of a congregational visit, see "Gilbert Moore, "Christian Message Holds Final Answer," *Galesburg Register-Mail*, 6 May 1959, box 902B, folder 27, PT papers. This article records that Tillich, while at Knox College in Illinois, spoke at the nearby Central Congregational Church.

88. Malcolm Correll to PT, 19 October 1962, and 26 November 1962, PT papers.

89. Walter Lehmann to PT, 19 May 1965, PT papers.

90. Max Daskam to PT, 14 September 1951, 6 January 1956, 3 November 1958, and 21 March 1962, PT papers. For his part, Tillich expressed his gratitude at the opportunity to preach at Germantown, writing to Daskam in 1959 that he felt "a little bit like a member of your congregation." See PT to Max Daskam, 9 February 1959, PT papers.

91. Tillich met with eager and appreciative congregations at Bruton Parish Church, Williamsburg, Virginia (see Cotesworth Lewis to PT, 6 January 1957, PT papers); First Presbyterian Church, New Orleans, Louisiana, 7 April 1963; an unnamed church in New Orleans, in late April 1965 (see Lee S. Weaver to PT, 21 April 1965, PT papers); Fall River Ministerial Association, Fall River, Massachusetts, 14 October 1959 (see "Doctrine of Christ Topic of Professor's Talk," *Fall River Herald-News*, box 902B, folder 27, PT papers); Waiokeola Congregational Church, Honolulu, Hawaii (Teruo Kawata to PT, 5 February 1965, PT papers); and Auburndale Congregational Church, Auburndale, Massachusetts (Eugene Meyer to PT, 3 November 1958, PT papers). See also box 802D, folder 66, PT papers, for copies of Tillich's schedule in the late 1950s and early 1960s. The list of congregations that invited Tillich to preach is quite large and geographically and denominationally diverse. For example, requests came from First Baptist Church in America, Providence, Rhode Island; First Methodist Church, Philadelphia, Pennsylvania; First Plymouth Congregational Church, Lincoln, Nebraska; First Presbyterian Church, Auburn, Alabama; and First Baptist of Iowa City, Iowa City, Iowa.

92. Dody Zachmann to PT, n.d., PT papers [Ohio]. Zachmann likely wrote to Tillich sometime in the spring of 1959, as her letter mentions Tillich's 16 March 1959 *Time* cover appearance. For an archetypal male lay theologian, see Billy Mullins to PT, 16 February 1963, PT papers [Virginia]. Denominationally and geographically, Mullins resided outside the northeastern elite circles that Tillich supposedly ministered to. In regard to education, he explained, "I ain't got no education." Yet he had read four of Tillich's books and one volume of commentary regarding Tillich's theology. Reinhold Niebuhr, Søren Kierkegaard, and Friedrich Nietzsche rounded out his list of favorite thinkers. Mullins eagerly told of his educated friends who could not follow Tillich, including one religious professor who walked out of Tillich's Terry Lectures at Yale (what would later become *The Courage to Be*).

93. Zachmann to PT, n.d., PT papers.

94. Zachmann to PT, n.d., PT papers. On Tillich's concern with accessible language, see Pauck and Pauck, *Paul Tillich*, 227–32.

95. R. E. Bradstrum Jr. to PT, 19 October 1965, PT papers; "Revolution in Religion," *Chicago Tribune*, 7 November 1965, 14.

96. PT, "Courage and a Dynamic Faith," 194–98. Essays by Billy Graham and Norman Vincent Peale were also included in *Faith Is a Star*.

97. "Only in This Country," *Time*, 17 May 1963, 59–70; Henry Luce to PT, 26 April 1963, PT papers. Tillich's biographers, Wilhelm Pauck and Marion Pauck, use this occasion to speculate that Tillich began to believe in his fame, "glancing Narcissus-like at his own image." Pauck and Pauck, *Paul Tillich*, 275–76. Several of Tillich's contemporaries, including Tillich's dean at the University of Chicago Divinity School, Jerald Brauer, dispute the Paucks' account on this matter. See Brauer, "Tillich at Chicago," 8.

98. "Only in This Country," *Time*, 17 May 1963, 59–70; [Whittaker Chambers], "Faith for a Lenten Age," *Time*, 8 March 1948, 70–76.

99. PT to Donna Petrie, 25 June 1965, PT papers.

100. Ibid.

CONCLUSION

1. The phrase "lived theology" has also spawned the Project on Lived Theology at the University of Virginia. More information about this project can be found at http://livedtheology.org/wkgp—seminar.htm.

2. Gilkey, *On Niebuhr* (2001); Sifton, *Serenity Prayer* (2003); Halliwell, *Constant Dialogue* (2005).

3. Arthur Schlesinger Jr., "Forgetting Reinhold Niebuhr," *New York Times Book Review*, 18 September 2005, http://www.nytimes.com/2005/09/18/books/review/18 schlesinger.html?—r=1&scp=1&sq=%22forgetting%20reinhold%20niebuhr%22&st= cse; Martin Marty "Recalling Reinhold Niebuhr," *Sightings*, 1 December 2003, available online at http://marty-center.uchicago.edu/sightings. Since 2006, David Brooks has commented on Niebuhr in his column at least a half dozen times. For example, he advised all college freshmen to begin their education by reading Niebuhr: "Harvard Bound? Chin Up," *New York Times*, 2 March 2006, 27. For an excellent review of this twenty-first-century Niebuhr phenomenon, see Paul Elie, "A Man for All Reasons," *Atlantic Monthly*, November 2007. Stanley Hauerwas's criticisms of Niebuhr and Robin Lovin's ethical study of him have kept his thought alive in theological circles: Hauerwas, *With the Grain of the Universe*; Lovin, *Reinhold Niebuhr and Christian Realism*. Lovin is also an instrumental figure in the Niebuhr Society, http://www.niebuhrsociety.org, which, like the North American Paul Tillich Society, holds sessions at the American Academy of Religion's annual conference.

4. Giardina, *Saints and Villians*; Ben Brantley, "The Eternal Vaudeville of the Spiritual Mind," *New York Times*, 6 June 2007.

5. Searching online, I discovered Tillich's works featured in courses at Valparaiso University in Indiana, Princeton University Seminary in New Jersey, and Luther Seminary in Minnesota. At my home institution, my colleague Dan Peterson has offered a course dedicated entirely to Tillich's thought.

6. Bulman and Parrella, *Religion in the New Millennium: Theology in the Spirit of Paul Tillich*; Cooper, *Paul Tillich and Psychology*; Dourly, *Paul Tillich, Carl Jung, and the Recovery of Religion*.

7. Lisa Miller and Richard Wolffe, "Finding His Faith," *Newsweek*, 12 July 2008, 29.

8. Jon Meacham, "Pilgrim's Progress," *Newsweek*, 14 August 2006; Nancy Gibbs and Michael Duffy, "Pastor in Chief," *Time*, 9 August 2007.

9. Michael G. Long has been the scholarly voice most outspokenly critical, at times

irresponsibly so, with respect to Graham's career. See p. 208 n.57. Long has provided a more balanced treatment of Graham in his edited collection, *The Legacy of Billy Graham*. Other new projects include Aikman, *Billy Graham: His Life and Influence*; Gibbs and Duffy, *Preacher and the Presidents*; and Steven Miller, *Billy Graham and the Rise of the Republican South*. Grant Wacker of Duke Divinity School is currently at work on a book about the Graham phenomenon in the second half of the twentieth century.

10. David Chappell makes this point carefully and, to my mind, successfully in his *Stone of Hope*, especially page 185.

11. For an excellent history of the doctrine of original sin, see Jacobs, *Original Sin*. Among those who have continued to emphasize the doctrine's importance after Niebuhr, Graham, and Tillich are Karl Menninger, Martin Marty, Stanley Hauerwas, Robert Wilken, Theodore Hesburgh, George Marsden, and David Brooks.

12. Updike, *More Matter*, 852.

13. Updike, *Rabbit, Run*, 141–43.

BIBLIOGRAPHY

PRIMARY SOURCES

Archives

Billy Graham Papers, Archives of the Billy Graham Center, Wheaton, Ill.
Reinhold Niebuhr Papers, Collections of the Manuscript Division, Library of
 Congress, Washington, D.C.
Paul Tillich Papers, Andover-Harvard Theological Library, Harvard Divinity School,
 Cambridge, Mass.

Newspapers

Boston Globe	New York Times
Chicago Tribune	Wall Street Journal
Los Angeles Times	Washington Post

Periodicals

Atlantic Monthly	Outlook
Christian Century	Presbyterian Life
Christian Herald	Pulpit Digest
Christianity Today	Reader's Digest
Life	Reporter
Look	Saturday Review
McCall's	Saturday Evening Post
New Republic	Time
Newsweek	Zion's Herald
New Yorker	

Books and Articles

Ahlstrom, Sydney E. "Continental Influence on American Christian Thought since
 World War I." *Church History* 37 (September 1958): 256–72.
——, ed. *Theology in America: The Major Protestant Voices from the Puritans to Neo-
 Orthodoxy.* Indianapolis, Ind.: Bobbs-Merrill, 1967.
Arendt, Hannah. *Eichmann in Jerusalem: A Report on the Banality of Evil.* New York:
 Viking, 1963.
——. *The Human Condition.* Chicago: University of Chicago Press, 1958.

———. *The Origins of Totalitarianism*. New York: Harcourt, Brace, 1951.

Barth, Karl. *The Epistle to the Romans*. Translated by Edwyn C. Hoskyns. 1933. Reprint, London: Oxford University Press, 1972.

Bennett, John C. "Billy Graham at Union." *Union Seminary Quarterly Review* 9 (May 1954): 9–14.

Berger, Peter L. *The Noise of Solemn Assemblies: Christian Commitment and the Religious Establishment in America*. Garden City, N.Y.: Doubleday, 1961.

Bingham, June. *Courage to Change: An Introduction to the Life and Thought of Reinhold Niebuhr*. 1961. Reprint, New York: Charles Scribner's Sons, 1972.

Brooks, Cleanth. *The Hidden God*. New Haven, Conn.: Yale University Press, 1963.

Brown, D. Mackenzie. *Ultimate Concern: Tillich in Dialogue*. New York: Harper and Row, 1965.

Brown, Elijah P. *The Real Billy Sunday*. Dayton, Ohio: Otterbein, 1914.

Bursk, Edward, ed. *Business and Religion: A New Depth Dimension in Management*. New York: Harper, 1959.

Butler, G. Paul, ed. *Best Sermons: 1946 Edition*. New York: Harper and Brothers, 1948.

———. *Best Sermons: 1947–1948 Edition*. New York: Harper and Brothers, 1948.

Carnell, Edward J. *The Theology of Reinhold Niebuhr*. 1950. Reprint, Grand Rapids, Mich.: Eerdmans, 1960.

Cherbonnier, E. La B. *Hardness of Heart: A Contemporary Interpretation of the Doctrine of Sin*. Garden City, N.Y.: Doubleday, 1955.

Conklin, Groff. *The New Republic Anthology, 1915–1935*. New York: Dodge, 1936.

Eckardt, A. Roy. *The Surge of Piety in America*. New York: Association Press, 1958.

Edwards, David L., ed. *The "Honest to God" Debate: Some Reactions to the Book "Honest to God."* London: SCM Press, 1963.

Edwards, Jonathan. *The Great Christian Doctrine of Original Sin Defended*. In *The Works of Jonathan Edwards*, vol. 3, edited by Clyde A. Holbrook. New Haven, Conn.: Yale University Press, 1970.

Ferm, Robert O. *Persuaded to Live: Conversion Stories from the Billy Graham Crusades*. Westwood, N.J.: Revell, 1958.

———. *The Psychology of Christian Conversion*. Westwood, N.J.: Revell, 1959.

———. *They Met God at the New York Crusade*. Minneapolis, Minn.: Billy Graham Evangelistic Association, 1957.

Fosdick, Harry Emerson. *Christianity and Progress*. Westwood, N.J.: Revell, 1922.

———. *Riverside Sermons*. New York: Harper and Brothers, 1935.

———. *The Secret to Victorious Living: Sermons on Christianity Today*. New York: Harper and Brothers, 1934.

Friedan, Betty. *The Feminine Mystique*. New York: Dell, 1963.

Fromm, Erich. *Man for Himself: An Inquiry into the Psychology of Ethics*. New York: Holt, 1947.

Gammon, Roland, ed. *Faith Is a Star*. New York: Dutton, 1963.

Goldman, Eric. *The Crucial Decade: America, 1945–1955*. 1956. Reprint, New York: Vintage Books, 1960.

Graham, Billy. *Just as I Am: The Autobiography of Billy Graham*. San Francisco: HarperSanFrancisco; Grand Rapids, Mich.: Zondervan, 1997.

———. *My Answer.* Garden City, N.Y.: Doubleday, 1960.

———. *Peace with God.* 1953. Reprint, Old Tappan, N.J.: Spire Books, 1968.

———. *The Secret of Happiness.* New York: Doubleday, 1955.

———. *The Seven Deadly Sins.* Grand Rapids, Mich.: Zondervan, 1955.

———. *World Aflame.* 1965. Reprint, New York: Pocket Books, 1967.

Graham, Billy, and others. *Revival in Our Time.* Wheaton, Ill.: Van Kampen, 1950.

Handy, Robert T. "The American Religious Depression, 1925–1935." *Church History* 29 (March 1960): 3–16.

Harkness, Georgia. *The Dark Night of the Soul.* New York: Abingdon-Cokesbury, 1945.

———. "A Symposium on Reinhold Niebuhr's *Nature and Destiny of Man.*" *Christendom* 6 (Autumn 1941).

Herberg, Will. *Protestant, Catholic, Jew: An Essay in American Religious Sociology.* Garden City, N.Y.: Doubleday, 1955.

Hill, David. "Paul's 'Second Adam' and Tillich's Christology." *Union Seminary Quarterly Review* 21 (November 1965): 13–25.

Hiltner, Seward. *Preface to Pastoral Theology.* New York: Abingdon, 1958.

Hinkle, Gerald H. "The Layman's Call and Ministry." *Theology and Life* 1 (May 1958): 122–26.

Hofmann, Hans, ed. *Making the Ministry Relevant.* New York: Charles Scribner's Sons, 1960.

Hordern, William. *A Layman's Guide to Protestant Theology.* New York: Macmillan, 1955.

Howe, Reuel L. "Problems of Communication between Clergy and Laity." *Pastoral Psychology* 25 (December 1964): 21–26.

Hoyt, Arthur S. *The Pulpit and American Life.* New York: Macmillan, 1921.

Hutchison, John A., ed. *Christian Faith and Social Action.* New York: Charles Scribner's Sons, 1953.

James, William. *The Varieties of Religious Experience.* 1902. Reprint, New York: Penguin, 1958.

Kegley, Charles W., and Robert W. Bretall, eds. *The Theology of Paul Tillich.* 1952. Reprint, New York: Macmillan, 1961.

———. *The Theology of Reinhold Niebuhr.* New York: Macmillan, 1956.

Kierkegaard, Søren. *The Concept of Dread.* Translated by Walter Lowrie. Princeton, N.J.: Princeton University Press, 1944.

———. *The Sickness unto Death.* Translated by Walter Lowrie. Princeton, N.J.: Princeton University Press, 1941.

Komarovsky, Mirra. *Women in the Modern World: Their Education and Their Dilemmas.* Boston: Little, Brown, 1953.

Landon, Harold, ed. *Reinhold Niebuhr: A Prophetic Voice in Our Time.* 1962. Reprint, Eugene, Ore.: Wipf and Stock, 2001.

Leibrecht, Walter, ed. *Religion and Culture: Essays in Honor of Paul Tillich.* New York: Harper and Brothers, 1959.

Leiffer, Murray H. *The Layman Looks at the Minister.* New York: Abingdon-Cokesbury, 1947.

Lisansky, Edith. "The Woman Alcoholic." *Annals of the American Political and Social Sciences* 315 (March 1958): 315.

Lowrie, Walter. *Our Concern with the Theology of Crisis*. Boston: Meador, 1932.

Machen, J. Gresham. *Christianity and Liberalism*. New York: Macmillan, 1923.

——. *The Christian View of Man*. New York: Macmillan, 1937.

Marty, Martin. *The New Shape of American Religion*. New York: Harper and Brothers, 1959.

Marty, Martin E., John G. Deedy Jr., David Wolf Silverman, and Robert Lekachman, eds. *The Religious Press in America*. New York: Holt, Rinehart and Winston, 1963.

May, Henry F. *The End of American Innocence*. Chicago: Quadrangle, 1959.

McKeehan, Hobart D. *Great Modern Sermons*. New York: Revell, 1923.

Menninger, Karl. *Man against Himself*. New York: Harcourt, Brace, 1938.

——. *Whatever Became of Sin?* New York: Hawthorn, 1973.

Miller, Perry, ed. *The Works of Jonathan Edwards*. New Haven, Conn.: Yale University Press, 1957.

Mitchell, Curtis. *God in the Garden: The Story of the Billy Graham New York Crusade*. Garden City, N.Y.: Doubleday, 1957.

Morgan, Edward P., ed. *This I Believe*. New York: Simon and Schuster, 1952.

Mudd, Emily. *The Practice of Marriage Counseling*. New York: Association Press, 1951.

Niebuhr, H. Richard. "The Idea of Original Sin in American Culture." In H. Richard Niebuhr, *Theology, History, and Culture: Major Unpublished Writings*, edited by William Stacy Johnson, 174–91. New Haven, Conn.: Yale University Press, 1996.

——. *The Kingdom of God in America*. 1937. Reprint, New York: Harper and Row, 1959.

Niebuhr, Reinhold. *Beyond Tragedy*. 1937. Reprint, New York: Charles Scribner's Sons, 1964.

——. "Biblical Thought and Ontological Speculation in Tillich's Theology." In *The Theology of Paul Tillich*, edited by Charles W. Kegley and Robert W. Bretall, 216–27. 1952. Reprint, New York: Macmillan, 1961.

——. *The Children of Light and the Children of Darkness*. New York: Charles Scribner's Sons, 1944.

——. "The Cultural Crisis of Our Age." *Harvard Business Review* 32 (January-February 1954): 33–38.

——. *Discerning the Signs of the Times*. New York: Charles Scribner's Sons, 1946.

——. *Faith and History: A Comparison of Christian and Modern Views of History*. New York: Charles Scribner's Sons, 1949.

——. "From Progress to Perplexity." In *The Search for America*, edited by Huston Smith, 135–46. Englewood Cliffs, N.J.: Prentice-Hall, 1959.

——. "The Hazards and the Difficulties of the Christian Ministry." In *Justice and Mercy*, edited by Ursula Niebuhr, 128–37. San Francisco: Harper and Row, 1974.

——. "Intellectual Autobiography." In *Theology of Reinhold Niebuhr*, edited by Charles W. Kegley and Robert W. Bretall, 3–23. New York: Macmillan, 1956.

——. *An Interpretation of Christian Ethics*. New York: Harper and Brothers, 1935.

——. *Leaves from the Notebook of a Tamed Cynic*. 1929. Reprint, Cleveland, Ohio: World, 1965.

——. *Man's Nature and His Communities: Essays on the Dynamics and Enigmas of Man's Personal and Social Existence*. 1965. Reprint, London: Bles, 1966.

———. *Moral Man and Immoral Society: A Study in Ethics and Politics*. New York: Charles Scribner's Sons, 1932.

———. *The Nature and Destiny of Man*. 2 vols. 1941–43. Reprint, New York: Charles Scribner's Sons, 1964.

———. *Pious and Secular America*. New York: Charles Scribner's Sons, 1958.

———. *Reflections on the End of an Era*. New York: Charles Scribner's Sons, 1934.

———. "The Security and Hazard of the Christian Ministry." *Union Seminary Quarterly Review* 13 (November 1957): 19–23.

Niebuhr, Ursula, ed. *Justice and Mercy*. San Francisco: Harper and Row, 1974.

Oates, Wayne E. "The Cult of Reassurance." *Religion in Life* 24 (Winter 1954–55): 72–82.

Peale, Norman Vincent. *The Power of Positive Thinking*. New York: Prentice-Hall, 1952.

———. *Sin, Sex, and Self-Control: A Practical, Common-Sense, Inspiring Challenge to the Individual*. Garden City, N.Y.: Doubleday, 1965.

———. *The Tough-Minded Optimist*. Englewood Cliffs, N.J.: Prentice-Hall, 1961.

Rauschenbusch, Walter. *Christianity and the Social Crisis*. 1907. Reprint, New York: Macmillan, 1910.

———. *A Theology for the Social Gospel*. 1917. Reprint, Louisville, Ky.: Westminster John Knox Press, 1997.

Religious Book Week May 7–14. New York: National Conference of Christians and Jews, 1944.

Rieff, Philip. *The Triumph of the Therapeutic: Uses of Faith after Freud*. New York: Harper and Row, 1966.

Riesman, David, Nathan Glazer, and Reuel Denney. *The Lonely Crowd: A Study of the Changing American Character*. 1950. Reprint, New Haven, Conn.: Yale University Press, 1961.

Robinson, John A. T. *Honest to God*. Louisville, Ky.: Westminster John Knox Press, 1963.

Rosten, Leo. *Religions of America*. New York: Simon and Schuster, 1955.

Rowland, Stanley J. *Land in Search of God*. New York: Random House, 1958.

Scherer, Paul. "Reinhold Niebuhr—Preacher." In *Theology of Reinhold Niebuhr*, edited by Charles W. Kegley and Robert W. Bretall, 312–32. New York: Macmillan, 1956.

Schlesinger, Arthur M. *The Vital Center: The Politics of Freedom*. Boston: Houghton Mifflin, 1949.

Schneider, Louis, and Sanford M. Dornbusch. *Popular Religion: Inspirational Books in America*. Chicago: University of Chicago Press, 1958.

Smith, H. Shelton. *Changing Conceptions of Original Sin*. New York: Charles Scribner's Sons, 1955.

Smith, Huston, ed. *The Search for America*. Englewood Cliffs, N.J.: Prentice-Hall, 1959.

Spence, Hartzell. *The Story of America's Religions*. New York: Holt, Rinehart and Winston, 1960.

Sykes, Gerald, ed. *Alienation: The Cultural Climate of Our Time*. New York: Braziller, 1964.

Tillich, Hannah. *From Time to Time*. New York: Stein and Day, 1973.

Tillich, Paul. "Courage and a Dynamic Faith." In *Faith Is a Star*, edited by Roland Gammon, 193–98. New York: Dutton, 1963.

———. *The Courage To Be*. New Haven, Conn.: Yale University Press, 1952.

———. *The Dynamics of Faith*. New York: Harper and Row, 1957.

———. *The Eternal Now*. New York: Charles Scribner's Sons, 1963.

———. *The Irrelevance and Relevance of the Christian Message*. Edited by Durwood Foster. Cleveland, Ohio: Pilgrim Press, 1996.

———. *My Search for Absolutes*. New York: Simon and Schuster, 1967.

———. *My Travel Diary: 1936*. Edited by Jerald C. Brauer. New York: Harper and Row, 1970.

———. *The New Being*. New York: Charles Scribner's Sons, 1955.

———. *On the Boundary: An Autobiographical Sketch*. New York: Charles Scribner's Sons, 1966.

———. "The Person in Technical Society," In *Christian Faith and Social Action*, edited by John A. Hutchison, 137–53. New York: Charles Scribner's Sons, 1953.

———. *The Protestant Era*. Translated by James Luther Adams. Chicago: University of Chicago Press, 1948.

———. *The Religious Situation*. 1932. Reprint, New York: Meridian Books, 1956.

———. *The Shaking of the Foundations*. New York: Charles Scribner's Sons, 1948.

———. *Systematic Theology: Three Volumes in One*. 1951, 1957, 1963. Reprint, Chicago: University of Chicago Press, 1971.

———. *Theology of Culture*. Edited by Robert C. Kimball. New York: Oxford University Press, 1959.

———. "Vertical and Horizontal Thinking." *American Scholar* 15 (Winter 1945–46): 102–5.

Updike, John. *Rabbit, Run*. Greenwich, Conn.: Fawcett, 1960.

Weiman, Henry N. "Religion and Illusion." In *American Protestant Thought in the Liberal Era*, edited by William Hutchison, 183–89. New York: Harper and Row, 1968.

"What the Layman Expects from His Minister." *Religion in Life* 24 (Spring 1955): 361–67.

Whitelaw, Thomas. "The Biblical Conception of Sin." In *Fundamentals: A Testimony to Truth*, edited by George M. Marsden, vol. 4. New York: Garland, 1988.

Whyte, William. *The Organization Man*. New York: Simon and Schuster, 1956.

Williams, C. B. "Paul's Testimony to the Doctrine of Sin." In *Fundamentals: A Testimony to Truth*, edited by George M. Marsden, vol. 3. New York: Garland, 1988.

Williams, George H. *The Harvard Divinity School: Its Place in Harvard University and in American Culture*. Boston: Beacon, 1954.

Williams, J. Paul. *What Americans Believe and How They Worship*. New York: Harper and Brothers, 1952.

Wilson, Sloan. *The Man in the Gray Flannel Suit*. New York: Simon and Schuster, 1955.

Winter, Gibson. *The Suburban Captivity of the Churches: An Analysis of Protestant Responsibility in the Expanding Metropolis*. Garden City, N.Y.: Doubleday, 1961.

SECONDARY SOURCES

Books and Articles

Ahlstrom, Sydney E. *A Religious History of the American People*. Vol. 2. Garden City, N.Y.: Image Books, 1975.

Aikman, David. *Billy Graham: His Life and Influence*. Nashville, Tenn.: Nelson, 2007.

Allitt, Patrick. *Religion in America since 1945: A History*. New York: Columbia University Press, 2003.

Bains, David R. "Conduits of Faith: Reinhold Niebuhr's Liturgical Thought." *Church History* 73 (March 2004): 168–94.

Baughman, James L. *Henry R. Luce and the Rise of the American News Media*. Boston: Twayne, 1987.

Berkman, John, and Michael Cartwright, eds. *Hauerwas Reader*. Durham, N.C.: Duke University Press, 2001.

Blake, Casey Nelson. *Beloved Community: The Cultural Criticism of Randolph Bourne, Van Wyck Brooks, Waldo Frank, and Lewis Mumford*. Chapel Hill: University of North Carolina Press, 1990.

Boyer, Paul. *By the Bomb's Early Light: American Thought and Culture at the Dawn of the Atomic Age*. New York: Pantheon Books, 1985.

Branch, Taylor. *Parting the Waters: America in the King Years, 1954–63*. New York: Simon and Schuster, 1988.

Brauer, Jerald C. "Tillich at Chicago." *North American Paul Tillich Society Newsletter* 15 (October 1989).

Brown, Charles C. *Niebuhr and His Age: Reinhold Niebuhr's Prophetic Role in the Twentieth Century*. Philadelphia: Trinity, 1992.

Bruns, Roger A. *Preacher: Billy Sunday and Big-Time American Evangelism*. New York: W. W. Norton, 1992.

Bulman, Raymond, and Fredrick Parrella, eds. *Religion in the New Millennium: Theology in the Spirit of Paul Tillich*. Macon, Ga.: Mercer University Press, 2001.

Butler, Jon. "Jack-in-the-Box Faith? The Religion Problem in Modern American History." *Journal of American History* 90 (March 2004): 1357–78.

Cali, Grace. *Paul Tillich First-Hand: A Memoir of the Harvard Years*. Chicago: Exploration Press, 1996.

Carey, John J. *Paulus Then and Now: A Study of Paul Tillich's Theological World and the Continuing Relevance of His Work*. Macon, Ga.: Mercer University Press, 2002.

——, ed. *Kairos and Logos: Studies in the Roots and Implications of Tillich's Theology*. Macon, Ga.: Mercer University Press, 1978.

Carpenter, Joel. *Revive Us Again: The Reawakening of American Fundamentalism*. New York: Oxford University Press, 1997.

Carter, Paul. *Another Part of the Fifties*. New York: Columbia University Press, 1983.

——. *The Spiritual Crisis of the Gilded Age*. DeKalb: Northern Illinois University Press, 1971.

Castronovo, David. *Beyond the Gray Flannel Suit: Books from the 1950s That Made American Culture*. New York: Continuum, 2004.

Cauthen, Kenneth. *The Impact of American Religious Liberalism*. New York: University Press of America, 1983.

Chafe, William. *The Unfinished Journey: America since World War Two*. New York: Oxford University Press, 1986.

Chappell, David. *A Stone of Hope: Prophetic Religion and the Death of Jim Crow*. Chapel Hill: University of North Carolina Press, 2004.

Chartier, Roger. *The Cultural Origins of the French Revolution*. Durham, N.C.: Duke University Press, 1991.

Clark, Henry B. *Serenity, Courage, and Wisdom: The Enduring Legacy of Reinhold Niebuhr*. Cleveland, Ohio: Pilgrim Press, 1994.

Coontz, Stephanie. *The Way We Never Were: American Families and the Nostalgia Trap*. New York: Basic Books, 1992.

Cooper, Terry D. *Paul Tillich and Psychology*. Macon, Ga.: Mercer University Press, 2005.

Cornwell, Patricia. *Ruth, a Portrait: The Story of Ruth Bell Graham*. 1983. Reprint, New York: Doubleday, 1997.

Cort, David. *The Sin of Henry R. Luce: An Anatomy of Journalism*. Secaucus, N.J.: Lyle Stuart, 1974.

Cotkin, George. *Existential America*. Baltimore, Md.: Johns Hopkins University Press, 2003.

Davidson, Cathy N., ed. *Reading in America: Literature and Social History*. Baltimore, Md.: Johns Hopkins University Press, 1989.

Delbanco, Andrew. *The Death of Satan: How Americans Have Lost the Sense of Evil*. New York: Farrar, Straus and Giroux, 1995.

Donaldson, Gary A. *Abundance and Anxiety: America, 1945–1960*. Westport, Conn.: Praeger, 1997.

Dorrien, Gary. *The Making of American Liberal Theology: Idealism, Realism, and Modernity, 1900–1950*. Louisville, Ky.: Westminster John Knox Press, 2003.

———. "Niebuhr and Graham: Modernity, Complexity, White Supremacism, Justice, Ambiguity." In *The Legacy of Billy Graham: Critical Reflections on America's Greatest Evangelist*, edited by Michael G. Long, 141–59. New York: Palgrave Macmillan, 2006.

———. *The Remaking of Evangelical Theology*. Louisville, Ky.: Westminster John Knox Press, 1998.

Dourly, John P. *Paul Tillich, Carl Jung, and the Recovery of Religion*. New York: Routledge, 2008.

Dower, John. *War without Mercy: Race and Power in the Pacific War*. New York: Pantheon Books, 1986.

Drummond, Lewis A. *The Canvas Cathedral*. Nashville, Tenn.: Nelson, 2003.

Eagleton, Terry. *Literary Theory: An Introduction*. 1983. Reprint, Minneapolis: University of Minnesota Press, 1986.

Elie, Paul. *The Life You Save May Be Your Own: An American Pilgrimage*. New York: Farrar, Straus and Giroux, 2003.

Ellwood, Robert. *The Fifties Spiritual Marketplace: American Religion in a Decade of Conflict*. New Brunswick, N.J.: Rutgers University Press, 1997.

———. *1950: Crossroads of American Religious Life*. Louisville, ,Ky.: Westminster John Knox Press, 2000.

———. *The Sixties Spiritual Awakening: American Religion Moving from Modern to Postmodern*. New Brunswick, N.J.: Rutgers University Press, 1994.

Epp, Roger. "The Ironies of Christian Realism: The End of an Augustinian Tradition in International Politics." In *The Christian Realists: Reassessing the Contributions of Niebuhr and His Contemporaries*, edited by Eric Patterson, 199–226. Lanham, Md.: University Press of America, 2003.

Farber, David. *The Age of Great Dreams: America in the 1960s*. New York: Hill and Wang, 1994.

———. *The Sixties: From Memory to History*. Chapel Hill: University of North Carolina Press, 1994.

Flowers, Ronald B. *Religion in Strange Times: The 1960s and 1970s*. Macon, Ga.: Mercer University Press, 1984.

Fox, Matthew. *Religion USA: An Inquiry into Religion and Culture by Way of TIME Magazine*. Dubuque, Ill.: Listening Press, 1971.

Fox, Richard W. "The Niebuhr Brothers and the Liberal Protestant Heritage." In Lacey, *Religion and Twentieth-Century American Intellectual Life*, 94–115.

———. *Reinhold Niebuhr: A Biography*. 1985. Reprint, Ithaca, N.Y.: Cornell University Press, 1996.

Gambone, Michael D. *The Greatest Generation Comes Home: The Veteran in American Society*. College Station: Texas A&M University Press, 2005.

George, Carol V. R. *God's Salesman: Norman Vincent Peale and the Power of Positive Thinking*. New York: Oxford University Press, 1993.

Giardina, Denise. *Saints and Villains*. Ballantine Books, 1999.

Gibbs, Nancy, and Michael Duffy. *The Preacher and the Presidents: Billy Graham in the White House*. Boston, Mass.: Center Street, 2008.

Gilbert, James. *Another Chance: Postwar America, 1945–1968*. Philadelphia: Temple University Press, 1981.

Gilkey, Langdon. *Gilkey on Tillich*. Eugene, Ore.: Wipf and Stock, 1990.

———. *On Niebuhr: A Theological Study*. Chicago: University of Chicago Press, 2001.

Gitlin, Todd. *The Sixties: Years of Hope Days of Rage*. 1987. Reprint, New York: Bantam Books, 1993.

Graebner, William. *The Age of Doubt: American Thought and Culture in the 1940s*. Boston, Mass.: Twayne, 1991. Halberstam, David. *The Fifties*. New York: Villard Books, 1993.

Hale, Nathan. *The Rise and Crisis of Psychoanalysis in the United States: Freud and the Americans, 1917–1985*. New York: Oxford University Press, 1995.

Hall, David D., ed. *Lived Religion in America: Toward a History of Practice*. Princeton, N.J.: Princeton University Press, 1997.

Hall, Douglas John. *Remembered Voices: Reclaiming the Legacy of "Neo-Orthodoxy."* Louisville, Ky.: Westminster John Knox Press, 1998.

Halliwell, Martin. *The Constant Dialogue: Reinhold Niebuhr and American Intellectual Culture*. Lanham, Md.: Rowman and Littlefield, 2005.

Harries, Richard. *Reinhold Niebuhr and the Issues of Our Time*. Grand Rapids, Mich.: Eerdmans, 1986.

Hart, D. G. *The University Gets Religion: Religious Studies in American Higher Education.* Baltimore, Md.: Johns Hopkins University Press, 1999.

Hauerwas, Stanley. *With the Grain of the Universe.* Grand Rapids, Mich.: Brazos, 2001.

Heinze, Andrew R. *Jews and the American Soul: Human Nature in the Twentieth Century.* Princeton, N.J.: Princeton University Press, 2004.

Herman, Ellen. *The Romance of American Psychology.* Berkeley: University of California Press, 1995.

Herzstein, Robert E. *Henry R. Luce: A Political Portrait of the Man Who Created the American Century.* New York: Charles Scribner's Sons, 1994.

Hoge, Dean R. *Vanishing Boundaries: The Religion of Mainline Protestant Baby Boomers.* Louisville, Ky.: Westminster John Knox Press, 1994.

Holifield, E. Brooks. *A History of Pastoral Care in America: From Salvation to Self-Realization.* Nashville, Tenn.: Abingdon, 1983.

——. *Theology in America: Christian Thought from the Age of the Puritans to the Civil War.* New Haven, Conn.: Yale University Press, 2003.

Homans, Peter. *Theology after Freud: An Interpretive Inquiry.* New York: Bobbs-Merrill, 1970.

Hudnut-Beumler, James. *Looking for God in the Suburbs: The Religion of the American Dream and Its Critics.* New Brunswick, N.J.: Rutgers University Press, 1994.

Hulsether, Mark. *Building a Protestant Left:* Christianity and Crisis *Magazine, 1941–1993.* Knoxville: University of Tennessee Press, 1999.

Hunt, Lynn, ed. *The New Cultural History.* Berkeley: University of California Press, 1989.

Hutchison, William R. *The Modernist Impulse in American Protestantism.* Cambridge, Mass.: Harvard University Press, 1976.

——. *Religious Pluralism in America: The Contentious History of a Founding Ideal.* New Haven, Conn.: Yale University Press, 2003.

——, ed. *American Protestant Thought in the Liberal Era.* New York: Harper and Row, 1968.

——. *Between the Times: The Travail of the Protestant Establishment in America, 1900–1960.* Cambridge: Cambridge University Press, 1989.

Jackson, Kenneth T. *Crabgrass Frontier: The Suburbanization of the United States.* New York: Oxford University Press, 1995.

Jacobs, Alan. *Original Sin: A Cultural History.* New York: HarperOne, 2008.

Jezer, Marty. *The Dark Ages: Life in the United States, 1945–1960.* Boston: South End Press, 1982.

Kammen, Michael. *American Culture, American Tastes: Social Change and the Twentieth Century.* New York: Knopf, 1999.

King, William McGuire. "An Enthusiasm for Humanity: The Social Emphasis in Religion and Its Accommodation in Protestant Theology." In Lacey, *Religion and Twentieth-Century American Intellectual Life,* 49–77.

Kloppenberg, James T. *Uncertain Victory: Social Democracy and Progressivism in European and American Thought, 1870–1920.* New York: Oxford University Press, 1986.

Korda, Michael. *Making the List: A Cultural History of the American Bestseller, 1900–1999.* New York: Barnes and Noble Books, 2001.

Lacey, Michael J., ed. *Religion and Twentieth-Century American Intellectual Life.* Cambridge: Cambridge University Press, 1989.

Lears, T. J. Jackson. *No Place of Grace: Antimodernism and the Transformation of American Culture, 1880–1920.* Chicago: University of Chicago Press, 1981.

——. *Something for Nothing: Luck in America.* New York: Viking, 2003.

Leuchtenburg, William E. *A Troubled Feast: America since 1945.* Boston: Little, Brown, 1973.

Levine, Lawrence W. *Highbrow/Lowbrow: The Emergence of Cultural Hierarchy in America.* Cambridge, Mass.: Harvard University Press, 1988.

Lindbeck, George A. *The Nature of Doctrine: Religion and Theology in a Postliberal Age.* Louisville, Ky.: Westminster John Knox Press, 1984.

Lippy, Charles H. *Being Religious, American Style: A History of Popular Religiosity in the United States.* Westport, Conn.: Praeger, 1994.

——. "Billy Graham's 'My Answer': Agenda for the Faithful." *Studies in Popular Culture* 5 (1982): 27–34.

——, ed. *Religious Periodicals of the United States.* Westport, Conn.: Greenwood, 1986.

Long, Michael G. *Billy Graham and the Beloved Community: America's Evangelist and the Dream of Martin Luther King, Jr.* New York: Palgrave Macmillan, 2006.

——. *The Legacy of Billy Graham: Critical Reflections on America's Greatest Evangelist.* Louisville, Ky.: Westminster John Knox Press, 2008.

Lovin, Robin. *Reinhold Niebuhr and Christian Realism.* New York: Cambridge University Press, 1995.

Lyons, James R., ed. *The Intellectual Legacy of Paul Tillich.* Detroit, Mich.: Wayne State University Press, 1969.

Macquarrie, John. *Twentieth-Century Religious Thought.* 1961. Reprint, Harrisburg, Pa.: Trinity Press International, 2001.

Mahan, Wayne W. *Tillich's System.* San Antonio, Tex.: Trinity University Press, 1974.

Marsden, George M. *Fundamentalism and American Culture: The Shaping of Twentieth-Century Evangelicalism, 1870–1925.* Oxford: Oxford University Press, 1980.

——. "Human Depravity: A Neglected Explanatory Category." Unpublished essay, 2003. [Author's personal copy.]

——, ed. *Evangelicalism and Modern America.* Grand Rapids, Mich.: Eerdmans, 1984.

——, ed. *The Fundamentals: A Testimony to Truth.* 4 vols. New York: Garland, 1988.

Martin, William. *A Prophet with Honor: The Billy Graham Story.* New York: William Morrow, 1991.

Marty, Martin. "Hell Disappeared. No One Noticed. A Civic Argument." *Harvard Theological Review* 78 (1985): 381–98.

——. *Modern American Religion.* 3 vols. Chicago: University of Chicago Press, 1986–96.

——. "Reinhold Niebuhr: Public Theology and the American Experience." In *The Legacy of Reinhold Niebuhr*, edited by Nathan A. Scott, Jr., 8–35. Chicago: University of Chicago Press, 1975.

Massa, Mark. *Catholics and American Culture: Fulton Sheen, Dorothy Day, and the Notre Dame Football Team.* New York: Crossroad, 1999.

Matusow, Allen J. *The Unraveling of America: A History of Liberalism in the 1960s.* New York: Harper and Row, 1984.

May, Elaine Tyler. *Homeward Bound: American Families in the Cold War Era*. 1988. Reprint, New York: Basic Books, 1999.

May, Rollo. *Paulus: Reminiscences of a Friendship*. New York: Harper and Row, 1973.

McBride, James. "Paul Tillich and the Supreme Court." *Journal of Church and State* 30 (Spring 1988): 245–72.

McCarraher, Eugene. *Christian Critics: Religion and the Impasse in Modern American Social Thought*. Ithaca, N.Y.: Cornell University Press, 2000.

McLoughlin, William G. *Revivals, Awakenings, and Reform*. Chicago: University of Chicago Press, 1978.

McPherson, James. *For Cause and Comrades: Why Men Fought in the Civil War*. New York: Oxford University Press, 1997.

Merkley, Paul. *Reinhold Niebuhr: A Political Account*. Montreal: McGill-Queen's University Press, 1975.

Meyer, Donald. *The Positive Thinkers: Religion as Pop Psychology from Mary Baker Eddy to Oral Roberts*. 1965. Reprint, New York: Pantheon Books, 1980.

———. *The Protestant Search for Political Realism, 1919–1941*. 1960. Reprint, Middletown, Conn.: Wesleyan University Press, 1988.

Miller, Donald, and Marion Nowak. *The Fifties: The Way We Really Were*. New York: Doubleday, 1975.

Miller, Robert Moats. *Harry Emerson Fosdick: Preacher, Pastor, Prophet*. New York: Oxford University Press, 1985.

Miller, Steven P. *Billy Graham and the Rise of the Republican South*. Philadelphia: University of Pennsylvania Press, 2009.

Minus, Paul M. *Walter Rauschenbusch: American Reformer*. New York: Macmillan, 1988.

Moore, R. Laurence. *Selling God: American Religion in the Marketplace of Culture*. New York: Oxford University Press, 1994.

Moskowitz, Eva. *In Therapy We Trust: America's Obsession with Self-Fulfillment*. Baltimore, Md.: Johns Hopkins University Press, 2001.

Mouw, Richard J. "The Bible in Twentieth-Century Protestantism: A Preliminary Taxonomy." In *The Bible in America: Essays in Cultural History*, edited by Mark Noll and Nathan Hatch, 139–62. New York: Oxford University Press, 1982.

Noll, Mark. *America's God: From Jonathan Edwards to Abraham Lincoln*. New York: Oxford University Press, 2002.

———. *The Old Religion in a New World: The History of North American Christianity*. Grand Rapids, Mich.: Eerdmans, 2002.

Noll, Mark, and Nathan Hatch. *The Bible in America: Essays in Cultural History*. New York: Oxford University Press, 1982.

Nourie, Alan, and Barbara Nourie. *American Mass-Market Magazines*. Westport, Conn.: Greenwood, 1990.

Novick, Peter. *That Noble Dream: The "Objectivity Question" and the American Historical Profession*. Cambridge: Cambridge University Press, 1988.

Oakley, J. R. *God's Country: America in the Fifties*. New York: Dembner Books, 1986.

O'Neill, William L. *Democracy at War: America's Fight at Home and Abroad in World War II*. Cambridge, Mass.: Harvard University Press, 1993.

Oppenheimer, Mark. *Knocking on Heaven's Door: American Religion in the Age of Counterculture*. New Haven, Conn.: Yale University Press, 2003.

Pagels, Elaine. *Adam, Eve, and the Serpent*. New York: Vintage Books, 1989.

Patterson, Eric, ed. *The Christian Realists: Reassesing the Contributions of Niebuhr and his Contemporaries*. Lanham, Md.: University Press of America, 2003.

Pauck, Wilhelm, and Marion Pauck. *Paul Tillich: His Life and Thought*. New York: Harper and Row, 1976.

Pells, Richard H. *The Liberal Mind in a Conservative Age: American Intellectuals in the 1940s and 1950s*. New York: Harper and Row, 1985.

Peyser, Joan. *Bernstein: A Biography*. New York: Billboard Books, 1998.

Plaskow, Judith. *Sex, Sin, and Grace: Women's Experience and the Theologies of Reinhold Niebuhr and Paul Tillich*. Lanham, Md.: University Press of America, 1980.

Pokki, Timo. *America's Preacher and His Message: Billy Graham's View of Conversion and Sanctification*. Lanham, Md.: University Press of America, 1999.

Pollock, John. *Billy Graham: Evangelist to the World*. New York: Harper and Row, 1979.

Radway, Janice A. *A Feeling for Books: The Book-of-the-Month Club, Literary Taste, and Middle-Class Desire*. Chapel Hill: University of North Carolina Press, 1997.

Reinitz, Richard. *Irony and Consciousness: American Historiography and Reinhold Niebuhr's Vision*. London: Associated University Presses, 1980.

Reynolds, David S. *Faith in Fiction: The Emergence of Religious Literature in America*. Cambridge, Mass.: Harvard University Press, 1981.

Richey, Russell E., and Donald G. Jones. *American Civil Religion*. New York: Harper and Row, 1974.

Roozen, David A., Jackson W. Carroll, and Wade Clark Roof. "Fifty Years of Religious Change in the United States." In *The Post-war Generation and Establishment Religion: Cross-Cultural Perspectives*, edited by Roozen, Carroll, and Roof, 59–86. Boulder, Colo.: Westview, 1995.

Rossiter, Clinton, ed. *The Federalist Papers*. 1961. Reprint, New York: Mentor Books, 1964.

Rubin, Joan Shelley. *The Making of Middlebrow Culture*. Chapel Hill: University of North Carolina Press, 1992.

Rubin, Julius H. *Religious Melancholy and Protestant Experience in America*. New York: Oxford University Press, 1994.

Russell, Jeffrey Burton. *Paradise Mislaid: How We Lost Heaven—and How We Can Regain It*. New York: Oxford University Press, 2006.

Sandeen, Ernest R. *The Roots of Fundamentalism: British and American Millenarianism, 1800–1930*. Chicago: University of Chicago Press, 1970.

Saum, Lewis O. *The Popular Mood of Pre–Civil War America*. Westport, Conn.: Greenwood, 1980.

Scott, Nathan A., ed. *The Legacy of Reinhold Niebuhr*. Chicago: University of Chicago Press, 1975.

Sifton, Elisabeth. *The Serenity Prayer: Faith and Politics in Times of Peace and War*. New York: W. W. Norton, 2003.

Silk, Mark. *Spiritual Politics: Religion and America since World War II*. New York: Simon and Schuster, 1988.

Sittser, Gerald. *A Cautious Patriotism: The American Churches and the Second World War*. Chapel Hill: University of North Carolina Press, 1997.

Smith, Michael J. *Realist Thought from Weber to Kissinger*. Baton Rouge: Louisiana State University Press, 1986.

Stenger, Mary Ann, and Ronald H. Stone. *Dialogues of Paul Tillich*. Macon, Ga.: Mercer University Press, 2002.

Stokes, Allison. *Ministry after Freud*. New York: Pilgrim Press, 1985.

Stone, Ronald H. *Paul Tillich's Radical Social Thought*. Atlanta, Ga.: John Knox Press, 1980.

———. *Professor Reinhold Niebuhr: A Mentor to the Twentieth Century*. Louisville, Ky.: Westminster John Knox Press, 1992.

Swanberg, W. A. *Luce and His Empire*. New York: Charles Scribner's Sons, 1972.

Sweet, Leonard I. "The 1960s: The Crisis of Liberal Christianity and the Public Emergence of Evangelism." In *Evangelicalism and Modern America*, edited by George Marsden, 29–45. Grand Rapids, Mich.: Eerdmans, 1984.

Taylor, Mark K. *Paul Tillich: Theologian of the Boundaries*. San Francisco: Collins Liturgical, 1987.

Thomas, J. Heywood. *Paul Tillich: An Appraisal*. Philadelphia: Westminster, 1963.

———. *Tillich*. London: Continuum, 2000.

Tompkins, Jane P., ed. *Reader-Response Criticism: From Formalism to Post-structuralism*. Baltimore, Md.: Johns Hopkins University Press, 1980.

Toulouse, Mark G. "Christianity Today and American Public Life: A Case Study." *Journal of Church and State* 35, no. 2 (1993): 241–84.

Tweed, Thomas A., ed. *Retelling United States Religious History*. Berkeley: University of California Press, 1997.

Updike, John. *More Matter: Essays and Criticism*. New York: Knopf, 1999.

Walls, Jerry L. *Hell: The Logic of Damnation*. Notre Dame, Mich.: University of Notre Dame Press, 1992.

Weber, Timothy P. *Living in the Shadow of the Second Coming: American Premillennialism, 1875–1982*. New York: Oxford University Press, 1979.

Welch, Claude. *Protestant Thought in the Nineteenth Century*. Vol. 2, *1870–1914*. New Haven, Conn.: Yale University Press, 1985.

White, Ronald C., Jr. *Lincoln's Greatest Speech: The Second Inaugural*. New York: Simon and Schuster, 2002.

Whitfield, Stephen J. *The Culture of the Cold War*. Baltimore, Md.: Johns Hopkins University Press, 1991.

Wiley, Tatha. *Original Sin: Origins, Developments, Contemporary Meanings*. New York: Paulist Press, 2002.

Wuthnow, Robert. *After Heaven: Spirituality in America since the 1950s*. Berkeley: University of California Press, 1998.

———. *The Restructuring of American Religion: Society and Faith since World War II*. Princeton, N.J.: Princeton University Press, 1988.

Theses and Dissertations

Bergman, William Carl. "Living the Questions, Telling the Truth: Paul Tillich's Theology in His Apologetic Preaching." Ph.D. diss., Boston University, 2001.

Burkhead, Howell W. "The Development of the Concept of Sin in the Preaching of Billy Graham." Ph.D. diss., Southwestern Baptist Theological Seminary, 1998.

Johnson, Barclay D. "How Americans Respond to Tillich: A Case Study." B.A. thesis, Harvard University, 1960.

Kolb, Frances A. "The Reaction of American Protestants to Psychoanalysis, 1900–1950." Ph.D. diss., Washington University, 1972.

Morris, Aubrey Leon. "A Study of Psychological Factors in the Evangelistic Preaching of Billy Graham." Ph.D. diss., Southern Baptist Theological Seminary, 1966.

Newbill, James G. "The Theology of Billy Graham, Its Practical Applications, and Its Relative Position in the Contemporary Religious Scene." Master's thesis, University of Washington, 1960.

Sanders, William Terrell. "Paul Tillich: Apologetic Preacher of the Christian Faith." Ph.D. diss., Florida State University, 1983.

Silva, William. "The Expression of Neo-Orthodoxy in American Protestantism, 1939–1960." Ph.D. diss., Yale University, 1988.

Voskuil, Dennis. "From Liberalism to Neo-Orthodoxy: The History of a Theological Transition." Ph.D. diss., Harvard Divinity School, 1974.

INDEX

Eckardt, A. Roy, 8, 41, 59, 203 (n. 82)
Edwards, Jonathan, 48, 127–28
Eisenhower, Dwight D., 108–9, 140
Ellwood, Robert, 177, 198 (n. 5), 204
(n. 97), 207 (n. 41), 222 (n. 27)
Eternal Now, The, 167, 172–73
Evil, 31–32, 34–35, 37–45 passim, 50,
54, 66, 69, 70–71, 83, 86, 111, 115,
185–86; banality of, 20
Existentialism, 20, 92

Faith and History, 210 (n. 13)
Farmer, William R., 27–28
Ferm, Robert O., 139–40, 143
Ferré, Nels, 64
Finite freedom, 70–74
Finney, Charles G., 48
First Great Awakening, 48
Ford, Henry, 50
Fosdick, Harry Emerson, 39–40, 44, 49
Fox, Richard, 93, 104, 106, 116, 121, 209
(n. 1), 213 (n. 2), 216 (n. 45)
Francis, Saint, 116
Frank Sinatra Show, The, 39
Fuller Theological Seminary, 78

George, Carol, 24–26
Gilkey, Langdon, 193
Gill, Theodore, 173
Goldman, Eric, 43
Goldwater, Barry, 184
Graham, Billy: on Adam and Eve, 69–
70; anti-intellectualism of, 86, 150;
career of, 5, 125, 128; as cold warrior,
129; conversion of, 51–52; critics of,
59–63, 119–20, 137, 140; crusades of,
46, 125–42; early life, 4–5, 51–52;
and Harlem, 140; on Jesus, 60, 78,
81, 85–88, 127–49 passim; large
audiences of, 5, 46, 126, 129, 135; lay
response to, 126, 130–31, 137–39,
144–49, 151–53; as leader of theological revival, 8, 15, 26, 46, 67, 88; moralism of, 59–60, 82–83, 136, 143–44;
My Answer column, 5, 58, 143–50;

Newsweek covers, 133, 194; vs. Norman Vincent Peale, 3, 15, 23–25, 59;
pastors' views of, 132–33; and race
relations, 140–42; respect for Reinhold Niebuhr, 62; and "Sinners in the
Hands of an Angry God," 127–28, 221
(n. 17); social message of, 140–41;
Time covers, 1–2, 133, 194; at Union
Theological Seminary, 63, 150–51;
views of sin, 69–70, 73–75, 77–78,
81–83, 90, 189–90
Graham, Ruth, 128
Great Depression, 2, 88, 108, 192

Ham, Mordecai. *See* Graham, Billy: con-
version of
Harrington, Michael, 18
Harris, T. George, 45
Hegel, G. W. F., 71
Heidegger, Martin, 55, 206 (n. 28)
Hell, 7–8, 146
Herberg, Will, 8, 29, 41–42, 214 (n. 13)
Hiroshima, 16
Homrighausen, E. G., 152–53
Hoover, J. Edgar, 184
Hope, Bob, 184
Hordern, William, 114
Hour of Decision, 5, 58
Hudnut-Beumler, James, 31–32, 42, 207
(n. 41)
Hutchinson, Paul, 25

Interpretation of Ethics, The, 72

James, William, 21–22
Jesus Christ: crucifixion of, 85–88; in lib-
eral thought, 36; in suburbs, 27. *See also*
Graham, Billy: on Jesus; Niebuhr, Rein-
hold: on Jesus; Tillich, Paul: on Jesus
Johnson, Lyndon B., 184
Jones, Bob, 52, 140, 142
Jones, Howard O., 143
Journal of Pastoral Care, 21
Jung, Carl, 78, 142
Justification by faith, 156, 170

Khrushchev, Nikita, 82
Kierkegaard, Søren, 20, 40, 51, 54, 70–74, 78, 195
King, Martin Luther, Jr., 44, 141–42
Kobler, John, 158
Korean War, 13, 16

Layman Looks at the Minister, The, 33
Lay theologian, 6–9, 88–90, 108, 119, 121–22, 153, 172, 176, 177–78, 182–83, 186, 189–91
Leaves from the Notebook of a Tamed Cynic, 50, 102
Leiffer, Murray H., 33
Leonard (Cali), Grace, 158, 209 (n. 70)
Lewis, C. S., 31, 41
Liberal theology, 32, 35–36, 48–51, 53–54
Liebman, Joshua Loth, 21–22, 38
Life, 4, 20–34 passim
Long, Michael G., 208 (n. 57), 232–33 (n. 9)
Look, 4, 32–33, 43–44
Los Angeles crusade. *See* Graham, Billy: crusades of
Luce, Henry, 2, 34, 112–13, 184–85, 218 (nn. 65, 66)
Luther, Martin, 7, 44, 47, 58, 75–76, 79, 120, 180

MacArthur, Douglas, 184
Macdonald, Dwight, 29
Machen, J. Gresham, 49
Macintosh, D. C., 50
Mackay, John A., 124
Madison, James, 48, 205 (n. 5)
Madison Square Garden, 134, 138
Man in the Gray Flannel Suit, The, 16–17
Man's Nature and His Communities, 46, 69, 192, 209 (n. 2)
Marty, Martin, 8, 41, 59, 193, 215 (n. 27), 217 (n. 53), 233 (n. 11)
Marx, Karl, 71, 76
Marxism, 54, 56, 122
Mather, Cotton, 47

Mather, Increase, 47
May, Rollo, 65
McCarraher, Eugene, 209 (n. 68), 217 (n. 53)
McIntire, Carl, 140
Meyer, Donald, 88, 151–53, 200 (n. 24)
Miller, William Lee, 24, 34, 112–13
Moody, Dwight, 49, 51–52
Moral Man and Immoral Society, 22, 51, 72, 101, 119, 205 (n. 5), 215 (n.29)
Moskin, J. Robert, 43–44

Nature and Destiny of Man, The, 31, 57, 72, 87, 101–8, 115, 209 (n. 2)
Neo-evangelical, 4, 56, 67
Neo-orthodoxy, 34, 36, 43, 56, 67, 197 (n. 2)
New Being, The, 167, 172–73
Newsweek, 4, 14, 35–36, 109, 133, 194
New York City crusade. *See* Graham, Billy: crusades of
Niebuhr, Gustav, 49–50
Niebuhr, H. Richard, 51, 56, 114
Niebuhr, Reinhold: career of, 4, 50; as cold war liberal, 57, 206 (n. 35); as critic of Billy Graham, 60–63, 119–20, 208 (n. 59); as critic of Norman Vincent Peale, 24, 108, 110; death of, 96, 192; early life and education, 49–51; Gifford lectures, 98; influence on pastors, 100–103; on Jesus, 85–88, 94, 107; lay response to, 96, 98–99, 105–8, 110–11, 117–22; as leader of theological revival, 8, 14, 26, 30, 37, 46, 56–57, 67, 88; liberal theology and, 36, 50–51; newspaper column, 104, 216 (n. 39); as pastor, 50, 58, 96–98, 190; preaching of, 97–100; as public intellectual, 5, 58, 93, 104, 114–16, 193; relationship to Paul Tillich, 56, 64, 72; religious revival and, 108–12; and Serenity Prayer, 116–17; and *Time* cover, 1–2, 105; view of laity, 7, 89, 93–95; views of sin, 47, 57–58, 69–73, 75–77, 80–81, 90, 189–90, 210 (n. 13)

Nietzsche, Friedrich, 71, 74
Nixon, Richard, 82, 194
Noll, Mark, 198 (n. 7)
North American Paul Tillich Society, 193

Obama, Barack, 193
Original sin, doctrine of, 2–4, 6, 9, 33, 35, 189–90, 194–95; in American history, 47–49; definition of, 69–70, 204 (n. 1). *See also* Graham, Billy: views of sin; Niebuhr, Reinhold: views of sin; Tillich, Paul: views of sin

Parent-Teacher Association, 122
Pascal, Blaise, 47, 51, 74–75, 78
Pastoral Psychology, 21
Pauck, Marion and Wilhelm, 54, 209 (n. 70), 232 (n. 97)
Peace with God, 5, 73, 85, 136
Peale, Norman Vincent, 2–3, 14–15, 21–26, 28–29, 35, 37–39, 43, 59, 108, 110
Perfectionism, 22, 80, 105, 119, 143–44, 148, 178, 184–85, 190. *See also* Sanctification, doctrine of
Perkins School of Theology, 162
Pious and Secular America, 9, 61–62, 112
Pittenger, W. Norman, 168
Playboy, 64
Pollock, John, 62
Power of Positive Thinking, 2, 15, 22, 24, 26
Power of Prayer on Plants, 3, 29
Pray Your Weight Away, 26
Psycho, 20

Rauschenbusch, Walter, 34, 49
Reflections on the End of an Era, 72
Religious Emphasis Week, 176, 180, 229 (n. 68)
Religious Situation, The, 55–56
Rice, John R., 140
Rieff, Phillip, 45
Riesman, David, 18–19
Rietmulder, James, 40
Robinson, John A. T., 170, 208 (n. 66)
Rockefeller, Nelson, 184

Rogers, Roy, 184
Roland, Stanley, Jr., 8, 27
Romney, George, 184
Rusk, Dean, 184
Russell, Bertrand, 7

Sanctification, doctrine of, 85, 87, 120, 149. *See also* Perfectionism
Saturday Evening Post, 4–5, 17, 62, 157
Saum, Lewis, 48
Schelling, Friedrich, 53–54, 71
Schlesinger, Arthur, Jr., 193
Schneider, Louis, 38–40
Scopes trial, 51
Screwtape Letters, The, 31
Self and Dramas of History, The, 95
Seven Deadly Sins, The, 73
Shaking of the Foundations, The, 167, 172–74
Sheen, Bishop Fulton, 39–40
Sifton, Elizabeth, 193, 219 (n. 75)
Silk, Mark, 61
Smith, Huston, 115
Sockman, Ralph W., 30, 37
Sputnik, 37
Stengel, Casey, 184
Stone, Ronald, 100–101, 217 (n. 47)
Suburban Christianity, 26–28
Suburbs, 13, 16–18, 192
Sunday, Billy, 49–52
Systematic Theology, 4, 56, 64, 167, 178–79

Theological revival, 6, 8–9, 14–15, 25–26, 29–46 passim, 108, 114, 189–96, 198 (n. 5)
Thruelsen, Richard, 158
Tillich, Hannah, 65, 209 (n. 70)
Tillich, Paul: on Adam, 66, 71–72, 186; career of, 54–56, 63; death of, 64, 192; early life and education, 4, 52–54; influence on pastors, 89, 174, 179–80; intellectual biography, 54–55, 70–71; on Jesus, 64, 79, 85–88, 170, 173; lay response to, 160–67, 170–79, 181–